The
Irish Theatre

CHRISTOPHER FITZ-SIMON

The
Irish Theatre

with 202 illustrations, 24 in color

THAMES AND HUDSON

For Ben

1 *Frontispiece Waiting for Godot* by Samuel Beckett. Ciaran Hinds as Estragon and Barry McGovern as Vladimir in the 1982 revival by the Irish Theatre Company, directed by Ben Barnes and designed by Monica Frawley.

© 1983 Thames and Hudson Ltd, London

First published in the USA in 1983 by Thames and Hudson Inc., 500 Fifth Avenue, New York, New York 10110

Library of Congress Catalog Card Number 82-74547

Printed and bound in Japan

Contents

Introduction

Ireland possesses the oldest written literature in western Europe. The Irish language was the earliest in 'modern' Europe into which works of classical Greece and Rome – such as Virgil's *Aeneid* – were first translated. Geographical circumstances – a remote island surrounded by boisterous seas – seem to have promoted rather than hindered the desire for learning and travel. The succession of invasions with which the course of Irish history is notably punctuated did not impede the flow of scholarly or artistic enterprise, until the suppressive measures which followed the Tudor conquest practically extinguished the old Gaelic tradition. Irish literature from earliest times to the sixteenth century reveals a rich and vital imagination, influenced and replenished by the invading or trading cultures.

Yet for all this originality and versatility, several of those arts which would normally be considered as essential to the self-expression of a comparatively civilized people did not flourish in Ireland – and one of these was the theatre. There are two interdependent reasons for this. The first is the very nature of the Gaelic literary tradition; and the second concerns the absence of a concentrated population. Gaelic literature, whether epic or lyric, directs itself to the single reader or hearer. When it was 'performed' – if indeed this be the correct term, for anything in the character of a performance would only have taken place before a small group of listeners gathered in traditional manner round the hearth or in the open air – the bard, *file* or *ollamh* merely recited or sang. There was no attempt to employ performers as interpreters or creators of roles. Dialogue did exist – as in the famous and witty exchanges supposed to have taken place between Oisin and St Patrick – but this was philosophical disquisition, in no way dramatic.

Western drama developed in cities, whether the Graeco-Roman metropolis, the medieval cathedral town, or Shakespeare's London. In Ireland, there were no cities in the European sense until the busy, organizing Normans created their own administrative and commercial centres after Díarmuid MacMurchú, King of Leinster, had invited Henry II of England over to Ireland to settle a private feud. The Anglo-Normans remained; they invested their own stalwart talents in the development of the society which they found. It was only natural, once an Anglo-Norman urban administrative structure had been furnished, that the same administration should seek inspiration for its public entertainments from the other side of the Irish Sea. This became even more logical after the Elizabethan and Jacobean settlements.

And so it came about that when eventually a formal metropolitan theatre was established, it served what was virtually a colonial audience – those persons associated in one way or another with the regime centred in Dublin Castle – and was run by appointees of the colonial government. Even the writers, and most of the actors, were imported (in a manner of speaking) from England.

Gradually the balance changed. The quality which Lady Gregory was later to call 'the Irish genius for mythmaking' found it could adapt itself to dramatic myth-making. Many Irishmen who took to play-writing in the seventeenth and eighteenth centuries were the descendants of settlers, and the term 'Anglo-Irish' is appropriate to describe their ancestry and the outlook expressed in their work. Other playwrights, however, sprang from the 'native Irish', yet used the English

2 The Irish noblemen is entertained by his harper and his bard, from Derricke's *Image of Irlande*, an English cautionary work of the late sixteenth century. There being no Gaelic theatrical tradition, this was the nearest equivalent to a dramatic performance.

language which their forebears had assimilated over a period of time. They were fortunate heirs to a dual tradition, revelling in their choice of words, in unusual juxtaposition of images and inventive turn of phrase. These playwrights quite literally enjoyed the best of both worlds. We find an obvious example in the Sheridan (O Sireadáin) theatrical dynasty.

A very large proportion of Irish (or Anglo-Irish, if the distinction still has to be made) theatrical talent found its way to England owing to economic pressures. After the dissolution of the Irish parliament and the Act of Union of 1801, Dublin lost its official status as a capital city, and it became even more natural that Irishmen in all walks of life should seek work or patronage in the British capital. At the same time, however, a curiosity about the 'hidden' Ireland began to develop in intellectual and artistic circles; this was manifest in research into the legends and sagas of what came to be known as 'Celtic' antiquity. The rediscovery of Ireland's remote past, allied to successive (and largely abortive) movements of insurrection, led to a change in perspective among writers. Irish themes and subjects were sought. In the theatre, an Irish audience was envisaged, rather than an international English-speaking one. While this inevitably led to inward-looking, parochial and 'folksy' writing, it also produced Yeats, Joyce, Synge and O'Casey.

Yeats, Synge and Joyce were, in their highly disparate and individual ways, closely involved with European literature, particularly with French. They, together with Samuel Beckett, form a discernible school which can certainly not be labelled 'English', nor indeed purely 'Irish', but which must be positively recognized as 'European'. It is wrong, therefore, to regard the Irish dramatic movement from 1898 to the present day as being Irish in a narrowly ethnic sense; and absurd to see it as a provincial offshoot of the British. It is arguable that the twentieth-century Irish theatre is in the European mainstream.

Note on dating
The year given against the title of a play is generally that of the first public performance, as this usually precedes publication. Where production was long delayed, or where a production is not known, the year of publication is given. Occasionally, the year of composition or completion of writing is given, and in such instances the reader's attention is drawn to the fact.

1
Inhospitable soil

1171–1649

Religious drama, John Bale, earliest colonial theatre, John Ogilby

An unacknowledged source quoted by the early twentieth-century scholar W. F. Dawson gives the year 1171 as that of the first organized dramatic performances in Ireland, when Henry II taught the Irish 'to take their part in miracle plays, masques, mummeries and tournaments'. This date is surprisingly soon after the Anglo-Norman invasion of 1169; one would have supposed that Henry II had rather more urgent matters on his mind in relation to the activities of his new Irish subjects. Be that as it may, there is no further record of plays of any kind until the fourteenth century. The fourteenth-century manuscript of the Eastertide processional play of *The Three Maries*, which belonged to the Church of St John I the Evangelist and was probably performed there, is now preserved in Marsh's Library, Dublin.

The Three Maries takes the form of the European liturgical play (in fact it should be described as one, for there is nothing specially Irish about it) in relating a well-known scriptural incident, in this case the visitation of the three Marys to the tomb, which they find empty and guarded by an angel; they tell their news to St Peter and St John, who confirm that Christ has risen, and the play ends with a joyful chorus – the *Te Deum*.

In 1891 part of a fifteenth-century morality play, now known as *The Pride of Life*, was discovered, written in the blank sections of the accounts for Holy Trinity Priory, the precursor of Christ Church Cathedral. As is usual in moralities, the characters are personifications – Health and Strength, Mirth, and Death; the King, Queen, Bishop and a Herald complete the cast. The manuscript was destroyed when the Public Records Office was burned during the Civil War of 1922.

In the later part of the fifteenth century Dublin followed the lead of the English cities of York, Chester, Coventry and Wakefield in presenting religious pageants at Corpus Christi, when the weather was most likely to be suitable for outdoor festivities. The city Corporation was the official sponsor, and each trade guild was made responsible for producing a scene from the Old or New Testament, and occasionally from the life of a saint. These 'processional' plays were mounted on carts, with the actors miming the stories as they moved through the streets. It is probable that as time went on dialogue was introduced, the waggons coming to rest in selected quarters of the city where the local inhabitants could gather round and listen to the words – as occurred at York, where the plays are still regularly revived in all their splendid simplicity. As no Dublin scripts survive, the theory has been put forward (by W. S. Clark) that these scenes were acted entirely in

9

dumb show. This seems unlikely in a city where the citizens have always been noted for their loquacity.

In Dublin, as in Britain, the guilds were deputed to enact stories which had some relevance to their own members' craft or trade. Thus the story of Noah was presented by 'Maryners, Vynters, Ship Carpendyres and Samountakers' – the latter ('salmon-takers') being the fishermen of the River Liffey. Presumably Noah laid in a quantity of wine to justify the participation of the vintners. The Twelve Apostles were symbolically represented by the 'Fisshers', and the Prophets were cast from the 'Marchauntes of Dublin', presumably because of their superior social standing. It was left to the 'Bouchers' to officiate at the crucifixion. Later in the fifteenth century somewhat similar performances were given on St George's Day. By the early sixteenth century it had become customary for the several guilds to invite the 'Chief Governour' of the city to see plays performed in St George's chapel. The attention given to St George indicates the way in which the Dublin drama took its cue from England: St Patrick is never mentioned. When vernacular dialogue was introduced into Irish theatrical performances, it was in English, which the vast proportion of the population outside Dublin would have been unable to understand. This underlines the completely foreign nature of the theatre at this period.

The Tudor conquest, which lasted from 1534 until the Battle of Kinsale in 1601, was as savage as the Cromwellian campaign half a century later. Performances of plays and interludes continued in Dublin through the war and famine, and in 1589 the Queen's Players and the Earl of Essex's players both appeared, in what was probably the first of many visits. Their repertoire is not known; and there is no record of any of Shakespeare's plays being performed in Ireland during the play-wright's lifetime.

The other towns of Anglo-Norman foundation, like Kilkenny and Youghal, though situated closer to the theatre of war, also let the turmoil pass them by. It was in Kilkenny and Youghal that the first formal theatrical presentations outside the capital took place. On the day of the accession of Mary I in 1563, a performance was given in Kilkenny of a play written and probably produced by John Bale (1495–1563), Bishop of Ossory, as a token to the supporters of the new Roman Catholic Queen that Protestantism would ultimately triumph. Bale's play is known as *God's Promises*. We have his own description of the event: '. . . the yonge men, in the forenoon, played a tragedye of God's promyses in the olde law, at the Market Cross, with organe plainges and songs very aptly . . .' – and in the afternoon: '. . . a comedie of Sanct Johan Baptiste's preaching of Christe's baptisynge and of his temptacion in the wildernesse; to the small contentacion of the prestes and other papistes there'.

The characters in *God's Promises* are 'Pater Coelestis, Justus Noah, Moses sanctus, Esias propheta, Adam primus homo, Abraham fideli, David rex pius, Joannes baptista, and Baleus proculator' – Bale must have spoken the prologue and epilogue himself. The play, which is in seven scenes, is written in a free though not unrhythmic verse, the larger proportion in rhyme. It is didactic in tone, and one admires the fortitude of the Kilkenny public in standing through such a production, for it is also extremely long-winded.

Open-air performances in Kilkenny were given at Corpus Christi and Mid-summer until the Rebellion of 1641 and the consequent closing of the theatres all over the British Isles. The scheme of presentation differed from the processional method favoured in Dublin. Stages were set up at vantage-points along the High Street, and were railed-off to prevent the crowd obstructing the action. The

3 John Bale. Shortly after his arrival in Ireland Bale began to encourage the performance of religious drama in English. Two of his own plays were performed in Kilkenny.

performers took their participation very seriously and, as in Dublin, the Corporation provided a substantial subsidy. The Kilkenny Corporation Records from 1580 to 1639 show successive entries concerning payment to actors, and for costumes and properties. New gloves for members of the Holy Family seem to be a major preoccupation:

> Patrick Morgan freren balife, You shall deliver James Krininge the sum 20s. Stg for the setting forth of the Maries and 16d. Stg for Six paire of Gloves for Christe, John Evangeliste, Mary Mother, and the other three Maryes, for which this shall be yor. Warrant the 9th of June 1584. Arthur Shee, Souvraine.

One of the last entries shows the Corporation's concern for the well-being of the players:

> Receaver of the Corporation Revenues faile nott to deliver and pay to Mary Roth Twentie Shillings Sterlg. which She disbursed for a Breckfaste which was for the Young Men that acted uppon the Stage uppon Corpus Christi day last 1637, for which this shalbe Yr. Warrant. Dated 8th July 1637. Jas. Cowley, Maior Kilkenny. Thos Archer.

In Youghal, Sir Richard Boyle, the 'Great' Earl of Cork, was an enthusiastic local patron. The plays – whatever they may have been – were performed indoors in the Tholsel, as we know from a record of 1620 describing how the building was almost wrecked by the large numbers of people trying to gain admittance. In 1635 the King's Players, the most important English company, performed at Youghal, having left London on account of an outbreak of plague.

The rise of Puritanism resulted in a decision of the Youghal town council in the same year to ban performance of plays in council property. It is interesting to note the general change in attitude over eighty years: at the beginning of the period a rabidly Protestant bishop used the medium of the drama as a means of spreading anti-Popish feeling, and thereby encouraged the annual theatrical festivities; at the end of the period, the overwhelming belief among extreme Protestants was that plays of their essence savoured of Popery, and that they should not be permitted to take place at all.

4 John Ogilby, who became known as the 'father of the Irish theatre'.

The establishment in 1633 of a resident court in Dublin Castle, with a Lord Deputy directly responsible to the reigning monarch, gave the city a political and cultural status which it had hitherto lacked. Charles I's Deputy was Thomas Wentworth (soon to become the Earl of Strafford), an energetic man much concerned for England's glory and also to satisfy his own social ambitions. He provided for entertainments at the Castle, and in the early 1630s engaged the services of a Scottish-born dancing master, John Ogilby (1600–1676), as tutor to his children. It has been suggested that Ogilby was brought over from London specifically to organize court theatricals, but this is unlikely, though his designation as 'gentleman of the household' was vague enough to include this duty.

It is probable that Ogilby immediately saw the potential for dramatic shows, not only in the court but also in the city at large. At this time the earlier type of religious drama still continued; the 'bachelors' of Trinity College and the students of 'the Inns' (the law schools) presented their own plays; there were the sporadic visits of companies from London; and the Lord Deputy's retainers sometimes entertained their master and his guests by producing plays in the Parliament House; the Mayor of Dublin presided at performances in the Tholsel. There was activity, but no organization; and there was no proper theatre building.

It seems that Ogilby himself raised the money to build Ireland's first theatre – which was to be the only theatre in the British Isles outside London. The site which he chose in Werburgh Street was almost opposite St Werburgh's Church, two hundred paces from the Castle, and the same distance from Christ Church Cathedral. The interior was designed on the Elizabethan plan, with a large forestage or apron and an inner stage which could be concealed by a curtain. Over this was a gallery which could be used by musicians, or for scenes requiring battlements or, indeed, Heaven. The Werburgh Street Theatre, unlike Southwark's famous Globe, was covered. W. S. Clark suggests that the floor of the small auditorium was raked, and that boxes were provided for the Lord Deputy and his retinue.

The same outbreak of plague which had encouraged the King's Players to visit Youghal made it easy for Ogilby to engage actors, and in the autumn of 1637 his theatre opened, its entire company recruited from London. Ogilby also engaged a dramatist, James Shirley (1596–1666), who probably felt that a paid position in Ireland was preferable to an uncertain career at home, where the Puritan element was becoming more and more influential. *The Royal Master*, the first play Shirley wrote for the Dublin theatre, was probably also the first play to be produced there.

On 28 February 1638 Ogilby was appointed Master of the Revels. The title was created by the Lord Deputy without a Royal patent, though, as will be seen, this was granted to Ogilby by Charles II thirty years later. Plays by Middleton, Fletcher and Jonson were performed, sometimes altered by Shirley, who also wrote prologues and epilogues, from the content of which we obtain some idea of what Ireland's first theatre was like. Attendances were not always high – a complaint to be often heard over the next one hundred and fifty years. Shirley wrote at least eight plays for Werburgh Street, but only one of them is of special interest, and that more in an historical than a theatrical sense.

St Patrick for Ireland (1639) is cleverly devised to appeal to the patriotic instincts of the Dublin public without giving offence to the Lord Deputy, who could afford to look indulgently upon the mildly nationalistic sentiments expressed in it. It is very much the work of the visitor to Ireland, ready to accept the local way of life, eager to praise whatever he found admirable, yet mindful all the time that he

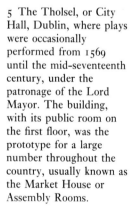

5 The Tholsel, or City Hall, Dublin, where plays were occasionally performed from 1569 until the mid-seventeenth century, under the patronage of the Lord Mayor. The building, with its public room on the first floor, was the prototype for a large number throughout the country, usually known as the Market House or Assembly Rooms.

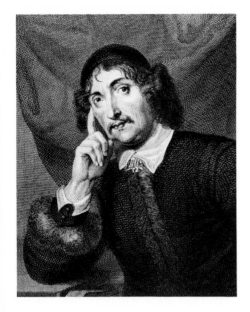

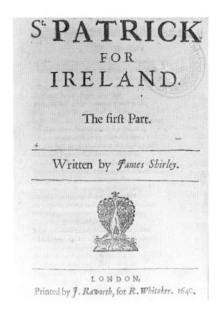

speaks from a superior standpoint as the representative of a master nation. The tone is completely 'un-Irish', though whether its hearers would have made such an observation is doubtful. The late nineteenth-century critic John Eglinton makes the point that by 1639 the 'Anglo-Irish' identified themselves closely with their adopted country – they were ready to take up arms against the English five years later – and any nationalistic sentiments (no matter how spurious on the part of the author) expressed by certain characters would have struck home.

The plot concerns the overthrow of the pagan religion (shown, with its adherents, as wildly ridiculous and barbaric) and the foundation of a Christian era of peace and plenty. There is an important secondary plot in which Emeria, daughter of Milcho, King Loegarius' deputy, is wooed by Corybreus (a character invented by Shirley). This story, or love-interest, is in the conventional vein of Jacobean drama, and characteristically ends with the lady murdering her suitor. There is a scene, taken directly from Patrician myth, in which the Saint is beset by serpents, and drives them off, forever ridding the country of everything reptilian.

Commentators have wondered how the serpents were represented. It is perfectly possible that they were portrayed by actors or by dancers, considering Ogilby's professional background. The scene may have been performed in the manner of a masque, a form of theatre fashionable at the time.

St Patrick for Ireland was the first Irish play of the modern theatre, albeit written by an Englishman. In seeking the first Irish playwright the claims of three authors should be considered. They are John Denham (1615–69), Richard Flecknoe (*fl.* 1656–64) and Henry Burnell (*fl.* 1641). Denham and Flecknoe, though of Irish birth, spent most of their lives in England. Denham is remembered as a poet rather than as a playwright. His best play, *The Sophy*, set in Persia, was acted at Blackfriars in 1641. In spite of some bloodcurdling incidents and a corpse-strewn finale which recalls *The Duchess of Malfi*, the play succeeds in being amazingly dull. Dullness, according to Dryden, was the quality of Flecknoe's work also. His only play to be acted was *Love's Dominion*, which came out at the theatre in Lincoln's Inn Fields in 1664.

Burnell's claim to be regarded as the earliest Irish playwright is stronger, for his only extant play, *Landgartha*, was performed in Dublin, and may have been

6, 7 *St Patrick for Ireland* was printed in London in the year following its first Dublin performance. It is the earliest known play on an Irish theme. *Left* The play's author, James Shirley, who was in Dublin from 1636 to 1640.

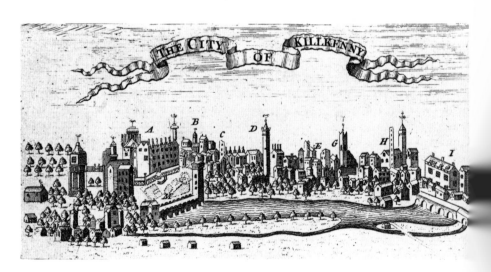

8 The earliest extant Irish
playbill.

expressly written for Werburgh Street. It contains one Irish character – Marisa, 'a humorous gentlewoman', some dialogue which may be taken as Irish, and some topical Irish allusions. It was performed on St Patrick's Day (17 March) 1639, and clearly was intended as no more than entertainment. Described by the author as an 'ancient story', it is set in Norway.

Marisa and her husband provide most of the comic interest, and even perform an Irish country dance – 'the whip of Dunboyne'; this has the same function as the mechanicals' dances in Shakespearian comedy. Marisa is dressed in 'an Irish gowne, tuck'd up to mid-legge, with a broad basket-hilt sword on'. W. S. Clark surmises that this is a satire on the native Irish squire. It is not impossible that *travesti* was intended, and as we must suppose there were no actresses in the company, the joke would have been fortified by casting a burly actor in the part.

Landgartha was one of the last, if not the last, play to be acted at Werburgh Street. The theatre had been in action for barely four years when it was closed by the Lords Justices due to the Cromwellian regime.

During the interregnum some troupes of English strolling players, presuming that the authorities would be less watchful in Ireland, visited provincial towns. Dr Peter Kavanagh has drawn attention to the incidence of religious plays written and performed by Jesuit scholars within their colleges in Kilkenny, Cashel and New Ross. One of these plays, *Titus; or, The Palme of Christian Courage*, provides the earliest known Irish playbill, printed in Waterford in 1644 for a performance given in Latin in Kilkenny.

The only other significant theatrical event of the period is the publication, also in Kilkenny, of a play called *The Tragedie of Cola's Furie; or, Lirenda's Miserie*, by Henry Burkhead (1645). 'Lirenda' is an anagram of 'Ireland', and Cola is the personification of perfidious Albion. This ill-constructed drama is little more than political wish-fulfillment, showing Ireland's enemies being tortured or murdered on the stage. C. G. Duggan in *The Stage Irishman* gives the personifications as follows: the character Theodoric is intended for Eóin Ruadh O'Neill, Guyroa for The Maguire, Pitho for Sir William Parsons, Berosus for Sir John Borlace, Osirus for the Duke of Ormonde, Meneus for Lord Mountgarret, Clanbrick for Crawford, and Cola for Sir Charles Coote. Coote and Borlace are still accorded the villain's roles in the popular Irish view of history, while O'Neill is one of the great heroes.

9 Kilkenny was the scene of annual religious pageant-plays from 1553 until the Rebellion of 1641. They were presented out-of-doors at a number of points between the Castle and the Cathedral.

2
French polish in a sink of sin

1662–1700

Roger Boyle, Thomas Southerne, the Smock Alley Theatre

In 1660 Charles II was restored to the throne after the dismal eighteen-year Protectorate of Oliver Cromwell. The ban on theatres and theatre-going was lifted, but in the place of the fifteen or so playhouses which had flourished in London from Elizabethan times up to the interregnum, only two, those managed by Thomas Killigrew and William Davenant, were opened to the public. Both, in time, were to provide a ready platform for Irish writers and actors.

Londoners had lost the theatre-going habit, though the court circle, certain fashionable or well-to-do persons and the students of the law schools provided a small but attentive public. The new theatre buildings were closed to the elements, painted scenery was used, and women instead of boys took the female parts. As the court had spent its years of exile in France, it was natural that it should bring back a taste for things French. Corneille was still the most esteemed playwright, though Racine's reputation was growing; the comedies of Molière were something quite new and somewhat alarming in their covert criticism of authority. Shakespeare seemed altogether old-fashioned; Beaumont and Fletcher, and Shirley, were still acceptable; but it was some time before a new school of British dramatists emerged, championed by Dryden, whose *Essay of Dramatic Poesie* appeared in 1668.

The same year saw the publication of two new plays by a young Irish author who had been in France, Roger Boyle (Baron Broghill). Boyle's first play, *Altemera*, had been given a private performance in Dublin in 1662, and may be regarded as one of the very earliest in the 'Restoration' mode.

Boyle was born at Lismore, Co. Waterford, in 1621, the third son of the 'Great' Earl of Cork, and brother of the Robert Boyle who was to become the scientist celebrated as the originator of 'Boyle's Law'. In 1638–9 he was in Paris where he saw plays by Corneille – possibly even Joseph Rutter's English version of *Le Cid*. He then spent two years in England, and was received at the court of Charles I 'with respect and delight'. He married Lady Margaret Howard.

Returning to Ireland in 1641, Boyle proved a ruthless associate of Oliver Cromwell in the suppression of Catholicism, but after Cromwell's death, impatient with Parliament's lack of purpose, he returned his support to the Royalist interest. He ingratiated himself so well with Charles II that he was created Earl of Orrery, a barony in north Cork. He became one of the Lords Justices of Ireland, and President of Munster. His mobility of political allegiance recalls a celebrated clergyman of the same period: 'For whatsoever King shall reign,/I'll be the Vicar of Bray still!' However, the same could be said of Dryden, and many others.

It was shortly after the Restoration that Boyle wrote *Altemera* (later retitled

10 Roger Boyle, who introduced rhymed tragedy.

11 Title page of the second volume of Boyle's plays.

THE DRAMATICK
WORKS
OF
ROGER BOYLE
EARL of ORRERY.

VOLUME II.

CONTAINING
HEROD THE GREAT.
ALTEMIRA.
GUZMAN, *a Comedy*.
ALSO
AS YOU FIND IT, *a Comedy*,
By CHARLES late Earl of *Orrery*.

LONDON:
Printed for R. DODSLEY, in *Pall-Mall.*
M.DCC.XXXIX.

The Generall) on the suggestion of Charles II, who passed the manuscript to Killigrew (manager of the King's Players). The private Dublin performance already referred to followed when Killigrew proved dilatory and did not put it into rehearsal.

Boyle sent his next play, *Henry the Fifth*, to Davenant, manager of the Duke's Players, in 1662, but it was not performed until two years later. It was reasonably successful, and that is probably why Killigrew at last decided to give the first public performances of *The Generall*. Boyle greatly enjoyed the praise lavished on him by the court circle, and by those who hoped through his influence to gain access to it.

In 1665 *Mustapha*, a play set in Hungary during the Turkish conquest, was produced, and then Charles II commanded a further historical work, *The Black Prince*: this failed. *Tryphon* (1668) did not do much better. Boyle then turned to the writing of comedies, with *Guzman* (1669) and *Mr Anthony* (1671), but these plays fared as disappointingly, and Samuel Pepys wrote in his Diary that *Guzman* was 'very ordinary' – a kind criticism. Of *Tryphon* he said that the play possessed 'the very same design, on words and sense and plot, as every one of his plays have'. Boyle's later plays were not acted.

In spite of his subsequent lack of success with audiences, and an undeniable monotony of style, Boyle has the distinction of being the first playwright in the English language to adopt the rules of French heroic drama. In introducing Cornelian rhymed tragedy, he started a fashion which was followed assiduously by Dryden and many other British playwrights. The recurring themes of the conflict of love and duty, of honour and passion, became inseperable from the idea of stage tragedy, and lengthy tirades in which characters publicly debated the merits of their inmost feelings replaced the dramatic action of earlier plays.

The trouble is that such high-flown verbiage can become extremely boring, and when allied to speeches descriptive of events which have occurred offstage (usually delivered by messengers, or persons bearing letters which then have to be read out) tedium can become unbearable, especially with inexperienced actors – and most actors were inexperienced, after an eighteen-year-long interval.

Mustapha is Boyle's most interesting play. The Sultan of Turkey, Solyman, besieges the city of Buda; the Queen of Hungary, Isabella, and her retinue visit the Turkish camp to treat for peace. Solyman's sons Mustapha and Zanger (who do not share the same mother) both fall in love with Isabella; a moral code dictates that each present the other's suit to her. Zanger's mother Roxolana, determined that her son shall obtain the Hungarian throne by marriage, falsely accuses Mustapha of treachery, and Solyman has him executed. Zanger heroically kills himself rather than dishonour his stepbrother; Solyman banishes Roxolana, and Isabella immures herself in a convent.

Pepys said that *Mustapha* was 'exceedingly well written'. Nahum Tate hailed the play as a model of how a tragedy should be constructed, but Dryden was critical of the ending, believing that it should close with the death of Zanger, thus preserving a greater unity of action. That critics of such eminence should take *Mustapha* so seriously shows the high regard in which the new heroic drama was held: certainly there is no hint in their comments that they found the play risible.

Roger Boyle died at Castlemartyr, Co. Cork, in 1679. He is ever associated in the Irish mind with the cruelty of the Cromwellian campaign, though it was his wish to be remembered as a man of letters.

While most of Boyle's plays received their first production in London, where their author liked to keep himself in the eye of the King, official duties required him to be in Dublin, and indeed he took an active interest in the revival of the Dublin theatre. John Ogilby had become a publisher and bookseller in London, but at the time of the Restoration was engaged in the preparation of street-decorations and civic pageantry for the coronation. This occupation may have prevented him from noticing Davenant's petition to Charles II to be appointed Master of the Revels in Ireland, and for the exclusive right to build and operate a theatre in Dublin. When Ogilby became aware of Davenant's undoubtedly under-hand application, which Charles had granted, he requested the King to reconsider the position, drawing His Majesty's attention to the fact that Charles I's Lord Deputy had bestowed this title upon himself, Ogilby, as long ago as 1637. A complicated court intrigue followed, resulting in the King's recognition of the unfairness of Davenant's petition, and the rescinding of his appointment and reinstatement of Ogilby. Here we have the entertaining spectacle of a British monarch adjudicating between rival Scottish and English claimants for an Irish incumbency.

It is interesting to note that Ogilby's new warrant permitted greater powers to the Master of the Revels than heretofore. To himself, his heirs and assignees was granted 'full and soul power licence and authoritie to erect and build one or more Theatres in what place or places to him shall seeme most fitt and convenient in our Citie of Dublin or elsewhere in our said Kingdome of Ireland'. Ogilby thus obtained the right to licence other companies or individuals to open theatres or perform anywhere in the whole island.

The patent was granted in May 1661, but it was more than a year before the new theatre was ready. When it opened in October 1662, it had the distinction of being the first purpose-built 'Restoration' theatre in the British Isles, those in London having been remodelled earlier structures. Its correct title was 'Theatre Royal', but it came to be known as 'the theatre in Smock Alley', or simply 'Smock Alley', from the name of the narrow street in which it was situated. Much was made, by those with lingering puritan sympathies, of the unsavouriness of the location, which was said to be 'a sink of sin' where persons met to make 'lewd bargains'. The exterior, to judge from the only surviving print, was somewhat forbidding, ironically resembling one of the grim stone chapels or meeting-houses favoured by the opponents of theatrical and musical enterprise. The rear portion of the church of St Michael and St John which now occupies the site is not unlike the old theatre in elevation, though it cannot be supposed that more than random stonework from the theatre was incorporated in the church fabric.

The stage was about thirty feet in depth, half being hidden when the curtain was lowered, the other half forming a forestage. It was lighted by floats (wicks floating in a trough of oil) and candelabra. At both sides of the forestage a door led behind the scenes, and over each door was a latticed aperture from which characters in a play looked down upon the stage-setting, as it were from a window overlooking a garden or town-square. When not required to represent Juliet's balcony or Titania's bower, these chambers were let out as boxes in which persons who did not wish to be recognized – such as the ladies of the town, or clergymen – could sit concealed by the latticework. The theatre historian W. S. Clark has shown that the term 'lattice' (or 'lettice' as it was sometimes spelled on the playbills) was unique to Dublin, as was the practice of actors describing the stage area as 'east upper' and 'west lower', etc. As in some of the Elizabethan playhouses in London, the musicians were placed in a gallery over the proscenium arch. The auditorium consisted of a pit and three galleries – the lowest containing the boxes being the most expensive, the uppermost traditionally accommodating those of low degree but high enthusiasm.

12 The only surviving picture showing the exterior of the Theatre Royal, Smock Alley, Dublin, the first 'Restoration' theatre in the British Isles. The Smock Alley company was in existence for over a hundred years, and produced many fine players.

The first play presented at Smock Alley was a revival of Fletcher's *Wit Without Money*, which Ogilby had produced previously at Werburgh Street. He was evidently anxious to open the theatre as early as possible in the season, and in so doing disappointed the playgoers who expected the new stage-scenery to be ready. *Othello* was also given, but there is no record as to whether the 'painted scenes' were yet available, though bizarre costumes are described. Then a Mrs Katherine Philips, who, from her letters, appears to have been a person of astonishing social as well as literary energy, was encouraged by Boyle to translate a play by Corneille, *La Mort de Pompey*. Mrs Philips was known in London as the poet 'Orinda', and in Dublin founded a 'Society of Friendship' which probably gained its inspiration from the *précieux* circle of the Marquise de Rambouillet in Paris, which had been satirized by Molière in *Les Précieuses Ridicules* three years earlier.

Boyle, then one of the Lords Justices and the principal public figure next to the Lord Lieutenant, the Duke of Ormonde, was so pleased with *Pompey* that he gave £100 to Ogilby for the acquisition of 'Roman and Egyptian habits'. This was the first direct English-language translation of a Cornelian tragedy to be performed in Ireland or England after the Restoration – but Corneille might have been somewhat surprised by the production, for Mrs Philips had introduced songs and dances between the scenes – the former composed by members of her accomplished circle, the latter choreographed by Ogilby.

With the exception of Boyle's *Altemera* (or *The Generall*) and Mrs Philips' *Pompey*, Corneille's *Nicomède* and Quinault's *Agrippa* (none of which can be reasonably be described as original), the only new plays known to have been produced in Ireland between the Restoration of 1660 and the Rebellion of 1680 were *Hic et Ubique; or, The Humours of Dublin* by Richard Head, *The Merchant of Dublin* by Ogilby, and *Belphegor* by John Wilson. This illustrates how far Dublin depended upon London for its stage-material. It was also dependent upon the London theatres for its players – all the leading actors, and almost all of those who took the supporting roles, being imported by Ogilby.

Ogilby's business interests necessitated frequent sojourns in London, and after 1669 he did not return to Ireland, leaving the management of Smock Alley to the Deputy Master of the Revels, his relative William Morgan. In the same year, that enlightened patron of the arts, the Duke of Ormonde, resigned as Lord Lieutenant and was replaced by the dour Baron Roberts, who so disapproved of the Theatre that he had it closed. This melancholy situation was redressed a year later, when Charles II appointed Lord Berkeley as his representative, but Smock Alley received another blow when on 26 December 1670 the galleries collapsed during a performance of *Bartholomew Fair* in the presence of the Lord Lieutenant, killing four people and injuring many others. This mishap was seen by the puritan element in Dublin as a just manifestation of the Lord's wrath upon the players and playgoers, particularly as Jonson's fifty-year-old play satirized nonconformist attitudes.

Morgan joined Ogilby in London in 1675, leaving as Manager at Smock Alley Joseph Ashbury, an English actor who had been entrusted with most of the leading parts there, and a new era of enterprise began in Ireland. Ogilby died in London in the following year. Though latterly he was separated from Irish affairs, his earlier achievements in Dublin earned this redoubtable Scotsman the title 'father of the Irish theatre'.

If at this time the impetus for theatrical endeavour in Ireland still came from the other side of the Irish Sea, the post-Restoration period marks the beginning of a movement of talent in the opposite direction. Roger Boyle had already con tributed his series of engagingly pretentious plays which tickled the fancy of an effete London society. A far better playwright was Thomas Southerne, whose *Oroonoko* (1696) may be accounted one of the great tragedies of the era.

Thomas Southerne was born in 1660 in what was then an outlying village to 16 the north-west of Dublin, Oxmantown. He was educated at Trinity College, and subsequently went to London to study law, but gradually found himself drawn into the literary coterie presided over by Dryden. He had the satisfaction of seeing his first play, *The Loyal Brother; or, The Persian Prince*, produced at Drury Lane when he was only twenty-two. James II, to whom the play was dedicated, presented him with a commission in the army. Southerne was far less pragmatic in his political affiliations than Boyle, and with the 1688 revolution found himself out of favour. He resigned his commission and for the rest of his life devoted himself entirely to writing.

His second play, *The Disappointment; or, The Mother of Fashion* (1684), was, like his first, a tragedy, though he described it simply as 'a play'. Both are deficient in the studied moral tone of Boyle's dramas, and this is to their advantage. In 1691 he turned to comedy with *Sir Antony Love; or, The Rambling Lady*, set at 'Mompelier', where the lively Lucia disguises herself as a young man journeying in France; this deception creates several amusing situations of a mildly licentious nature which caused the author's comedies to be ill-regarded in later eras when audiences professed to more delicate tastes.

The Lover's Excuse; or, Cuckolds Make Themselves (1692) was less popular, though informed contemporaries, including Dryden, thought it a superior work. *The Maid's Last Prayer; or, Anything Rather Than Fail* was the final comedy in the trilogy.

Southerne's first major success came in 1694 with the production of his tragedy in blank verse and prose, *The Fatal Marriage; or, The Innocent Adultery* – the title proves his awareness that public interest could be aroused by a hint of the scandalous; but there is little that can be described as salacious in the play. Were it not for *Oroonoko*, this would be considered his greatest work in the theatre, and it remains one of the most important conventional tragedies of the period. It concerns the supposedly widowed Isabella who, believing her husband to have died in battle, remarries, and kills herself when he returns unharmed. Garrick rewrote this play as *Isabella*, with the comic sub-plot removed.

Oroonoko; or, The Royal Slave (1696) has been reprinted in several modern 15 collections of seventeenth- and eighteenth-century theatre, and deservedly. It is probably the earliest play in English to take a reforming stance, and while didacticism can have a damaging effect on drama, here the 'message' is skilfully embedded in the action. Oroonoko, a West Indian chief sold into slavery, meets his wife Imoinda who has suffered the same fate and is about to become the concubine of the white colonial Governor. Imoinda entreats Oroonoko to kill her, but he cannot bring himself to do so, and she kills herself. Oroonoko stabs the Governor to death before committing suicide.

If the anti-slavery theme breaks new ground by introducing an overtly social purpose in a stage play, the treatment of the setting, Surinam, is also unique. Foreign locations had previously been mere exotic adjuncts to historical subjects. Southerne obtained his plot from Aphra Behn's novel *The History of the Royal Slave* which was based on her own experiences and observations in the Indies. The torrid colonial atmosphere and genuine sense of contemporaneous happenings beyond the seas combine to render the tragedy quite plausible – which is not the case with most heroic dramas. As in *The Fatal Marriage* there is a comic

13 Nahum Tate's version of *King Lear*, with its happy ending, was preferred to Shakespeare's for at least a century.

14 Title page of Nicholas Brady's *The Rape* of 1692.

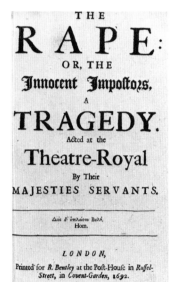

sub-plot – omitted without loss in some editions – yet it is amusing in its own right and might have made an actable afterpiece. It concerns Charlotte and Lucy Weldon, who have come out to Surinam in search of husbands.

Southerne's other plays are *The Fate of Capua* (1700), a spare tragedy without any comic relief; *The Spartan Dame* (1719) and *Money the Mistress* (1723), a tragedy and a comedy respectively. None of these is of great interest. He was greatly admired by his English contemporaries, including Pope, who praised his Irish wit, and Dryden, who declared him to be the equal of Otway (which he surely was not). He seems to have been a congenial companion, though unusually careful of his money. He drove a very hard bargain with the theatre managers, and charged exorbitantly for prologues – a source of ready income for inventive writers over two centuries.

Southerne wrote with certain players in mind. He took advantage of the vogue for frequent changes of scenery, and for incidental music. *Oroonoko* stands among the half-dozen best tragedies of the age, and it is certainly the most original.

Two Irish-born dramatists whose names are for ever inextricably linked on account of their collaboration on the metrical version of the *Psalms of David* – 'appointed to be sung in churches' – are Nahum Tate (1652–1715) and Nicholas Brady (1659–1726). Except for two early plays, *Brutus of Alba* (1678) and *The Loyal General* (1679) – both produced soon after his arrival in London from Dublin – Tate's work for the theatre consists of adaptations of earlier (and superior) dramatists. He is best remembered for Pope's mocking portrait of him in *The Dunciad*, and as the author of the revised version of *King Lear*, at the end of which those characters who remain, live happily ever after. *The History of King Lear* was preferred to Shakespeare's version for at least a century, and is skilfully adapted to the French-polished taste of the times. Tate's introductory remarks to *The History of King Lear* are audacious:

> 'Twas my good fortune to light on one Expedient to rectify what was wanting in the Regularity and Probability of the Tale, which was to run through the Whole, as Love betwixt Edgar and Cordelia; that never chang'd Word with each other in the Original. This renders Cordelia's indifference, and her Father's Passion in the first scene, probable . . .

Nicholas Brady was born in Bandon, Co. Cork, and though he went to Westminster School, he returned to Ireland, and did not leave it to settle in London until he was in his thirties. The fact that he was in holy orders did not deter him from writing a play entitled *The Rape; or, The Innocent Imposters* (1692), a consequential drama in blank verse set in a medieval 'Gothish' court.

Tate and Brady are typical of an increasing number of Irish writers in seeking to make a living in London. While Irish writers were beginning to find acceptance in England, Joseph Ashbury continued the tradition begun by Ogilby of running the Dublin theatre on English lines. It was said of him that he was 'esteemed not only the best actor but also the best teacher in the three kingdoms'. If we assume that the term 'teacher' signifies what we should now call 'director', then it is not surprising that several unknown actors whom he brought over and trained in Dublin found favour when they returned to Drury Lane and Covent Garden. Some of his 'discoveries' were, however, Irishmen, among them Robert Wilks and James Quin. Ashbury was also responsible for what the eighteenth-century historian William Chetwood called 'the Dublin school of clear and bold elocution'.

In 1677 the Duke of Ormonde was reappointed Lord Lieutenant, much to the joy of the actors. It was a tribute to the standard of Ashbury's theatrical adminis-

tration, as much as to the Duke's enterprising patronage, that the Smock Alley players were invited to perform in Oxford. Ormonde was Chancellor of Oxford University, and when the King's Players disgraced themselves during a theatrical season there and were banned from returning, Ormonde suggested that they should be replaced by the troupe which had pleased him so much in Dublin. As it turned out, the first 'foreign' season by an Irish company brought honour to the players, to their noble and learned patron, and to their country.

The visit lasted three weeks, with two performances almost every day. It is not known what plays were produced, but they were probably the staple Shakespeare from the repertoire; almost certainly none of the original Smock Alley scripts or French adaptations was presented.

The possibility of a return visit to Oxford vanished when the King's Players were pardoned and readmitted to perform in the University; but in July 1681 a company of thirty from Smock Alley set out for Scotland, under the patronage of the Earl of Roscommon. So enthusiastic was the response that the company remained in Edinburgh until November, long after the date when the Dublin season should have opened. Some performances were given before royalty, and Ashbury was engaged to direct a private performance of Racine's *Mithridate* at Holyrood House, in which the future Queen Anne, then a girl of sixteen, played the part of Senandra. Nothing more clearly indicates how closely the players were identified with their royal or vice-regal patrons in Ireland, Scotland and England alike, and how genuine was the interest of the court in involving itself in theatrical affairs.

The prosperity of the Dublin company continued until the death of Charles II and the appointment of the Earl of Clarendon as Lord Lieutenant. The absence

15, 16 A scene from Thomas Southerne's tragedy *Oroonoko*, set on the island of Surinam *(left, above)*. Its contemporary theme and social intent make it unique among plays of its genre. Southerne *(top)* was the earliest of a long line of Irish dramatists to receive a university education at Trinity College, Dublin.

17 The 1st Duke of Ormonde *(above)* was a noted patron of the arts. During his terms of office as Lord Lieutenant the Smock Alley Theatre flourished.

St. Stephen's-Green
OR THE
Generous LOVERS.
A
COMEDY,
As it is Acted at
The Theatre - Royal,
IN
DUBLIN.
Written by *WILL. PHILIPS*, Esq;

DUBLIN,
Printed by *John Brocas* in *School-House-Lane* ;
And are to be Sold by the Bookfellers, 1700.

18 Title page of *St Stephen's Green*. William Phillips' plays were produced in Dublin; had he entered the more competitive London theatrical scene he might have become a first-rate dramatist.

of official local encouragement under the new regime, and the subsequent wars fought between James II and William of Orange on Irish soil, resulted in poor attendances, and eventually in closure.

At Christmas 1691 Ashbury tested the public mood by organizing a private performance of *Othello*. Evidently he was satisfied that the time had come to re-open the theatre, and three months later the Smock Alley playbills proclaimed that *Othello* would be the first play in a new season. Ashbury must also have been satisfied that the young Irishman who had played the part of the Moor was talented and skilful enough to try the role professionally. This was Robert Wilks, who had performed small parts as an amateur or 'gentleman', but found the lure of the stage too compelling to disregard, even in these sparse times for the theatre, and so gave up his position in the civil service. He stayed with the company till 1693 when he was taken on at Drury Lane, and spent the rest of his life acting alternately in London and Dublin. His name was to become inseparably linked with that of George Farquhar.

The century, and the reign of William III, closed with a fair degree of prosperity at Smock Alley. However, the only play known to have been written by an Irishman for an Irish audience was *St Stephen's Green; or, The Generous Lovers* by William Phillips of Derry. A typical minor comedy of manners, it has the distinction of being set in contemporary Dublin, and its dedication reveals that the author was very much aware of the absence of any Irish identity in the work of Irish playwrights.

Phillips wrote another play on an Irish theme, the rather turgid drama *Hibernia Freed*. It is a pity that he did not attempt another Irish comedy, for *St Stephen's Green* displays a talent which would certainly have developed with experience, and Ireland badly needed a resident playwright to interpret or satirize the national scene. As it was, the year which saw the first production of *St Stephen's Green* at Smock Alley found William Congreve at work on *The Way of the World* and George Farquhar completing *The Constant Couple*: but Congreve and Farquhar were writing in London. The most talented Irish playwrights automatically offered their work to London managements; and this was to continue, with only a few significant departures, for the next two hundred years.

3
The lure of London

1693–1707

William Congreve and George Farquhar

As has been seen, the professional theatre was securely established in Ireland by the final quarter of the seventeenth century. English writers and actors had helped to create it; in the course of time Irish men and women took an increasingly important part in its development and continuance.

Critics over the centuries have deemed it strange that tyro dramatists like Southerne, Tate or Brady should have commanded almost instantaneous recognition upon their arrival in London. Yet Southerne, Tate and others were theatregoers in Dublin, and regarded theatregoing as a natural activity. Indeed, as 'the College' provided a sizable and partisan section of the Dublin audience, it would have been extraordinary had young men of literary understanding not attended the theatre during their student days.

The span of fourteen years between 1693 and 1707 contains the first performances of all the plays William Congreve and George Farquhar ever wrote. All their plays were first produced in London; both men had Irish Protestant backgrounds and both went to Trinity College, Dublin (though not at the same time), yet it is unlikely that they ever met, so different were their private circumstances. Different, too, were their attitudes to playwriting. Congreve was a gentleman, and the theatre was to him a diverting pastime – a pastime easily relinquished when the public failed to respond enthusiastically enough to his greatest play. Farquhar came from a clerical background, and entered the theatre as a professional; he never experienced the social confidence that financial independence would have brought.

William Congreve was long honoured in the pantheon of Irish playwrights, until the twentieth-century critic Andrew Malone revealed (without any very painstaking research) that he was born in Yorkshire on 24 January 1670. This caused understandable dismay among Hibernophiles who had heretofore claimed that the playwright was an Irishman by birth. (It is interesting, however, to note that he is still classed as 'Irish' in the *Revels History of English Drama*, 1975, and in *World Playwrights*, 1978.) His early education was probably at the Free School in Youghal, where his father had a commission in the army. The family moved to Carrickfergus and thence to Kilkenny where, in 1681, William was enrolled at Kilkenny College, his father having joined the regiment of the Duke of Ormonde. II

Kilkenny was then the most prosperous and sophisticated inland city in Ireland, and for this the Ormondes were totally responsible, holding ducal sway over matters civil and military, patronizing the College, and also the visits of the Smock Alley players. When William Congreve entered the College at the age of twelve, Jonathan Swift was in his final year; the two became and were to remain friends for the rest of their lives.

19 William Congreve, after Sir Godfrey Kneller.

Congreve studied classical literature assiduously. The scholars produced plays, but Congreve did not take part; he was said to have been of shy disposition and slow of speech. The scholars also attended the plays presented by visiting professionals at Kilkenny Castle. After he went to Trinity (in 1686) Congreve 'frequented the Playhouse', and is on record as regularly neglecting the Saturday afternoon study-period when there was a performance at Smock Alley. Plays by Brome, Dryden, Otway and the recently graduated Southerne were in the repertoire, and the actors Dogget, Norris, Quin, and Wilks were members of the company. An intriguing insight into Congreve's interest in the theatre is provided by a list of books which he bought at this time: Horace's *Ars Poetica*, Dryden's *Essay of Dramatic Poesy*, and Hadelin's *Whole Art of the Stage*.

As a result of the rebellion of 1689 the students were advised to leave the College, and Congreve went to visit his well-to-do relatives in England. There he remained, entering the Middle Temple in London in 1691. He saw plays by Etherege, Shadwell and Wycherley, became acquainted with Dryden (for whom he made verse translations), and published a work of prose fiction, *Incognita* (1692). A hesitant showing of a half-written play to Dryden caused considerable fluttering in the heart of that elderly dramatist, who immediately advised upon the editing of certain scenes, and the rearrangement of others. Thomas Southerne was also helpful, and introduced the young playwright to Thomas Davenant, lessee of the Theatre Royal, Drury Lane, who resolved to present his play, *The Old Bachelor*, as soon as possible.

21

The murder of one actor in the company, and the natural death of two others, delayed production until 1693. Anne Bracegirdle spoke the Prologue (Southerne wrote another, for publication) and played Araminta; Thomas Betterton was the eponymous hero; and Thomas Dogget, with whom Congreve had been friendly in Dublin, took the comic part of Fondlewife. Colley Cibber, the actor-manager, said that it was to Dogget that the play 'probably owed the greatest part of its success'. It ran for fourteen nights, a record for the London theatre, and went through three printings in four weeks. The Earl of Cork wrote to Congreve's parents at Lismore: 'Your son's play was acted on Thursday last, and was by all hearers applauded to be the best that has been acted for many years.'

Though Dryden and Southerne were probably responsible for the play's construction and for the neat arrangement of its sub-plots, the comedy is wholly Congreve's. It abounds in lively metaphor, and contains a notion that is novel – surprisingly, considering the innumerable changes already rung on the sexual theme by Restoration playwrights – of the young gallant (Vainlove) who, though irresistible to women and relishing the pursuit of those who languish for him, abandons the pursuit to another (Bellmour) almost at the moment of consummation.

Few new playwrights can have been as greatly encouraged by the theatrical establishment, or as well served by the actors, as was Congreve for *The Old Bachelor*. Almost the same cast appeared in his second play *The Double Dealer* (1694). Dryden wrote a prologue, Betterton played Maskwell, Dogget was Sir Paul Plyant, and Mrs Bracegirdle (with whom Congreve was in love, and for whom he henceforth created all his heroines, comic or tragic) was Cynthia. The satire in this comedy is more bitter, less exuberant, than that of *The Old Bachelor*, and the play was not quite so popular, demonstrating how well the public had recognized the originality of his first work. However, Queen Mary was amused, and a large following saw nothing wrong in agreeing with her. When the Queen died some months later, Congreve wrote a panegyric which earned him £100 from

20

the sorrowing William III. This, and several other poems on public matters, consolidated his position as a rising writer in the Whig interest. He was given, in due course, a number of *sine cure* appointments (the first was the commissionership for Hackney Coaches) but, contrary to general belief, he was never more than comfortably off until the final years of his life.

In 1695 Betterton left Drury Lane and founded his own company at the theatre in Lincoln's Inn Fields. The season opened with Congreve's new comedy *Love for Love*. If any debt of gratitude was due to Betterton for bringing out his first two plays, Congreve now repaid that debt in full. *Love for Love* is the most easily entertaining and actable of his comedies; and if *The Way of the World* surpasses it in intensity of wit and subtlety of characterization (as indeed it surpasses any comedy of the period written in English), *Love for Love* was nevertheless received with acclamation and ran for thirteen nights on its first showing.

Congreve made an arrangement with Betterton to supply one play a year 'if his health permitted'. The first production resulting from this contract was of an unexpected nature. *The Mourning Bride* is described as a tragedy, but is more in the vein of lachrymose melodrama. Audiences were naturally surprised that Congreve could write convincingly in this genre. Indeed, *The Mourning Bride* became the most frequently performed of his plays during his lifetime, and held the stage until the late nineteenth century. It follows the pattern set by earlier Restoration writers of tragedy in taking a highly moral standpoint – a curious reversal for writers whose comedies were often intemperately licentious. The rather staid blank verse is relieved by rhyming couplets and triplets in moments

20–1 *Left* A scene from Congreve's satiric comedy *The Double Dealer*, a play much admired by Mary II when first produced in London by Thomas Davenant in 1694. *Right: The Old Bachelor*, Congreve's first play, and one of his most successful. Fondlewife became a popular role with the leading English comedian Samuel Foote, seen here at centre.

22

of tension and at the conclusion of scenes, a trait inherited from the Elizabethans. The setting is exotic – Granada; and the plot operatic – though far less complicated than those of his comedies. The play contains the often mis-quoted couplet:

Heav'n has no Rage like Love to Hatred turn'd
Nor Hell a Fury like a Woman scorn'd.

Congreve did not keep his promise to produce a play a year, even though his health was good, and Betterton had to wait till 1700 before *The Way of the World* had been revised and re-polished enough to satisfy its author's sense of perfection. In the meantime Congreve had been reading other authors' plays with a view to new productions at Lincoln's Inn Fields. It pleased him to be able to help Charles Hopkins of Derry to have *Pyrrhus* and *Boadicea* performed – but if these were among the more promising works reviewed, the standard of submissions must have been low. He also gave much time to refuting the arguments of the Rev. Jeremy Collier in *A Short View of the Immorality and Profaneness of the English Stage*. Congreve's reply – *Amendments to Mr Collier's False and Imperfect Citations* – is disappointing, dealing with the broader issues. Some passages in *The Double Dealer* were altered as a result of Collier's attack, and this rather weakens Congreve's argument.

At some stage during this period Congreve travelled to Dublin with Southerne for both to receive, belatedly, their Masters' degrees. It is supposed that he visited his parents in Ireland on a number of occasions – his father had left the army and had become chief agent to the Earl of Cork and Burlington, elder brother of the playwright Roger Boyle.

The Way of the World (1700) was not as successful as Congreve's earlier and, admittedly, lesser plays. Whether the public had been unduly influenced against him by the Collier controversy, or the first production was deficient in some respect, or audiences simply found the plot too difficult to follow and the ending too perfunctory, remains unclear. It is usually suggested that the poor response resulted in Congreve's forsaking the stage – but he did not forsake it entirely. The following year he produced the masque *The Judgement of Paris*, and in 1707 undertook a brief foray into management with Vanbrugh at the Haymarket Theatre, London. His libretto for Handel's opera *Semele* was published in 1710. It may be that he simply wished to devote his time to other matters – the minor government posts which he held, and the enjoyment of membership of the Kit-Kat Club.

Even an extensive outline of *The Way of the World* gives no indication of the wit, the sparkle and the vivacity of the piece, and may serve rather to confuse. The chief characters are Lady Wishfort, guardian to a clever niece Millamant, and 'enemy to Mirabell' – Millamant's suitor – 'for having falsely pretended love to her'. Lady Wishfort is undoubtedly Congreve's greatest comic creation: a woman of sharp intelligence with a laceratingly polite command of language. She is not, however, devoid of finer feeling, and the scene where she accepts the advances of 'Sir Rowland' (who is really Mirabell's servant Waitwell in disguise) should evoke sympathy. She can even bring herself to mock her own situation when made aware that she has been deceived, by placing herself in an absurdly literary pastoral context, proposing retirement to 'Desarts and Solitudes, and [to] feed harmless Sheep, by Groves and purling Streams'. Her niece, Millamant, appears at first a well-bred coquette, adept at fashionable repartee; but she too has her serious side which reveals itself nowhere more strongly than in the scene in which she and Mirabell bargain on the subject of their proposed marriage. Mirabell, too, is much

22 Mrs Siddons as Zara in a nineteenth-century revival of Congreve's *The Mourning Bride* (1697).

more than the conventional Restoration gallant: his nimble wit conceals a remarkable gravity of disposition.

The intertwined relationships of the several characters go back some considerable period of time before the action of the play begins. Marriage in Restoration comedy is not a conclusion (as in Shakespeare's comedies) but a beginning: a signal, as it were, for the commencement of indiscretions, quarrels and misunderstandings of the most modish kind. When Mirabell and Millamant finally do marry, it is after much legal and financial negotiation. The difference between their situation and that of the lovers in most Restoration plays is that their marriage is obviously going to work. Mirabell's declaration that he 'may prove a tractable and complying husband', and Millamant's 'if I continue to endure you a little longer I may by degrees dwindle into a wife', should be spoken ironically, in knowing reference to the accepted *mores* of the age, to which they have no intention of subscribing. They will, no doubt, continue their mutually derisive banter – they could hardly do otherwise, for they are sardonically witty by nature – but we must suppose that their marriage will feed and grow on such *facetiae*, rather than disintegrate as a result of them.

In other comedies of the period a true love-match was a thing to be ridiculed. Congreve rises above the popular practice in treating the subject seriously within the comic convention. The incisive quality of the dialogue, the balance of the phrasing, the clarity of the ideas expressed, far from creating a 'literary' effect, render the lines manageable (in spite of terms which may now seem archaic) when spoken by the trained actor. 'Ses pièces sont les plus spirituelles et les plus exactes . . .', said Voltaire in the *Lettres Philosophiques*, and there could hardly be greater praise from a critic brought up on the principles of seventeenth-century French classicism. 'Les règles du théâtre y sont rigoureusement observées; elles sont pleines de caractères nuancés avec une extrême finesse . . .'.

'Extrême finesse': this sums up Congreve's art. Yet Congreve laid no great store by his own theatrical achievement – once the plays had been written and performed, that was that, and he seems to have been genuinely content to retire from the scene after the public had shown less than usual interest. Voltaire was shocked by this attitude when he visited him in 1726, believing Congreve to be affecting aristocratic disinterest, probably out of pique. Congreve remarked that he hoped Voltaire would regard him simply as a gentleman who lived very modestly; to which Voltaire retorted that he wouldn't have troubled to visit him if he were nothing more than a gentleman.

Congreve died in London on 19 January 1729. The critic John Dennis wrote that 'Mr Congreve quitted the stage early, and that comedy left it with him'. Comedy of a certain sharply intellectual kind did so, indeed; but fashion was changing, and a different view was required by the larger metropolitan audience which was less concerned with fashions set by royalty. The courtier-dramatist was superseded by the bourgeois professional, and George Farquhar fitted this description perfectly.

Farquhar has been wrongly described as 'the last of the Restoration dramatists'. 23 In fact he is not a Restoration dramatist at all, either in regard to the period during which he was active in the theatre, or in the style of his plays. True, his earliest comedies derive from the 'Restoration' in their structure – but hardly in their feeling. Farquhar brought a whiff of country air to a stage which had been excessively urban and urbane. Warmth and good-humour replace cynicism and cold caustic wit; his work has far more in common with that of his fellow-countryman Oliver Goldsmith, writing half a century later. If nothing distinctively

Irish may be discerned in the plays of Congreve, the tone of Farquhar's plays is very Irish indeed.

George Farquhar is universally described as having been born in Derry in 1778. His father was the Rev. John Farquhar, but as no John Farquhar appears in the list of clergy for the Diocese of Derry at that period, it is more likely that he was born at Stranorlar in the neighbouring Diocese of Raphoe, where a John Farquhar was curate. Stranorlar is only twenty-five miles from Derry City, and it is perfectly possible that when asked where he came from, in later life, he mentioned Derry, as few people in Dublin – let alone in London – would ever have heard of Stranorlar.

At the age of sixteen he entered Trinity College, Dublin, where he was supported by a relative of his mother, Bishop Wiseman of Dromore – the Farquhars had seven children, and would have found it difficult to maintain a son in Dublin on a clergyman's stipend. Dr Wiseman – and no doubt Rev. Farquhar as well – intended that George should study Divinity, and this he did, although possessed of 'a volatile disposition' according to the eighteenth-century theatre historian Thomas Wilkes. Alas for Farquhar's projected career in the Church of Ireland; the Bishop died when the student was only in his second year, leaving no provision in his Will for the continuance of his protegé's studies. In order to keep himself in Dublin, Farquhar took a position as 'corrector' in the College Press. The Church lost a potential divine, but the Theatre gained a promising playwright.

It must be assumed that Farquhar was leading something of a double life in studying for holy orders and at the same time consorting with the theatrical circle. On the other hand, Smock Alley depended very much upon the patronage of the 'college wits', and it may have been that the puritanical attitude to the theatre prevalent in schools of divinity in English universities was less severe in Ireland. In any event, what may have been an uneasy situation was suddenly cut short, for he seems to have lost his position at the printing-house. He joined the Smock Alley company in 1696 on the recommendation of the actor Robert Wilks, at a salary of twenty shillings a week.

There may have been some sudden crisis at Smock Alley, such as the illness or resignation of an actor, for Farquhar's debût was in the unlikely part of Othello. He may have been engaged merely as an understudy, realizing the understudy's dream of stepping into a major role at short notice. He later played Lennox in *Macbeth*, Rochford in John Bank's *Vertue Betrayed*, Lord Dion in Beaumont and Fletcher's *Philaster*, Bellair in Etherege's *The Man of Mode*, Careless in Howard's *The Committee*, Loveless in Beaumont and Fletcher's *The Scornful Lady*, and Guyomar in Dryden's *The Indian Emperor*, all under Joseph Ashbury's direction.

It was while Farquhar was playing the part of Guyomar that the accident occurred which Thomas Wilkes describes as being the reason for his leaving the stage 'forever' – in fact he did not leave it forever, but he left the Smock Alley company. Farquhar forgot to change his sword for a foil, and dangerously wounded the actor Price who played Basquez. Price recovered, but Farquhar turned to writing – an occupation which had been previously suggested to him by Robert Wilks, who may have divined that his friend would never make a successful actor. His first play was *Love and a Bottle*: Wilks gave him ten guineas, and Ashbury organized a benefit-performance in order to help him to reach London; but Ashbury cannot have had much confidence in Farquhar's prowess as a writer, for he does not appear to have made any attempt to produce the play in Dublin. On the day after the benefit Farquhar left for London, to find a certain degree of fame but, as matters turned out, no fortune.

Love and a Bottle was produced at Drury Lane in 1698. Nine performances were given, a great encouragement to the novice playwright. He had intended the chief character, Roebuck – 'an Irish gentleman, of a wild, roving temper' – for Wilks, in the way that many dramatists to this day write with a specific performer in mind; unfortunately Wilks could not be released from his contractual commitments at Smock Alley, but he came to London the following year and Farquhar wrote an Epilogue for him which he spoke in a subsequent production. In 1700 Wilks was cast as Sir Harry Wildair – a character distinctly related to Roebuck – in Farquhar's second play *The Constant Couple*, and it was this collaboration which confirmed the reputations of the two emigrés.

23 George Farquhar, by Clamp.

Love and a Bottle would hardly be remembered if it were Farquhar's only play. It is a mildly amusing piece, borrowing heavily from *Le Bourgeois Gentilhomme* – Lyrick the poet, Pamphlet the bookseller, Rigadoon the dancing master, and Nimblewrist the fencing instructor, all derive from similar characters in Molière's comedy. *The Constant Couple; or, A Trip to the Jubilee*, however, shows the mark of a more mature craftsman. It is based on a novelette which Farquhar had published in 1698 called *The Adventures of Covent Garden* (in turn loosely based on Antoine Feretière's *Le Roman Bourgeois*). Sir Harry Wildair, 'an airy gentleman, affecting humorous gaiety and freedom', has recently returned from Paris with his head full of fashions and fashionable life which he feels should be transported to London. Far from being the type of the Restoration rake, in his pursuit of female companionship he lacks the ruthlessness of the beaux of Etherege or Wycherley, and his part in the story ends with his betrothal to Angelica, 'a woman of honour'. Lurewell, a 'lady of jilting temper proceeding from a resentment of her wrongs from men', has several suitors, and much of the comedy is derived from rival attempts to capture her; she finally accepts the advances of an old admirer, Standard, 'a disbanded colonel, brave and generous'.

The part of Sir Harry became a favourite with actresses, and was later one of Peg Woffington's most famous roles. In 1701 Farquhar wrote a sequel, *Sir Harry Wildair*. The play's run of nine nights was not considered sufficiently successful, and it was unfavourably compared to *The Constant Couple*.

25

24

Military service in the Low Countries and the English provinces kept Farquhar in bread and butter over the next few years. In 1702 the Irish peer Charles Boyle, Earl of Orrery (nephew of the playwright Robert Boyle), presented him with a lieutenant's commission in recognition of the fact that, despite his talent, he was unlikely to make a permanent living from the theatre: patronage of the arts of this order was quite usual at the time. In 1703 Farquhar married Margaret Pemell of Yorkshire, a widow with three children who was so much in love with him that she let him know she was the possessor of a considerable fortune; he married her, it must be assumed for love, for he never chided her when she subsequently admitted that she was as poorly off as himself. They had two daughters.

Farquhar's works of this period comprise his published *Miscellanies*, which include his *Discourse upon Comedy*. This otherwise conventional critical essay contains the notion, foreign to Restoration writers of comedy, that virtue should be seen to triumph. It also contains the intriguing assertion that as Aristotle was not a playwright he was unqualified to formulate rules governing the composition of drama! A curious paradox emerges when one considers Farquhar's next play, *The Twin Rivals*, in which he attempts to construct his comedy in the regular Aristotelian form.

In 1704 Farquhar returned to Dublin in the hope of publishing his collected works, but he could not find enough subscribers. The Smock Alley management

24–7 *Left to right* Scenes from *The Constant Couple* and its unsuccessful sequel *Sir Harry Wildair*. *Opposite* Scene from *The Recruiting Officer*, in which Captain Plume addresses a chicken-seller, Rose, and *The Beaux' Stratagem*, whose breezy country humour anticipates Goldsmith.

came to the rescue by offering him a benefit performance, but as he was a commissioned officer he had to obtain permission from the Lord Lieutenant of Ireland in order to take even so temporary a step from military into civil life. Fortunately the Lord Lieutenant of the time was the Duke of Ormonde, who granted the necessary formalities and attended the resulting performance with a large court entourage. *The Constant Couple* was a Dublin favourite – in 1700 alone it had received twenty-three performances. The house was packed with well-wishers and admirers, but the applause was for the writer rather than the player: Farquhar had unwisely cast himself as Sir Harry Wildair. Thomas Wilkes wrote that 'his friends blushed to see him act'. This dismal venture earned him £100, and he left his native capital for ever.

Had Farquhar's career in the theatre ceased in 1705 he would now be regarded as an agreeable minor playwright, and not as one of the chief dramatists to write in English in the early eighteenth century. *The Recruiting Officer* (1706) and *The Beaux' Stratagem* (1707) ensure his lasting reputation.

26   *The Recruiting Officer* shows how much more at home its author was in the provinces than in the city. The hero is the debonair Captain Plume who has come to Shropshire to 'beat up' volunteers for Her Majesty's overseas service (the play had a particular topicality at the time of Marlborough's campaign). His private mission, however, is in making love to the local ladies – and this has the advantage of securing their followers for the army – while his special objective is to win the hand of Justice Ballance's daughter Sylvia. Sylvia makes it her business to observe Plume's constancy (or otherwise) at closer quarters, and to that end disguises herself as a young man. 'He' is arrested and brought to court before her own father, who has her committed to the army, under Plume. Plume is 'aided and abetted' by the devious Sergeant Kite. Captain Brazen (a braggadocio soldier in the tradition of Plautus and Italian comedy) is Recruiting Officer to a rival regiment and contributes to the misunderstandings; his hopes of marrying the wealthy

Melinda are destroyed when he finds himself contracted to her maid. The comedy is airy and whimsical, at times completely hilarious, and, as the author averred, 'painted from life'. Its gentle satire, freshness and rollicking humour captivated the London public.

The Beaux' Stratagem also has a rural setting. Aimwell and Archer, two impecunious young beaux, arrive at an inn with the intention of introducing themselves into county society in the expectation of finding rich and amiable wives. Aimwell masquerades as his own elder brother, and Archer as Aimwell's servant Martin. Thus the scene is set for conquests and misapprehensions both above and below stairs at the inn, and in the house of Squire Sullen, his wife, and his sister Dorinda.

A wide cross-section of society is portrayed. The nobility and gentry are represented by the Sullens, by Mrs Sullen's brother Sir Charles Freeman, by Lady Bountiful (the Squire's mother) and by a French prisoner of war, Count Bellair. The members of the lower orders sustain an equally important part in the action, to an extent unknown in the Restoration theatre, recalling Shakespeare and Ben Jonson. There is Foigard, an Irishman posing as a Jesuit from Brussels; Gibbet, a highwayman; Scrub, Squire Sullen's clownish manservant; Boniface, the landlord at the inn; his amorous daughter, Cherry; Gipsy, Mrs Sullen's maid; and sundry other rustics.

'Farquhar's characters are adventurers; but they are adventurers of a romantic, not a knavish, stamp, and succeed no less by their honesty than by their boldness.' So said William Hazlitt just over a hundred years after Farquhar's death. Aimwell and Archer (near relatives of Roebuck, Sir Harry Wildair and Captain Plume) are well contrasted: Aimwell is notable for his sensitivity, Archer for his light-hearted pragmatism. Aimwell is the forerunner of the sentimental hero of eighteenth-century comedy, and though Archer is closer to the philanderer of the Restoration, he is much more considerate.

28 *Below* The Irish actor John Moody in the 'stage-Irish' part of Foigard in *The Beaux' Stratagem*, in a late eighteenth-century revival.

The spectacle of a married couple who can no longer bear each other's company was a fairly familiar one on the stage, but Farquhar takes the case of Squire and Mrs Sullen a step further and allows the question of divorce: he had read (and indeed in some of his dialogue paraphrased) Milton's *Doctrine of Discipline and Divorce*, and suggests that incompatability might be resolved in another way than simply by taking lovers. Very few people could afford the cost of taking a process of separation through the ecclesiastical courts; the law should be changed:

> MRS SULLEN: Law! What law can search into the abyss of nature? What evidence can prove the unaccountable disaffections of wedlock? Can a jury sum up endless aversions that are rooted in our souls, or can a bench give judgement upon antipathies?

Such lines might pass for dull pleading rhetoric were they not placed in the mouth of Mrs Sullen, who is a person of spirit, as well as a woman of wit. In the earlier scenes she expresses her disaffection with a sardonic turn of phrase which disguises the presence of real feeling. We laugh at her description of Squire Sullen's arrival in the matrimonial bedchamber after a night at the tavern, but we sympathise with her predicament as well:

> MRS SULLEN: . . . He came home this morning at his usual hour of four, wakened me out of a sweet dream of something else by tumbling over the tea-table, which he broke all to pieces; after his man and he had rolled about the room, like sick passengers in a storm, he comes flounce unto bed, dead as a salmon into a fishmonger's basket; his feet cold as ice, his breath hot as a furnace, and his hands and his face as greasy as his flannel nightcap. O matrimony! He tosses up the clothes with a barbarous swing over his shoulders, disorders the whole economy of my bed, leaves me half naked, and my whole night's comfort is the tuneable serenade of that wakeful nightingale, his nose! . . .

This deeply introspective woman, conscious of the futility of her life in the country with a drunken sot for a husband and with no opportunity at all for intellectual stimulation, might well seek comfort of a kind in adultery: but Mrs Sullen is too scrupulous for this easy solution. She allows herself to fantasize about the charming personality of Archer, but further than this she will not permit herself to go. Mrs Sullen is a complex creation, far removed from the disappointed ogling wives of the conventional comedies of manners.

The Beaux' Stratagem is a serious comedy, a comedy with 'heart'. It was often revived throughout the eighteenth century, but practically disappeared from the stage during the Victorian era, when critics seemed unable to discern the difference between Farquhar's sexual honesty and the open licentiousness of his immediate forerunners. His reputation was gradually restored during the twentieth century, and productions of *The Recruiting Officer* in 1963 and *The Beaux' Stratagem* in 1970 (both directed by William Gaskill at the National Theatre in London) set a new tone of underlying seriousness, where earlier productions – in America and Ireland, as much as in Britain – had tended to treat the plays as little more than jovial period romps, the players continually curtseying and bowing, fluttering fans, and generally tripping about the stage as if a moment's pause would allow the attention of the audience to wander and reveal the superficiality of the material.

The first production of *The Recruiting Officer* in London coincided with a decline in the writer's health and fortune. It is not known how Farquhar came to be apprehended for debt: in any event, the Earl of Ormonde suggested he should sell his commission in order to pay his creditors. This Farquhar did, in the

29–30 *Left* Eve Watkinson as Millamant in a Dublin Gate Theatre revival of *The Way of the World*, 1958. *Right* Stella McCusker as Mrs Sullen in a Belfast Lyric Theatre revival of *The Beaux' Stratagem*, 1975.

expectation that Ormonde would provide him with a post in Ireland. No such post, however, was forthcoming, and, as Thomas Wilkes remarked, 'this distracting disappointment so preyed upon the mind of our author, who saw nothing but beggary and want before him, it occasioned his death a short time after'.

Robert Wilks found him in a garret in St Martin's Lane in 'the greatest agitation of mind'. Wilks' advice to him to write a play was perhaps given in the hope that the mental activity would divert his thoughts from his distressing situation, rather than in the expectation of a masterpiece. Yet as a masterpiece *The Beaux' Stratagem* was hailed at its first performance on 8 March 1707. Farquhar died on the night of his benefit, 20 or 23 May (accounts differ). His final letter to his friend and collaborator from Dublin days, Robert Wilks, is a touching memorial to his concern for others:

Dear Bob,
I have not anything to leave thee, to perpetuate my memory, but two helpless girls; look after them sometimes, and think of him who was to the last moment of his life thine,

G. Farquhar.

Wilks arranged two benefits for the 'helpless girls', and Edmond Challoner, to whom Farquhar had dedicated his *Miscellanies*, gave them £20 per annum; but the children remained in obscurity. Leigh Hunt was aware that one of them became a maidservant, ignorant of her father's fame.

As to Farquhar's character, he described himself as 'very splenetic, and yet very amorous'. The tradition is that he resembled the light-hearted heroes of his own comedies; but the critic A. J. Farmer suggests that he was much more likely to have been nothing other than 'a sadly harassed young playwright'.

4

Sentimental comedies
and unsentimental comedians

1709–1778

New Dublin theatres, Charles Shadwell,
Richard Steele, Arthur Murphy, James Quin,
Peg Woffington and others

Joseph Ashbury continued as Manager of the Smock Alley theatre throughout the
reign of Queen Anne and well into that of George I. Ashbury was an Englishman,
and as might be expected he continued to hold the opinion that, as Ireland was an
English dependency, the Dublin theatre was in some way subservient to that of
London, or at least should be so. When Irish playwrights offered suitable work he
produced it, but he never actively sought plays of Irish interest. His greatest contribution, as has been earlier noted, was in the directing of stage productions and
the training of actors. The British stage was constantly refurnished with fine
players who had spent their early years under his tutelage.

A gradual divergence of Court and Theatre is marked by the fact that when
Lord Wharton was appointed Lord Lieutenant in 1709 he installed Thomas
Clayton, composer of the operas *Rosamund* and *Arsinoe*, as his entertainments
officer. It is unclear whether all the performances arranged by Clayton took place
in the Castle, or if some were mounted at Smock Alley. Wharton's genuine
interest in the arts is shown by his appointment of Joseph Addison as his Secretary
of State. Addison's famous tragedy *Cato* was often given at Smock Alley from
1713 onwards, though there is no evidence to suggest that its first performance
there had anything to do with the author's important office.

At this period there were usually two performances each week during the
season, which ran from October to May, with additional nights given over to
benefits, galas, or other special occasions. The theatre was opened at 4 p.m., after
the conclusion of the day's rehearsal, so that the servants of those who wished to
have seats reserved could occupy the best places until the master or mistress
arrived in time for the curtain at 6 p.m. The play was followed by a light afterpiece,
and as the years passed, the evening was extended by up to three or four items –
an afterpiece or two, comic sketches, or dance displays.

About 1712 Charles Shadwell, son of the English dramatist Thomas Shadwell,
set himself up in Dublin as an insurance broker. He had already had three plays
produced in London, and shortly after arriving in Dublin took up playwriting
again. He was never (unlike James Shirley) engaged as the official 'playwright in
residence', but he regularly provided new plays for Smock Alley from 1715 to
1720, and five of these he set in Ireland.

The Hasty Wedding (1716) is no more than a conventional comedy of intrigue;
the epilogue informs us that the author had set out to expose the follies of Dublin

but there is little in the preceding play to support his assertion, which those who stayed for the epilogue might have been surprised to hear. *Irish Hospitality* (1717) is set in the country, and humorously exploits the traits of the squireen class. *The Plotting Lovers*, based on Congreve and Vanbrugh's *Squire Trelooby*, contains some rustic Irish speeches, which, rendered phonetically in the text, require some pains to decipher. *The Sham Prince* (1719) was written and produced in two weeks and a day: it was based on an incident which had taken place earlier in the same year when a young spark from Westmeath perpetrated a forgery which passed him off as the Prince of Passau – he had borrowed a large amount of money on the strength of the documents which purported to prove his title – but he disappeared before being apprehended.

Shadwell's most interesting 'Irish' play is *Rotherick O'Connor: King of Connaught; or, The Distressed Princess* (1718), a tragedy as unwieldy but as intriguing as its title. It is based on historical events at the time of the Anglo-Norman invasion in the twelfth century, and the main characters are Rotherick, King of Connaught; Avelina, his daughter; Dermot, King of Leinster; Eva, his daughter; Cothernus, his son; Strongbow, whom Eva eventually marries; Maurice Regan, Eva's lover; and Catholicus, Archbishop of Tuam. Disbelief has to be very willingly suspended if the amazing conglomeration of historical, quasi-historical and imaginary events are to be accepted by the reader. It is easy to smile at the naiveté of the work in the knowledge that 'history was not like that', but this is a romance, of a sort, and its audience would not have concerned itself with the accuracy of historical facts. Furthermore, there is a definite parallel between the conflict of the native Irish and the Anglo-Normans in the play, and the idealogical conflict of Irish and Anglo-Irish taking place at the time it was written. The recent Williamite wars are obviously recalled:

> *A horrid war long time has plagu'd this Isle*
> *And right and wrong are to confusion brought:*
> *Their lawless passions thirsting after Blood*
> *Have even depopulated all the land,*
> *Nobility is nowhere to be found*
> *The base Plebean lords it over all.*

Catholicus is, symbolically, the villain of the piece, as might be expected when the Protestant succession was still a matter for grave concern. One of his speeches, while disputing with the victorious Strongbow, ends with the wonderfully machiavellian couplet:

> *Observe that Prince sits easiest on his Throne*
> *Who strives to make the clergy all his own!*

When Ashbury died in 1720 at the age of eighty-one, Smock Alley was still the only theatre in Ireland. (A theatre had been opened in Cork in 'a great cellar or malt house' off North Main Street in 1713 to accommodate visits from the Smock Alley players, but it hardly survived its first season.) In 1729 a famous rope-dancer and tumbler, Madam Violante, appeared with her troupe at Smock Alley. Dublin lacked a variety theatre or music hall, as Madam Violante realized, and she shortly opened a theatre, or 'commodious booth' as it was described, of her own. She played pantomime, and also ran a childrens' company which for a time became too popular for Smock Alley's comfort. In 1732 she left Dublin, for by engaging 'legitimate' productions, she violated the Theatre Royal's exclusive patent, and was accordingly 'stop'd by the Lord Mayor'.

The Mayor also stopped the performances given by some freelance actors who took over Madam Violante's booth after her departure. This action annoyed a section of playgoers, who as a consequence encouraged the building of a small theatre outside the city boundary in Rainsford Street, where the Mayor had no jurisdiction. This theatre opened with Congreve's *Love for Love*. The managers were Mr Husband, who had been a pupil of Ashbury's some years before, and Mr Duval, who had come to Dublin as a dancer in Madam Violante's troupe.

Rainsford Street survived for two-and-a-half years. Thomas Elrington, the new Smock Alley manager (and also its leading actor) and his colleagues determined to fight this competition by building a completely new theatre. They took a plot of land in Aungier Street and engaged the architect Edward Lovett Pearce, who was at that time Surveyor General, to design it for them. Pearce had, with Alessandro Galilei, built Castletown House for William Connolly, Speaker of the Irish House of Commons – it remains the largest and most magnificent Palladian house in the country. Pearce also designed the new Irish Parliament House (now the Bank of Ireland), and several other important buildings. It is most unfortunate that no plans or other visual records of this theatre survive. The theatrical historian William Chetwood, writing fifteen years later, recalled:

> I think the Architect had more view to the Magnificent than Theatrical: The Audience Part is ornamented with rich Embellishment that gives it a superbe Countenance, but no Disparagement to the Architect in other Buildings, this might have been more convenient with less Cost. But I believe the contriver had an eye more to *Ridottos*, than the *Drama*, if so, indeed his Intentions were answered, for in that Shape, it may vie with that in the *Hay-market* in *London*.

The theatre in Aungier Street was opened on 9 March 1734 with a performance of Farquhar's *The Recruiting Officer*, in the presence of the Lord Lieutenant, the Duke of Dorset. A voluntary committee was formed from those 'noblemen and gentlemen of the first rank and consequence' who had subscribed towards the erection of the theatre. It was incumbent upon these public-spirited people to 'advance its interests, and fix it on the most permanent and flourishing basis without the least idea of emolument in return'. The day-to-day business of the new theatre was administered by Elrington of Smock Alley.

Shortly after the opening of Aungier Street, the old Smock Alley playhouse was demolished and quickly rebuilt. Hitchcock, the prompter, noted:

> Notwithstanding the uncommon expedition used, the architect studiously avoided the errors and mistakes of former builders, and erected a strong, elegant, commodious well-constructed theatre. The cavea, or audience part is remarkably well constructed for the first two requisites, of seeing and hearing. In these essentials it gives place to none that I ever saw, and I think may safely say is superior to most.

The Rainsford Street theatre closed as a consequence of the double competition from the elegant new houses – as had been intended. An arrangement had also been made enabling the Rainsford Street players to use the new Smock Alley stage, and this was honoured when the building was ready for occupation.

Dublin now had two fine new theatres and, as with Drury Lane and Covent Garden, the two houses vied with one another to attract the public with very similar repertoires, despite close managerial connection and frequent interchange of actors. Prosperity did not last long, and before a decade had passed Aungier Street was relegated to the position of a supporting venue. Its committee

31 Richard Steele, by Kneller, 1711.

32 A scene from *The Conscious Lovers*.

'noblemen and gentlemen' seems to have proved ineffective, as is often the way with such altruistically recruited bodies.

The 'sentimental comedy' which came into vogue in the reign of Queen Anne was a reaction against the equivocal morals of the 'old comedy', and also against its intellectuality. The new middle-class audiences, both in Dublin and in London, required something less rarefied, less remote from 'ordinary' life, and they found exactly what they were looking for in the plays of Richard Steele (1672–1729).   31

Steele was born in Dublin and was looked after by an uncle, Henry Gascoigne, as his parents died when he was very young. Gascoigne was secretary to the Duke of Ormonde, through whose influence Steele gained admittance to the Charterhouse School in Surrey, of which Ormonde was a governor. As Steele seems to have left Ireland permanently at the age of twelve he can hardly have received literary or dramatic influences from his native country, and his career belongs exclusively to England. His principal plays were *The Funeral* (1701), *The Lying Lover* (1703), *The Tender Husband* (1715), and *The Conscious Lovers* (1722) which was his best and which found its way across the Irish sea within weeks of its first production. *The Conscious Lovers* may be taken as the supreme example of the   32 sentimental comedy, for it is not very comic, and its characters are happily dedicated to the virtuous life.

37

33–4 Arthur Murphy, after Nathaniel Dance, 1805, and a scene from *Know Your Own Mind*, one of the best of his sentimental comedies. During his lifetime Murphy was considered the equal of Goldsmith and Sheridan.

If Steele was the chief instigator of the sentimental comedy, its principal perpetrator was Arthur Murphy (1727–1805), who came from a well-to-do mercantile family in Dublin. His father was drowned in one of his own ships on a voyage to Jamaica, and Murphy was brought up by his mother, one of the Frenchs of Cloonyquin in Co. Roscommon. He was educated at St Omer in France and remained there until he was seventeen, after which he worked as a clerk in a firm with which he had family connections in Cork. At the age of twenty-two he moved to a London firm of bankers, and while in London started a magazine called *The Gray's Inn Journal* which devoted much of its space to the theatre, and to which Murphy devoted more time than he did to his duties at the bank.

A disappointment in regard to an expected legacy, and the accumulation of personal debts led him, curiously, to leave the bank and take to the stage – an enterprise encouraged by Samuel Foote. He was playing leading parts, including Hamlet at Covent Garden for his own benefit, within a year of his debut. In 1756 his farce *The Apprentice* was brought out at Drury Lane, and in the following year, his debts paid off, he left the stage and returned to journalism. He also studied law at Lincoln's Inn.

Murphy's first full-length play was *The Orphan of China*, based on a tragedy of the same name by Voltaire. Though a mediocre work, it was popular, and remained in the Irish repertoire until at least 1810. Murphy wrote over twenty plays, none of them original, in the sense that he quite openly borrowed or adapted from the work of other writers.

Where the judgment of time is concerned, Murphy's best plays (*The Way to Keep Him*, *All in the Wrong* and *Know Your Own Mind*) have been overshadowed by those of Goldsmith and Sheridan, all of whose comedies appeared during the same period of two decades. Goldsmith and Sheridan despised the sentimental comedy even if they did not entirely succeed in ridding their own work of it.

34

influence; but it is worth recalling that Murphy was regarded by contemporary critics as on quite an equal footing with his younger compatriots; and it is also worth recalling that Murphy was perfectly well aware of the pitfalls of the genre to which his temperament as a writer was most suited.

The Way to Keep Him (1760) was first produced as a three-act afterpiece, and then expanded to five acts with the addition of two new characters, Sir Bashful and Lady Constant. Sir Bashful truly loves his wife, but behaves harshly towards her when others are present so as not to be ridiculed as a foolish husband. The central idea in the play is that, once married, ladies are at little pains to please the men although it was they who previously showed most affection. In spite of sentimental accretions, *The Way to Keep Him* is a comedy of manners, and should be played as such. It was revived by the Abbey Players in Dublin in 1978.

All in the Wrong (1761), a comedy on the effects of jealousy in a domestic situation, is based on a little-known play by Molière, *Le Cocu Imaginaire*. *Know Your Own Mind* (1778) is adapted from *L'Irresolu* by Destouches, and was overshadowed by the first production of Sheridan's *The School for Scandal* which it somewhat resembles, although Murphy had in fact drafted his piece nine years earlier. The moralizing tone takes away much of the sparkle which should be present in the comic scenes; the play was revived with reasonable success, however, at the Gate Theatre, Dublin, in the 1950s.

By the middle of the eighteenth century Ireland had given to the British theatre not only a number of first-rate dramatists, but also several actors of repute, some of them trained by Ashbury. The first Irish actor to rise to prominence was Thomas Dogget (1660–1721), who was born in Castle Street, Dublin, within a minute's walk of the site of the Smock Alley theatre, which opened when he was two years old. His name appears on a manuscript of the Smock Alley version of Fletcher and Shirley's *The Night Walker* in 1684: the part of 'the Boy' is assigned to 'Doggy'. Two years later, when Dogget was twenty, his name appears on the Drury Lane playbills. He quickly made a reputation as a character comedian, possessing, according to Colley Cibber, 'that peculiar art which so very few performers are masters of, *viz*. the arriving at the perfectly ridiculous without stepping into the least impropriety to obtain it'.

Cibber also notes that Dogget was 'the strictest observer of nature of any actor of his time'. Congreve, as has been seen, wrote Ben for him after his remarkable creation of Fondlewife. Dogget, as was so frequently the way with actors of the time, wrote a comedy, *The Country Wake* (1690); it was often revived. He rose to social prominence as part-proprietor of the Haymarket Theatre, London; and, as a supporter of the Hanoverian succession, he presented money for a perpetual trophy 'to be rowed for by six watermen from London Bridge to Chelsea' in commemoration of the accession of George I.

Farquhar's loyal friend and supporter Robert Wilks (1665–1732) seems to have been universally admired for his generosity. When in management in London he often favoured actors whose friendship he enjoyed, not seeming to notice absence of talent. He was born in Rathfarnham, then a village five miles from the outskirts of Dublin, went to London around 1795 and was back in Dublin three years later playing leading roles. A humorous story is told of the Duke of Ormonde issuing a warrant to prevent his leaving the country again, so valuable was his talent to Ireland.

His success as Sir Harry Wildair has already been mentioned. He was the original Elder Wouldbe in *The Twin Rivals* and Captain Plume in *The Recruiting Officer*. He created upwards of fifty roles in new plays in the course of his career,

Ne Sutor ultra
Crepidam

35 Thomas Dogget, the first Irish actor to achieve outstanding success in England.

including Lord Townley in *The Provoked Husband*, Masinissa in *Sophonisba*, Juba in *Cato*, Sir Charles Easy in *The Careless Husband* and Dumont in *Jane Shore*. As well as this he appeared in countless established plays. Though he won distinction in serious parts, he was chiefly regarded for his comic portrayals, especially as the light-hearted heroes of Farquhar.

> *Farquhar by writing gained himself a name*
> *And Wilks by Farquhar gained immortal fame.*

37   James Quin (1693–1766) was the illegitimate son of a barrister of the same name and grandson of the Lord Mayor of Dublin, Mark Quin. He may have spent some time at Trinity College. His first recorded appearance was at Smock Alley in 1714 as Abel in Robert Howard's *The Committee*. His talent must have been recognized very early, for in the same season he was given the leading role in Thomas D'Urfey's *The Comical History of Don Quixote*. In Shadwell's *Timon of Athens* he was cast as Cleon and in Rowe's *Tamerlaine* as the Prince of Tanais. In 1715 he went to London, where he was given a series of small parts at Drury Lane in which he evidently proved himself as far above the calibre of the 'bit-part' player. Then, in the time-honoured story-book fashion, the actor who was playing Bajazet in *Tamerlaine* fell ill and Quin, who had observed Thomas Elrington at close quarters in the Dublin production, read it 'in a manner which elicted great applause'. He then studied the lines overnight and played the part the following evening 'in a fashion that brought him into lasting favour'. In 1717 he moved to Lincoln's Inn Fields where he stayed for fourteen years, acting mainly in tragedy or the straight parts in comedy, though he is on record as having given a good account of Teague, the comic Irishman, in *The Committee*.

In 1746–7 one of those theatrical rivalries of the sort promoted more by the press and the public than by the protagonists themselves, came to notice, when Quin and Garrick were said to be pitted against each other for the favours of the audience. Quin played Sir John Brute in *The Provoked Wife* at Covent Garden while Garrick played the same role at Drury Lane. Garrick seems to have come out better, for having recollected throughout the play that Sir John was a gentleman! Great excitement was caused when the two actors appeared in the duel scene in *The Fair Penitent*: the shouts of their supporters unnerved both actors, neither of whom seems to have anticipated such partisan behaviour. Walpole, the Prime Minister, said that he preferred the acting of Quin to that of Garrick. In attempting Lear, Othello and Richard III, for which he was generally considered to be unsuited, Quin allowed Garrick an easy victory.

In spite of their alleged mutual jealousy, Garrick asked Quin to join him at Drury Lane, but Quin had no desire to do so, and used the invitation to obtain an annual salary of £1,000 from the managers of Covent Garden, who did not want to lose him. This was believed to be the highest salary ever paid to an actor. Towards the end of his career Quin became a greatly loved Falstaff. A Staffordshire
IV   pottery figurine depicting him in the role sold many thousand copies – a charming early example of the theatrical souvenir. Quin was noted for his somewhat gruff
36, III   and sardonic wit. When the actress Peg Woffington, who was well known for her affairs with a number of men, complained in the green-room that because of her continuing success as Sir Harry Wildair half the town believed her to be a man, Quin retorted, 'Madam, the other half knows you to be a woman!'

Peg Woffington (1714–60) was acknowledged as one of the greatest actresses of the century. She was the daughter of a Dublin bricklayer, who died when she was an infant. Her mother earned a meagre living as a street fruit-vendor. It was t

36–7 The actress Peg Woffington (left), and the actor James Quin. Quin excelled in tragic roles, though in private life he was famous as a wit.

Madam Violante that she owed her introduction to the stage, as that egregious entertainer used to carry two small children in baskets as part of her tightrope act – and one of these infants was Peg Woffington. She later acted as a member of Madam Violante's children's troupe in *The Beggar's Opera* and *The Devil to Pay*. She appeared at Rainsford Street, Aungier Street and Smock Alley. Elrington cast her in supporting roles until she was twenty-three, when he offered her Ophelia, after which, it may be said, she never looked back. Thereafter it was principally London and fame for the rest of her life, though she returned to act in Dublin much more frequently than most luminaries of the Irish stage. In spite of her very humble beginnings she excelled as high-born ladies.

From 1740 until her enforced retirement sixteen years later Peg Woffington was the most admired actress in the British Isles, rivalling Mrs Clive, who was also of Irish parentage, and whom she was said to hate more than any other woman. She also disliked Mrs Bellamy (another leading Irish actress) to such a degree that on one occasion she chased her off the stage and stabbed her behind the curtain! With men she got on rather better – so much so that she was accorded the honour of being elected President of the Beefsteak Club in Dublin during what was to be her last visit (1753); as she was the only woman ever admitted, her membership, let alone her presidency, was regarded askance in Dublin society. She had many amorous liaisons, and Garrick was her lover for some years. In 1757 she suffered a lapse of memory while playing Rosalind in *As You Like It* and had to leave the stage; it is probable that the cause was a severe stroke. She never recovered, and died three years later.

38 Don Felix: 'Pray let me go, Madam. Consider the gentleman wants you at the window.' A hilarious moment in Susannah Centlivre's comedy of intrigue *The Wonder! A Woman Keeps a Secret* (1714). Her plays enjoyed a greater success than their writing merited.

Peg Woffington's great rival Kitty Clive (1711–85) was a member of the Raftor (O Raiftéir) family from Co. Kilkenny. Her father had to leave Ireland when the family lost its property, having been on the 'wrong' side at the Battle of the Boyne. His daughter's story belongs to the English rather than to the Irish theatre, as her career was spent completely in England, but it is worth mentioning in the Irish context that one of her most admired comic roles was Nell in *The Devil to Pay* by Charles Coffey of Dublin – a work which would hardly have attracted notice had it not been for her performance. She wrote four short comedies, the last one entitled *The Faithful Irish Woman*.

An actress who enjoyed greater success as a playwright was Susannah Centlivre (*née* Freeman, 1667–1723), author of *The Wonder! A Woman Keeps a Secret*, *The Busy Body*, *A Bold Stroke for a Wife* and at least fifteen other comedies. She was born in Co. Tyrone. She ran away from home to escape the tyranny of a stepmother, and married successively two young men who were both killed in duels. She is said to have taken to writing as she knew of no other way to make a living. Her earliest appearance on the stage was in one of her own plays in Bath; she affected a vaguely French accent, said to be 'fetching in the extreme' – possibly to disguise her Ulster origin. Then while she was playing at Windsor, the castle cook, Joseph Centlivre, fell in love with her, and married her. The remainder of her life was happy and less fraught with incident. She gained a reputation as a blue-stocking, and was a member of the circle of Farquhar and Steele. Her plays, almost all of them comedies of manners, were much more popular (though much less accomplished) than those of Farquhar or Steele, and even at the close of the eighteenth century the three of her plays mentioned at the outset obtained nearly as many performances in Ireland as those of Richard Brinsley Sheridan.

5
Fifty pounds a night

1733–1768

Charles Macklin, Spranger Barry,
Thomas Sheridan, the decline of Smock Alley,
opening of Capel Street and Crow Street theatres

The greatest Irish actor of the eighteenth century was undoubtedly Charles
Macklin (?1697–1797). If he did not dominate the theatre in the British Isles,   V
that is only because David Garrick was a greater actor and, incidentally, a much
more agreeable person. History credits Macklin with the restoration of Shakespeare's *The Merchant of Venice* in place of Lansdowne's *The Jew of Venice*, and
the tale is often repeated of how a member of the audience (supposedly Alexander
Pope), on seeing his Shylock at Drury Lane, involuntarily exclaimed:

> *This is the Jew*
> *That Shakespeare drew!*

to which James Quin added:

> *Spew, reader, spew!*

George III, in discussing with his Prime Minister, Walpole, what might be the
most effective means of quelling the House of Commons, is said to have suggested
that the Members of Parliament be sent to Drury Lane 'to see that Irishman play
Shylock'!

Macklin was born Charles McLaughlin in Derry (some say Westmeath!), but
moved to Dublin with his mother in 1705. In 1713 he returned from a visit to
London where he may have done some acting, and took a menial position as a
badgeman or 'skip' in Trinity College; he devoted his spare time there to reading.
After about four years he joined an English touring company, and first came to
prominence when he played Brazen in a revival of *The Recruiting Officer* at Drury
Lane in 1733. There is no record of his playing in Ireland until 1748, by which
time he and the young Dublin actor Spranger Barry were Garrick's only serious
rivals.

Macklin was probably prevented from reaching the very top of the theatrical
ladder by his uncontrollable temper, which made him universally disliked in the
profession. He killed a fellow actor, Thomas Hallam, in a ridiculous quarrel over
a wig, and on other occasion physically assaulted Quin. Many of his engagements resulted in litigation.

Macklin preferred comedy, but appeared in most of the great tragic roles. He
did not create many important parts in new plays, except Sir Pertinax MacSyco-
phant in his own comedy *The True-born Scotchman* (first produced at Crow Street
Theatre in Dublin in 1766, and later rewritten as *The Man of the World*) and Sir

39 Macklin as Shylock

43

40 Scene from Macklin's comedy *The Man of the World*

41 Thomas Sheridan the Elder: clergyman, amateur playwright and wit.

41

42 Thomas Sheridan the Younger as Oedipus

Archy MacSarcasm in *Love à-la-Mode*. Macklin is said to have disliked Scotsmen ever since he was taught by one at his first school in Dublin.

Macklin often returned to Ireland. The outstanding theatrical personality in Ireland in the mid-eighteenth century, however, was Thomas Sheridan (1719–88), actor, playwright, manager and progenitor of a line of distinguished literary figures – the most famous being his second son Richard Brinsley Butler. The name Sheridan derives from O Sireadáin, and in earlier times the O Sireadáin had been Erinachs of Granard.

Although Thomas was the first in his family to enter the theatre professionally, his father, Rev. Dr Thomas Sheridan, had written plays that were performed by the boys of his school in Capel Street, Dublin. Jonathan Swift wrote a prologue and an epilogue for at least one of the school productions. Dr Sheridan published an amusing booklet on *The Art of Punning* – its verbal sallies most certainly had their influence on the writings of his son and grandson; but Thomas Sheridan the Younger later averred that it was from his godfather the Dean of St Patrick's (rather than from his father) that he gained his early interest in literature.

Thomas Sheridan the Younger was sent to Westminster School where he was awarded a King's scholarship. He was reprimanded by the school authorities for spending too much time in the London playhouses, where he saw Quin and Macklin. In 1735 he had to leave Westminster, as his father could not afford the £14 required to enable him to finish his year. He entered Trinity College, Dublin, and was awarded his Bachelor's degree in 1739. After Thomas Sheridan the Elder died in 1738 he showed sufficient expertise in rewriting one of the Capel Street school dramas, *The Faithful Shepherd*, to have it accepted at Smock Alley. Round about the same time he wrote a farce called *Captain O'Blunder* which was pre-

44

sented anonymously in 1743 – a year of great moment for him, for he also obtained his Master's degree, and decided not to become a school-teacher, but an actor.

During the summer of 1742 Garrick played in Dublin, and it became clear to Sheridan that in spite of his profession, Garrick was indeed 'a gentleman': this realization seems to have convinced him that he would not be disgraced among his academic and clerical friends if he were to join the Smock Alley company. During his first year he played Brutus, Hamlet, Othello and Richard III, it seems with amazing success. James Quin declared (humorously, one supposes) that he was forced to flee to London to avoid the competition; but Garrick, determined to make use of this burgeoning talent, invited Sheridan to join him there. This Sheridan declined, for he was already involved in managerial negotiations in Dublin.

A new company was being formed to take over the theatre in Aungier Street. Sheridan invited Theophilus Cibber to join him at Smock Alley – principally in order to prevent him from joining the rival company. Cibber agreed, but the two actors had a quarrel over a costume, and Sheridan was made to appear foolish in both the Dublin and London press, when an exchange of letters was published. Sheridan, in pique, removed himself from Smock Alley to perform Addison's *Cato* at Aungier Street – whether wearing the coveted costume or not we do not know.

A young member of the audience, Frances Chamberlayne, daughter of the Rev. Dr Philip Chamberlayne, Archdeacon of Glendalough, Prebend of Rathmichael and Rector of St Nicholas Without (all at the same time), wrote an anonymous pamphlet supporting Sheridan against his detractors. Her father disapproved of the education of women, and had forbidden her to learn to write, but an elder brother gave her surreptitious lessons. Her visits to Smock Alley were, needless to remark, equally surreptitious. Following a correspondence, she and Thomas Sheridan met secretly, and in 1747 they were married, her father 'having sunk into a state of mental imbecility'.

During their protracted period of courtship Sheridan moved frequently between Dublin and London. He appeared as guest at both Covent Garden and Drury Lane, but did not seek a permanent arrangement with either company. He played supporting roles to Garrick, and was often cast in productions with other Irish expatriates, including Peg Woffington, who at this time was Garrick's leading lady; he played Hamlet and Othello at his own benefits. Garrick was said to be jealous of Sheridan, but the Irish actress George Ann Bellamy declared that as their talents lay 'in a different line of acting' there was no need for such feelings.

While Sheridan was making his name in London, Dublin found a new favourite in Spranger Barry (1719–77), the son of a silversmith in Skinner's Row. Handsome and well-spoken, Barry made his debut at Smock Alley in 1744, just before Sheridan's first visit to London. When Sheridan returned the following year – less than three years after his own debut – he invited Barry to join him, and Barry accepted. Sheridan also invited Garrick, so three of the four most admired actors in the British Isles (Macklin being busy in London) were seen together on the Dublin stage for the winter season of 1745–6. No less than twenty command performances were given for the Lord Lieutenant.

The repertoire for the most brilliant season in the history of Smock Alley consisted of old and new plays in a selection which would do honour to any theatre director of that time or of the present day. Shakespeare, Dryden, Rowe, Milton, Vanbrugh and Addison were represented, and to these were added plays by the emigré Irish dramatists Southerne, Congreve and Farquhar. Dublin prologues of

43 Spranger Barry as Timon of Athens. A London critic described him as 'the wonder and darling of every audience'.

45

the period bewail the way in which the latter had become a part of the English theatre, and how Irish actors, finding it difficult to obtain a living in Dublin, moved to London, to return later as celebrities:

> *Hence prematurely driven, by conscious slight,*
> *Then here recalled, at fifty pounds a night!*

Thomas Sheridan's *Captain O'Blunder* is of little more than passing historical interest. It was rewritten as *The Brave Irishman* and relates the misadventures of a good-humoured Irish rustic on a visit to 'superior' relatives in London. The dialogue relies for comic effect on puns and mispronounced English words, and there are even examples of the malapropism, thirty-seven years before Richard Brinsley Sheridan's creation of Mrs Malaprop. Captain O'Blunder is purposely misdirected to a lunatic asylum, which he believes to be his cousin's house, and he presumes that two of the doctors are his relatives:

DOCTORS: Pray sir, be seated; we shall examine methodically into the nature of your case.

O'BLUNDER: Fat the devil do they mean by taking me by the wrists – may be 'tis the Fashion of Compliment in London.

DR CLYSTER: Brother, you plainly perceive that the Systole and the Diastole are obstructed.

O'BLUNDER: My Piss-hole and Arse-hole – Fat the Devil ails them? Eh! Sure de're mad . . .

DR GALYPOT: Pray sir, how do you rest?

O'BLUNDER: In a good Feather-bed, my Jewel – and sometimes I take a Nap in an Arm-chair.

DR CLYSTER: But do you sleep sound?

O'BLUNDER: Faith I sleep and snore all night, and when I awake in the morning I find myself fast asleep.

Thomas Sheridan was no great dramatist, but he was responsible for several administrative reforms which had repercussions in England. He was the first to pay regular salaries to actors, who up to his time had shared the takings, occasionally (if they were popular enough) obtaining the proceeds of a benefit performance. Sheridan also inaugurated a scheme 'for the support of maimed, reduced and superannuated Players'; but the reform for which he is best remembered is the banishment of members of the public from the stage.

Stage-seating was a survival from the British theatre of Elizabethan times, where the architectural intimacy of the buildings encouraged patrons to lean or sit on the apron stage; usually the men-about-town who wished to be seen took advantage of this and had their stools placed where they would be most conspicuous. In spite of the barrier created between the actor and the audience by the introduction of the proscenium arch, the *bels-esprits* still contrived to seat themselves on the forestage, and this often led to interruptions in the action of the play, when some over-vociferous or drunken *beau* answered the players or attempted to join in a scene. Peg Woffington was fondled 'with the utmost indecency' by a 'gentleman' while attempting to create a piteous effect during the death scene of Cordelia! Sheridan decided that the most effective way in which to prevent these irritating distractions was to increase the price of chairs to the outrageously high figure of 5s 5d; whereupon the demand for stage seats declined. Eventually the privilege was withdrawn altogether, but its loss rankled in the breasts of some of the more volatile patrons, and resulted in a series of incidents which were to become known in the annals of the Dublin theatre as the Kelly Riots.

THE
BRAVE IRISHMAN:
OR,
CAPTAIN O'BLUNDER.
A
FARCE.
As it is ACTED at the
THEATRE-ROYAL in Smock-alley:
WITH THE
GENUINE SONGS,
Not in any other EDITION.

Suppofed to be WRITTEN by
T----------S S----------N, Efq;

And REVISED with
Several CORRECTIONS and ADDITIONS.
BY
J----N P----S T----N.

BELFAST:
Printed by and for JAMES MAGEE, at the BIBLE
and CROWN in Bridge ftreet, M,DCC,LXI.

On 17 January 1747 a performance of Vanbrugh's *AEsop* in aid of the Royal Hospital for Incurables was interrupted when a Mr Kelly of Galway, much the worse for wine and cheered on by some young friends, clambered on the stage and chased the actress Mrs Dyer behind the scenes. Mrs Bellamy ran to her colleague's aid, and the two ladies managed to lock Kelly out of the dressing-room. Mrs Bellamy takes up the story:

> The play proceeded till we were come to the first scene of the last Act, when an orange, or an apple, was thrown at Mr. Sheridan, who played the character of AEsop, and so well directed that it dented the iron of the false nose which he wore, into his forehead. The curtain was then dropped and the piece left unfinished . . .

Ever apprehensive of his social position, Sheridan appeared and shouted 'I am as good a gentleman as you are!' – whereupon the audience fell into an uproar, sides being taken between those who wished the play to continue and those who felt that a patron had been insulted. Kelly followed Sheridan to his dressing-room where he found him attending to his wound; and Sheridan, taking up AEsop's sceptre, proceeded to belabour Kelly, breaking his nose.

Two nights later there was a benefit performance for a prisoner in the Marshalsea Gaol. Sheridan was too unwell (or too upset) to appear, and when this was announced a crowd of young men shouted 'Out with the ladies and down with the house!' The players escaped, but the internal fabric of the building was ruined and the theatre had to be closed. The Dublin *Journal* reported:

> Last Thursday Mr Sheridan was tryed at the Court of Oyer and Terminer, for assaulting Mr Kelly, and was acquitted. At the same time that Gentleman was tryed for assaulting Mr Sheridan, and found guilty of three Assaults.

44–5 *Left* Belfast edition of Thomas Sheridan's popular farce, printed in 1761. *Right* George Ann Bellamy, a leading actress in Thomas Sheridan's company at Smock Alley. Her autobiography (1785) provides many insights into the backstage life of Dublin and London.

47

46–8 *Opposite* Henry
Brooke, and a playbill for
his tragedy *The Earl of
Essex*, one of the few new
plays by Irish authors
presented by Thomas
Sheridan at Smock Alley.
Brooke's tragedy *Gustavus
Vasa* (*below, left*) was
banned from performance
in England because the
authorities believed,
wrongly, that one of the
characters was a satiric
portrait of the Prime
Minister, Walpole.

Kelly was fined £500. Sheridan, with a superb understanding of the value of good public relations, arranged for the fine to be revoked. Two weeks later he published a pamphlet entitled *A Full Vindication*. In due course theatre managements all over the British Isles followed Smock Alley's lead, and the practice of allowing members of the public to sit on the stage was universally discontinued.

Sheridan was also the first manager to have a description or synopsis of the play included on the playbills. He also increased the amount of press advertising from small announcements in the general news columns to display-advertisements in bold type. He inaugurated the season-ticket, charging three guineas admittance to cover all productions of the season, excluding benefits. He stopped the admission of patrons at half price for the second part of the evening's programme. He even arranged for a system of one-way traffic to operate in the adjacent streets which were (and still are) very narrow, on the evenings when a play was performed.

In 1748 Charles and Ann Macklin joined the company at a joint fee of £800 for two years. The presence of two such strong-minded – indeed overbearing – players in the same theatre caused much tension, especially as Sheridan insisted that as manager he should receive larger-type billing than Macklin when they appeared in the same play. Matters came to a head when Macklin, in a curtain speech, announced a benefit performance of *Twelfth Night* for himself and his wife, without having previously made arrangements with Sheridan. Sheridan immediately terminated their contracts, and Macklin sued Sheridan for dismissal without notice. The Macklins were then allowed the £300 which would have carried them to the end of their engagement.

Thomas Sheridan seems to have been one of those unlucky actors who, through force of youthful good looks and personality, captivate the audience in their early years but become the butt of critical stricture after their early bloom has faded, and the absence of genuine acting talent becomes more noticeable. Edmund Burke, the Irish politician and critic, said that as an actor Sheridan displayed poor carriage, effeminate gestures and a weak voice: a critic could hardly damn an actor more deeply.

Burke also criticized Sheridan's management-policy, especially the absence of encouragement for Irish actors and playwrights. This was not entirely fair, for a number of Irish players had been engaged (some, admittedly, via London) from time to time. The most recent acquisition was Henry Mossop (1729–74), a graduate of Trinity, who had tried to find theatrical employment in London, had been rejected by Garrick, and then presented himself to Sheridan. Later Garrick generously welcomed him to Drury Lane, where he played Richard III, Othello Macbeth, Coriolanus (his greatest part) and a host of others. Subsequently he managed Smock Alley and the theatre in Capel Street, but without much success

Burke's criticism of Sheridan's failure to promote Irish playwrights wa justified; but it must be said that Smock Alley could hardly offer better tha Covent Garden and Drury Lane. However, *The Earl of Essex* by Henry Brook proved to be very successful, and is one of the few plays first performed at Smo Alley to enter the London repertoire.

Henry Brooke had been a pupil of Thomas Sheridan the Elder in Capel Stree he may even have been related to the Sheridan family, for he came from the san part of Co. Cavan. He studied law, married his ward when she was only fourtee spent several years on the fringe of London literary society (where Pope prais his first substantial poem, *Universal Beauty*) and became the devoted parent twenty-two children. The Brookes returned permanently to Dublin in the ear

THIRD NIGHT.

This present *Thursday*, being the 9th of *February*, 1758, Will be presented, a TRAGEDY, called, The

EARL of ESSEX.

Written by *HENRY BROOKE*, Esq;

The Part of ESSEX to be performed by

Mr. SHERIDAN,

Burleigh, Mr. HURST,

Southampton by Mr. DEXTER,

Raleigh, Mr. STORER,

Nottingham by Mrs. KENNEDY,

Rutland by Miss KENNEDY,

And, the Part of Queen Elizabeth to be performed by

Mrs. FITZ-HENRY.

(Being her third Appearance in that Character)

The Characters drest in the Habits of the Times.

hich will be added, (the second Night) a *Pantomime Entertainment* called, The

M: Or, *Harlequin Villager.*

Scenes, *Musick* and other Decorations.

erof Harlequin by Mr. KING,

y Mr. SPARKS,

y by Mr. GLOVER,

Mr. HAMILTON,

Mr. MESSINK,

Miss MASON,

Mrs. KENNEDY,

NEW DANCE,

TIOLI,

AKER, &c.

49 Frances Chamberlayne
(Mrs Thomas Sheridan)

1740s, when he was appointed Barrack Master to Lord Chesterfield. On his death he left five unperformed tragedies, four unperformed comedies, and the libretto for an oratorio. His novel *The Fool of Quality* is the work upon which his reputation rests.

Brooke's performed plays were *Gustavus Vasa* (1739) and *The Earl of Westmoreland* (1741), as well as *The Earl of Essex*. The last mentioned gave Sheridan one of his favourite roles, which he played every season from 1750 to 1753, and again in 1757 and 1758; in one production at Smock Alley Peg Woffington played Queen Elizabeth. Ironically, when Barry later took on the part of Essex, he was regarded as far superior to Sheridan.

The years of Thomas Sheridan's management of Smock Alley in the early 1750s were notable for Peg Woffington's presence in the company. Sheridan and Woffington played Lord and Lady Townley in Colley Cibber's *The Provoked Husband*; and in *The Distressed Mother* by Ambrose Philips she played Andromaque to his Orestes. Among her other popular Dublin roles were Maria in Cibber's *The Non-Juror*, Constance in Shakespeare's *King John*, and Sir Harry Wildair in Farquhar's *The Constant Couple* – the part in which she had made her London debut and which few actors or actresses of the eighteenth century attempted while the memory of her dashing boyish interpretation lingered on. Her Smock Alley engagements realized a box-office return in excess of Garrick's.

Thomas Sheridan spent the years 1754–6 in England, acting mainly at Covent Garden, where Woffington was again the leading lady. He returned to Dublin in May 1756 as 'Deputy Master of the Revels and Masques of this Kingdom'. In spite of the prestigious title all was not well. During his absence Smock Alley attendances had dropped and the building had fallen into disrepair. Famine, and an unusually hard winter, naturally had their effect on theatregoing. Sheridan countered by providing spectacle; but the only real success of the 1756–7 season was the first production of the Scottish playwright John Home's *Douglas*, which had been rejected by Garrick, and in which Sheridan created the part of Young Norval, although he was really too old for it.

Matters were not improved by Barry's refusal to join the company, and by the announcement of his plans to build a new theatre in Crow Street. A series of disasters, including the drowning of Theophilus Cibber in a shipwreck on his way to rejoin Smock Alley, and the brilliant competition provided by Barry and his new company when Crow Street opened on 23 October 1758, caused Sheridan to lose heart completely, and give up all further ideas of theatrical management in Dublin.

Although he expressed a desire to quit the stage altogether, Sheridan often returned to accept leading roles during the remaining thirty years of his life, and he played an active part in the administration of Drury Lane while his son Richard was manager. For a time he ran an Academy of Elocution in Bath. He also published tracts and pamphlets on the theatre, language, and education, as well as a major pronouncing *Dictionary*, and a *Life* of Jonathan Swift.

Mrs Sheridan (Frances Chamberlayne) became a popular novelist, and her name was undoubtedly known to a much wider audience than that of her husband. In 1763 her comedy *The Discovery* was accepted by Garrick, who played in it, and revived it many times – one assumes that had Thomas Sheridan still been in management he would have produced it himself. She wrote another comedy, *The Dupe*; and a play which was never performed, *The Journey to Bath*. Almost a decade after her death her son Richard used part of the plot of *The Journey to Bath* as the basis for his comedy, *The Rivals*.

6
A very great man

1766–1773

Oliver Goldsmith

A visit to what has come to be known as 'the Goldsmith Country' will dispel any notions that the eighteenth-century poet, journalist, novelist and playwright has been forgotten in his native dwelling-place, for not only are all Oliver Goldsmith's real and supposed haunts carefully signposted, but people who probably know his literary works by nothing more than their titles still argue animatedly about the physical location of some incident in his life, or of a mirrored incident in one of his books.

One such argument still rages as to his place of birth. This is generally given as Pallas, Co. Longford, where his father, the Rev. Charles Goldsmith, was curate; but a tradition exists in the village of Elphin, in the neighbouring county of Roscommon, to the effect that he was born there while his mother was on a visit to her own family. A nineteenth-century house on the site of a much older farm-building is pointed out.

He was certainly brought up at Lissoy, Co. Westmeath, after his father had been appointed rector of the parish of Kilkenny West in 1730. Wayside notices, with quotations from *The Deserted Village*, identify such scenes as 'the busy mill' and

50 Lissoy parsonage, Co. Westmeath, as it appeared in the early nineteenth century. A few stones remain today.

'the decent church that topp'd the neighbouring hill'. Nothing is known of the family history beyond the fact that an ancestor in the previous century had relinquished the Church of Rome for the Church of Ireland, married, and had progeny, many of whom became clergymen or schoolteachers. Oliver Goldsmith was the great-great-grandson of this turncoat cleric.

His early years were spent in the kind of rustic simplicity which he later re-created with gentle irony in *The Vicar of Wakefield*, and with sad nostalgia in *The Deserted Village*. He went to school in Elphin, later in Athlone, and still later in Edgeworthstown – none of these places being more than a day's journey on horseback from one another, within the boundaries of the three midland counties.

51 Oliver Goldsmith

Goldsmith learned local ballads and folk tales, Irish country dances and the flute: his proficiency on the latter earned him many a night's lodging during his travels on foot through Holland, Belgium, Germany, Switzerland, France and Italy, with one shirt, and no money. He was fascinated, as a young man, by the work of the poet and composer Carolan (O Cearbhalláin), whom he was later to describe in *The British Magazine* as 'the last Irish bard'. He went to Trinity College as a sizar, for his father could not afford anything better, and lived in penury under an unsympathetic tutor, occasionally selling ballads to Dublin printers for five shillings. He obtained his Bachelor's degree in 1749.

After this there followed a period of frustrating vegetation in the country. He considered taking up teaching, and the Church. His uncle Contarine, his only benefactor of any consequence, helped him to go to Edinburgh to study medicine in 1752, but he stayed there only two years. Half of his life was over; and the remaining half was to be spent almost entirely in Grub Street. When he earned any considerable sum from writing, or when his friends in Dr Johnson's circle helped him to some material advantage, his generous nature led him to profligacy and back to poverty again.

Goldsmith settled permanently in London in 1756. From this date to that of his death only eighteen years later, he was to write the enormous body of work for which he is remembered, including the novel regarded the world over as a master-piece, *The Vicar of Wakefield*, the poem which is arguably the greatest and certainly the most popular in English in the eighteenth century, *The Deserted Village*, and *She Stoops to Conquer*, equally arguably the century's outstanding work in the theatre. Nevertheless, he was to live for the first three years of this period in what the nineteenth-century biographer Charles Read succinctly describes as 'gloom and misery', alternating as an usher at a private school, a 'corrector of the press', a chemist's assistant, and a menial contributor to *The Monthly Review*. In 1759 he was regularly engaged by Smollett on *The British Magazine*, and then he ran his own short-lived periodical, *The Bee*. In 1760 he contributed the *Chinese Letters* (later reprinted as *The Citizen of the World*) to the *Public Ledger*. Gradually his standing improved; he made the acquaintance of several writers, including his compatriots Edmund Burke, Isaac Bickerstaffe and Arthur Murphy, as well as Samuel Johnson (who became a loyal supporter and admitted him to 'The Club'), Joshua Reynolds (who painted the memorable portrait by which his profile is best remembered) and David Garrick (who failed to produce either of his plays).

It is repellent, though true, to think of Goldsmith as the pet leprechaun of this circle: his undisguisable Irish midland accent, his unprepossessing appearance, his constant flow of humorous repartee, all marked him out as the joker of the group; but it is quite likely that he traded upon these attributes, and exaggerated them when it suited him.

In 1766 Goldsmith started work on a comedy, *The Good-Natur'd Man*. He had not been on good terms with Garrick since he had published the critical essay 'Of The Stage' in the *Enquiry into the Present State of Polite Learning* in 1759, naively expecting that most self-centred of actors to take it in the kindly intentioned spirit in which it had been written. Reynolds arranged for the two to meet, in the hope of a reconciliation, and Garrick said he would read the play. He kept the manuscript for three months – in fact, until the end of the theatrical season when there was no longer any possibility of presenting it – and Goldsmith had to beg for its return. Goldsmith then gave it to George Colman. Colman doubted the play's suitability, probably finding it too farcical for an audience steeped in sentimental comedy. Burke and Reynolds persuaded him to accept it, and Colman reluctantly agreed. This annoyed Garrick, and ever the man to take advantage of a rival in a public controversy, he obtained the very willing consent of another Irish writer, Hugh Kelly, to present his new play *False Delicacy* at Drury Lane on the same night as that advertised for the premier of *The Good Natur'd Man* at Covent Garden.

Hugh Kelly (1739–77), who was born in Killarney and came to London at the age of twenty-one, had worked in much the same journalistic milieu as Goldsmith, though one finds in his work none of the latter's superlatively discursive style, nor the understanding of human nature. Critics have placed Kelly firmly in the sentimental school. *False Delicacy* is admirably constructed, and though the characters are absurdly conscious of their moral responsibilities, and the plot is fraught with tearful reconciliations, the play succeeds as a highly skilled piece of

52–3 Scenes from *The Good-Natur'd Man*, Goldsmith's first play (*left*) in which he attempted, not altogether successfully, to eschew the sentimental style, and *False Delicacy* by the Irish playwright Hugh Kelly (*right*), a truly sentimental comedy which was first presented at Drury Lane to draw the public away from *The Good-Natur'd Man*.

theatrical writing – more skilled, perhaps, then *The Good Natur'd Man*. If Gold-smith had not gone on to write *She Stoops to Conquer* Kelly would not be so unfavourably compared to him as a dramatist; but Kelly's other comedies, *A Word to the Wise* (1770), *The School for Wives* (1773), *The Romance of an Hour* (1774) and *The Man of Reason* (1776), do not survive the test of time.

Colman took fright at the confidence displayed by Garrick and the Drury Lane players, and at the pessimism of the members of his own company, and postponed the presentation of *The Good Natur'd Man* until the sixth night of the run of Kelly's play. As it turned out, Kelly made £700, while Goldsmith made about half that amount; but a profit of between £300 and £400, from what had appeared in prospect a dangerous adventure, was a surprisingly good result.

Johnson and other members of the Club attended the first night as a claque, Johnson having himself contributed the prologue. The performance passed off tolerably well, though members of the audience hissed at the indelicacy of the scene in Act III where Honeywell's house is taken over by the bailiffs. The comic actor Ned Shuter who played Croker (a part inspired by a passage in Johnson's *The Rambler*), was thought by Goldsmith to have carried the production by his zestful interpretation; but the evening had been an ordeal for the author, following the period of uncertainty before and during rehearsal. He appeared to enjoy himself at a first-night party, but after the other guests had departed broke down in tears when left alone with Johnson.

Goldsmith was trying to mock the sentimental comedy, but in doing so he almost wrote one himself. (Parody sometimes becomes indistinguishable from the thing it ridicules.) He wrote in the preface: 'When I undertook to write a comedy, I confess I was strongly prepossessed in favour of the poets of the last age, and strove to imitate them. The term *genteel comedy* was then unknown amongst us, and little more was desired by an audience than nature and humour, in whatever walks of life they were conspicuous . . .'

If one assumes that the 'poets of the last age' were those of the post-Restoration or Queen Anne period (rather than, as some critics have suggested, the Eliza-bethan), then Goldsmith must have been thinking of Farquhar, whose later plays his own resemble so closely in feeling and atmosphere. Yet if he had Farquhar in mind, he did not follow his predecessor's model sufficiently well, for Farquhar would never have allowed a comedy to stray from excessive *politesse* on the one hand to outrageous farce on the other: he eschewed the former and kept the latter in check, retaining a unity of comic spirit. Goldsmith allowed himself too many styles and moods, and *The Good Natur'd Man* suffers from this, as well as from the blurring of intention which makes it difficult for an audience to understand that the gentility of certain scenes is supposed to be ironic.

Goldsmith took the idea for the two pairs of lovers, and their hopes of being left a fortune, from Marivaux' play *Les Legs*. The character of Lofty is a borrowing from an earlier French comedy by Breuys. Sir William Honeywood closely resembles Sir William Thornhill in *The Vicar of Wakefield*, and it need not surprise us that Olivia of *The Good Natur'd Man* is very much the same Olivia as in the novel. Professor Lytton Sells has demonstrated that *Twelfth Night* was also a source, and says that 'Lofty's assurance of being loved is a reminiscence of Malvolio's illusions regarding Olivia; while Honeywood's pleading of Lofty's case is a parody of Viola's pleading with the Duke for Olivia'.

It is interesting that the first audience, and some of the critics, objected to the tone of the scene in which the bailiffs are introduced. In this scene the embarrassed Honeywood pretends to Miss Richards that the bailiffs, Flannigan and Twitch, are 'officers'; and an extremely amusing conversation ensues when she assumes that they are officers of the Navy, and the men spiritedly play up to the deception. It was the bailiffs' language which disgusted the audience, for Goldsmith was presenting their dialogue realistically, and not as the speeches of quaint members of the lower classes, to which the followers of sentimental comedy were used. The scene was tried again in one of the original nine performances, and was also given in the published version.

Goldsmith was so upset by the anxieties attendant upon the production of *The Good Natur'd Man* that he resolved never to write another play. Yet three years later, when living in a farmhouse at Hyde on the outskirts of London, he referred in a letter to the fact that he was 'trying to write a Comedy'. 'It is now finished, but when or how it will be acted, or whether it will be acted at all are questions I cannot resolve.'

He submitted the play to Colman, who took some months to ponder, and still refused to come to a decision. Then, in some perplexity, Goldsmith gave the manuscript to Garrick, but subsequently learned that Colman had the same day responded to pressure from Johnson and had agreed to take it on. He then had to go through the humiliating process of retrieving the play from Garrick, saying, as he did so, that he would much have preferred Garrick to produce it – this was no doubt a genuine sentiment.

Then some of the Covent Garden players refused to co-operate. The actor cast as Tony Lumpkin could not bear the character, and so it was given to a younger man, Quick, who had little experience but was, surely, more suited to the part, as Woodward, the original choice, was fifty-six! The actor Smith refused Marlow, and this equally fine role was then offered to a young man who had never spoken on the stage – until Ned Shuter put himself forward and, fortunately, was cast. There was also a prolonged and bitter row as to which of two actresses should speak the epilogue.

54 Scene from *She Stoops to Conquer*. Marlow: 'Madam, every moment that shows me your merit, only serves to increase my diffidence.'

Fearing that the public might again fail to understand his intentions, Goldsmith published *An Essay on the Theatre; or, a Comparison between Laughing and Sentimental Comedy* in *The Westminster Magazine* for 1 January 1773. Whether or not this smoothed the way for *She Stoops to Conquer* – as the play was called when it opened on 15 March, and which turned out to be a 'Laughing Comedy' if there ever was one – it clarifies some of Goldsmith's own ideas on the subject. His arguments in the *Essay* are entertainingly put forward, as when he says that 'if we are permitted to make Comedy weep, we have an equal right to make Tragedy laugh, and to set down in Blank Verse the Jests and Repartees of all the Attendants in a Funeral Procession'. Rather in the manner of Swift's satirical reflections, he bemoans the fate of comic players who would lose their livelihood if sentimental comedy were permanently established. 'It is not easy to recover an art when once lost; and it would be but a just punishment that when, by our being too fastidious, we have banished Humour from the Stage, we should find outselves deprived of the art of Laughing.'

54–5, 57

On the opening night Goldsmith felt quite redundant, and went for a walk in the Mall, where an acquaintance persuaded him to return to the theatre. As he entered the house (according to William Cooke in *The European Magazine* of 1793) he heard hissing, which increased his nervousness – members of the audience were objecting to Mrs Hardcastle's failure to recognize her own garden – but it was an isolated disturbance, and Colman, who by this time had realized that the play was a success, told its author not to be 'fearful of *squibs*, when we have been sitting almost these two hours on a barrel of gunpowder'.

55 The garden scene in
She Stoops to Conquer
with the cast of the first
production at Covent
Garden: Shutter as Hard-
castle, Mrs Green as Mrs
Hardcastle, and Quick as
Tony Lumpkin.

56 Zoffany's painting (*c.*
1768) of a scene from
Love in a Village, by the
Irish playwright Isaac
Bickerstaffe, a source of
material for *She Stoops to
Conquer.*

The performance was a triumph, even though none of the great actors of the day took part. Twelve performances were given before the close of the season, from which the author's financial return after three benefits amounted to £502 18s 6d. A discussion ensued in the press as to the merits or otherwise of the sentimental comedy genre (to which this play clearly did not belong), *The Monthly Review* maintaining the opinion that sentimental comedy was 'better suited to the principles and manners of the age'. Dr Johnson is quoted by Boswell as declaring – and Johnson always has the last word – that he 'knew of no comedy for many years that has so much exhilarated an audience, that has answered so much the great end of comedy – making an audience merry'. Goldsmith's attitude was of course the same. When he asked the painter James Northcote if the play had made him laugh, and Northcote answered 'exceedingly', Goldsmith observed, 'That is all I require'.

The idea of Marlow and Hastings mistaking Hardcastle's house for an inn came to Goldsmith when he recalled being misdirected to the home of the Featherstone family in Ardagh.* The story involving Marlow and Kate, and Hastings and Constance, comes from Marivaux' *Le Jeu de l'Amour et du Hasard*, but via Isaac Bickerstaffe's *Love in a Village*, which is closer to the original and has little originality' – whereas Goldsmith's treatment more than justifies the words of the epitaph which Johnson wrote in his memory – *nullum quod tetigit non ornavit*: 'he touched nothing which he did not adorn'.

57 The 1982 revival of *She Stoops to Conquer* at the Abbey Theatre, Dublin, directed by Joe Dowling and designed by Frank Conway.

56

* The house is now a college of domestic science.

58 Statue of Goldsmith by
Foley outside Trinity
College, Dublin.

Isaac Bickerstaffe (1735–1812) was a member of Garrick's staff at Drury Lane: he was paid a retainer to read and edit plays. His play with music *Love in a Village* was constantly revived at Covent Garden, and when Bickerstaffe moved to Garrick's management it was revived simultaneously at both houses. Bickerstaffe was born in Dublin – it may be that their shared Irish background threw Goldsmith and Bickerstaffe together in London. Bickerstaffe was either staying with Goldsmith at Hyde, or at least regularly visiting him there, at the time *She Stoops to Conquer* was being written, and the critic John Ginger has suggested that he may even have proposed to Goldsmith that he borrow part of the Marivaux plot which had served so well in *Love in a Village*.

Ginger also sees Bickerstaffe's 'satyr/peasant' Hodge as the immediate inspiration for Tony Lumpkin, and speculates convincingly that Colman's nervousness regarding *She Stoops to Conquer* being so easily recognizable as a 'pinch' from *Love in a Village* led him to avoid casting actors who had been in Bickerstaffe's play in the parallel roles. None of the critics commented on the similarity. (Bickerstaffe was not present for the opening performance as he had left in a hurry for France, following a case of blackmail arising from his penchant for guardsmen. He remained on the Continent for the rest of his life.)

There are distinct echoes of Lissoy in *She Stoops to Conquer*: clearly Goldsmith put a great deal of himself into this work, whether he knew it or not. The relationship between Mrs Hardcastle and her wayward son Tony – one minute 'poor boy' and the next a 'great ill-fashioned oaf' – recalls something of what we know of life at the Westmeath parsonage. The notion of the hero with a stammer and an 'awkward prepossessing visage', who is shy before young ladies of his own class but the opposite in encounters with those of the lower orders, has a suggestion of reality which Freudian critics probably find engrossing.

This is no 'artificial' comedy – it is miles away from the Marivaudage – and when played in an artificial way it does not succeed. Indeed, there is little verbal wit, beyond that which arises from the characters of the persons engaged in the dialogue. The humour is natural and unforced, and when the farcical element is introduced it is never taken too far, and is always truthful to the nature of those concerned; in other words, it is believable within the comic framework of the whole. Goldsmith had learnt a great deal from his experience with *The Good Natur'd Man*; he now allows the audience to be a step ahead of the people in the play, and this creates an overall atmosphere of true relish.

The death of his elder brother Henry, of whom he was very fond, probably extinguished Goldsmith's thoughts of ever returning to Lissoy, and his very real feelings of homesickness were sublimated in *The Deserted Village*. Anxiety about his increasing debts was believed by Reynolds to have hastened his decline; and there is no precise medical diagnosis of his final illness. He died on 4 April 1774 at his rooms in Brick Court, London, and was buried in the graveyard of the Temple church. Members of the Club contributed to the memorial by Joseph Nollekins in Westminster Abbey. In 1864 a statue by John Henry Foley was erected at Trinity College, Dublin, to match that of Edmund Burke. A memorial window was placed in the church at Forgney, Co. Westmeath, about a mile from the original church at Pallas. Only a few stones of Lissoy parsonage remain.

7

The best of its kind

1775–1779

Richard Brinsley Sheridan

Thomas and Frances Sheridan had five children. Their eldest son, Thomas, died young. Their second, Charles, entered the Irish civil service. The two girls, Alicia and Betsy, married within the Dublin literary and professional circle. The youngest son became one of the two greatest writers of comedy in the English language in the latter half of the eighteenth century – the other being Oliver Goldsmith.

Richard Brinsley Butler Sheridan was born at 12 Dorset Street, Dublin, in a solidly respectable neighbourhood situated close to the fashionable Mountjoy Square. A plaque adorns the house to this day, though the street is now sadly decayed. He and his brother Charles attended Mr White's Academy in Grafton Street. Mr White described Sheridan as 'an impenetrable dunce'. In due course Thomas Sheridan removed him to Harrow School in England, keeping Charles, whom he believed to be much brighter, at home. At Harrow, according to a contemporary, Sheridan 'formed no particular attachments, nor left behind him any pleasing remarks of remembrance'.

When Frances died in 1766 the family moved permanently to England, eventually settling in Bath where Thomas opened his Academy of Elocution.

It was only natural that the son of the Director of the Academy of Elocution should meet the daughter of the Director of the Academy of Music. Thomas Linley's daughter Elizabeth was the most accomplished and sought-after soprano of the day. She was also sought after by several gentlemen, including the wealthy (and elderly) Mr Long, a certain Captain Mathews, Nathaniel Halhed (a schoolfriend of Sheridan), Charles Sheridan, and Richard Brinsley Sheridan himself. The resulting intrigues lasted for several seasons, and delighted the people of Bath; so much so that the playwright Samuel Foote wrote a comedy, *The Maid of Bath*, in which the protagonists appeared under all too easily recognizable pseudonyms. In a sequence of events anticipating the plots of Sheridan's own comedies – including two law suits, the miscarriage of letters, and a midnight elopement – Sheridan emerged the victor and departed secretly with Elizabeth for London, and thence to Lisle, pausing at Calais to be married 'by a priest well known for his services on such occasions'.

The enraged Mr Linley followed them, but was somewhat mollified to find his daughter lodged in a convent. He was told nothing of the marriage, and arranged a concert tour of remote English cities where he felt Sheridan would be unlikely to follow. On returning to Bath Sheridan was challenged to a duel by Captain Mathews; they fought, and Sheridan courteously spared his rival's life. In due

59

59–60 *Left* The home of Thomas Sheridan the
Younger, and birthplace of Richard Brinsley
Sheridan in 1751: 12 Dorset St, Dublin. *Above*
Richard Brinsley Sheridan, by J. Russell.

course Richard and Elizabeth were publicly married. *The Morning Chronicle* of
13 April 1773 reports:

> Tuesday was married at Marlebone Church by Rev. Dr. Booth, the celebrated Miss
> Linley, to Mr Sheridan. After the ceremony they set out with her family and friends,
> and dined at the Star and Garter on Richmond Hill; in the evening they had a ball,
> after which the friends returned to town, and left the young couple in a gentleman's
> house at Mitcham, to consummate their nuptials . . .

It is odd that although Sheridan had been brought up among the families of
actors and entertainers he could not countenance the idea of his wife continuing
as a professional singer. Thomas Moore applauds this decision, stating that
Sheridan, 'instead of profiting by the display of his wife's talents, adopted the
manlier resolution of seeking an independence by his own'. On the other hand, it
is possible that Elizabeth was tired of the life of the touring artiste; or Sheridan

nay have been professionally jealous. Whatever the reason, Elizabeth never sang n public again. Perhaps it would have been better if she had, for their life together vas not entirely happy, and was marred by infidelities on both sides.

Sheridan, with no real qualifications for any profession, set himself to work in he only professional mode of which he had any knowledge, that of play-writing. He caused a flutter in the Sheridan and Linley dovecotes in Bath when he said the ubject of his first play was to be 'his own story'. The proposed title, *The Rivals*, uggested a reopening of the feud between himself and Captain Mathews. Sheridan had shown draft scenes – some of them taken directly from his mother's inperformed play *The Journey to Bath* – to Harrison of Covent Garden, who ncouraged him to proceed, and within two months of this discussion the play vas on the boards. Family fears were allayed at the opening night on 17 January 775 when nothing overtly autobiographical could be discerned.

The Rivals was not well received. The character of the Irishman, Sir Lucius)'Trigger, was universally disliked, most of the critics decrying the writing of the part as well as the casting. *The Morning Chronicle*, 18 January:

> What evil spirit could influence the writer and the managers to assign the part of Sir Lucius O'Trigger to Mr Lee, or Mr Lee himself to receive it? This representation of Sir Lucius is indeed an affront to the common sense of the audience, and is so far from giving the manners of our brave and worthy neighbours (the Irish) that it scarce equals the picture of a respectable Hottentot, gabbing in an uncouth dialect, neither Welsh, English, nor Irish . . .

The following day *The Morning Post* was jocularly cynical about the whole affair:

> The comedy of *The Rivals* at Covent Garden is withdrawn for the present, to undergo severe prunings, trimmings and patchings, before its second appearance.

Six days later the same paper reported:

> At the second representation of the new comedy of *The Rivals*, it was received with warm bursts of approbation by a crowded and apparently impartial audience. The author has very judiciously removed everything that could give offence in the character of Sir Lucius O'Trigger . . .

An early copy of *The Rivals* has been preserved. The character of Sir Lucius vas indeed coarse, and Sheridan softened his language. Some of the changes are imple excisions of the kind which are made after the first public exposure of almost every play. The 'malapropisms' spoken by some of the characters are emoved, so that this vein of verbal humour is left entirely to Mrs Malaprop. It is in extremely rare occurrence for a new play to fail so completely, and succeed so vell when revived ten days later. Sheridan, for his part, blandly stated that he had altered nothing', but simply advised that Sir Lucius be recast.

It is interesting to note how the reviewers concentrated their remarks on this aspect, and failed to notice the finer points of the play. Few even mention Mrs Malaprop, a character that has come down to us as one of the great comic creations of the theatre. It may be that Mrs Green was not a strong enough comedienne for the part which, in spite of its essential vulgarity, requires the expenditure of the same kind of comic energy as Lady Wishfort or Lady Bracknell. Perhaps the critics decided that they were not going to take this young upstart too seriously, even after the unusual second opening. Sheridan published the text himself, and had this to say in his Preface:

As for the little puny critics, who scatter their peevish strictures in private circles, and scribble at every author who has the eminence of being unconnected with them, a they are usually spleen-swollen from a vain idea of increasing their own consequence there will always be found a petulance and illiberality in their remarks which should place them as far beneath the notice of a gentleman as their dullness has sunk them below the level of the most unsuccessful author . . .

The Rivals is a fine if not a brilliant comedy. The characters display individual traits and absurdities which are exceptionally entertaining – in fact, they have a way of describing their own peculiarities which, in the end, contrives to weaken the action. Faulkland's casuistical jealousy, which he proclaims, fails to occasion any remarkable incident which might be expected to arise from the exercise of such a temperament; and Lydia's romantic ideas of herself do not produce the kind of extravagant love scenes which an audience might justly suppose should follow. Sir Lucius O'Trigger's belligerence is the only one of his several personal attributes which is developed to enhance the plot. Sir Anthony is the most proficiently sustained character, and his scenes with Captain Absolute are completely engaging. The dialogue has an amusingly homely quality which place *The Rivals* closer in feeling to Farquhar's *The Recruiting Officer*, and to Goldsmith's two comedies, than to the sharply destructive wit of Sheridan's later work. The actor Clinch, who replaced Lee in *The Rivals*, was rewarded by the author with another Irish part, O'Connor in *St Patrick's Day*, a two-act farce which was brought out with success at Covent Garden on 2 May 1775. It is based on Thomas Sheridan's *The Brave Irishman*, but is altogether more refined. Captain O'Blunder in the original becomes Lieutenant O'Connor, 'a very well bred and discerning young man' – perhaps Sheridan had learned a lesson from his earlier attempt to show his countrymen as uncouth in order to amuse.

Less than a year had passed since the opening of *The Rivals* when Sheridan's third play was produced. *The Duenna* is described as 'a comic opera' and is set in a highly Anglicized Seville. Its dialogue is very different from the stilted type of exchange usually placed between musical numbers by writers in this genre. It is light and easy, with no great attempt at anything more – though there are a few instances of the kind of incisive remark which Sheridan put to full use in *The School for Scandal*, such as the allusion to Isaac's religious neutrality, 'like the blank leaf between the Old and New Testament'.

Thomas Linley, with the help of his son, wrote the music. *The Duenna* was presented seventy-five times during its first season – a record in London in the eighteenth century. During its run it became known that Garrick intended to retire (he was sixty), if not from the stage, at least from management. Sheridan's star was by now very much in the ascendant – he had three plays to his credit, one of them making a great deal of money; he had an inherited knowledge of theatre business; and he was obviously possessed of initiative and vivacity. Garrick was impressed by the son of his erstwhile colleague of Dublin seasons, and offered him his half-share of the patent of the Theatre Royal, Drury Lane. Sheridan immediately set about raising funds, and persuaded Thomas Linley and the wealthy Dr Forde to join him in the transaction. Dr Forde was a famous obstetrician, and the Irish actress Kitty Clive wrote to Garrick: 'What a strange jumble of people! I thought I should have died laughing when I saw a man-midwife among them. I suppose they have taken him in to prevent miscarriages!'

The new patentees raised £75,000 between them. They took over the acting company as well as the building, and very soon the following persons were recruited to the staff: Accountant, Elizabeth Linley; Musical Director, Thomas

62 The Irish actress Dorothy Jordan (1761–1816) as Cora in Sheridan's tragedy *Pizarro*. This undistinguished play provided excellent acting roles.

61 The scene in Sheridan's comic opera *The Duenna* in which Donna Louisa and Donna Clara reveal themselves to Ferdinand: 'How is this! My sister! Clara too! I am confounded.'

Linley Senior; Assistant Musical Director, Thomas Linley Junior; Wardrobe Mistress, Mrs Linley. It is sad to think of Elizabeth poring over the ledgers when she could quite legitimately have been engaged as the leading singer. Later, Thomas Sheridan contributed in various capacities, including that of Stage Manager.

Richard Brinsley Sheridan found his time as manager – his position would be termed 'Artistic Director' in today's parlance – very much taken up with reading new plays and sending out old ones to hack dramatists ('Script Editors') for adaptation – exactly the same routine as that followed by his father at Smock Alley a quarter of a century earlier. He adapted *The Relapse* by Vanbrugh as *A Trip to Scarborough* because the more polite late eighteenth-century audience would have found the Restoration comedy too ribald. He translated Kotzebue's *Pizarro*, giving Mrs Siddons, as Elvira, and Mrs Jordan, as Cora, parts which they 62 repeated almost unceasingly for the rest of their careers. He also helped to write or adapt several pantomimes. He made a new version of Shakespeare's *The Tempest* as an opera for Linley.

Wherever one turns for a glimpse of Sheridan the man – as distinct from the overgilded pen-portraits with their repetitive use of words like 'elegant' and 'brilliant' – there is always a sense of intense movement, often of frenzy, behind the *bon mots* of the salon or greenroom. Everyone, it seems, desired his company, from the Prince Regent down. Everyone, that is, except his near-relations, to whom he gave decreasing attention as the years passed; and his close associates at Drury Lane, though they admired his skill as a playwright, found him difficult to deal with on business matters. Mrs Siddons stated that, for her part, he was 'uncertainty personified', and that, financially speaking, he was 'the drowning gulph'.

Sheridan dedicated his next play to the actress Mrs Crewe, with whom he was enjoying a liaison, though she did not take part when it was produced. The first sketch for *The Slanderers* was probably written while Sheridan was living in Bath – possibly even before his elopement. There was to have been a scene in a lodging-house in that city, run by a Mrs Surface – a scene borrowed directly from that useful source of inspiration to Sheridan, his mother's *A Journey to Bath*. He then decided to treat the subject of slander on what he considered to be a more universal level, and moved the setting to London, changing the title to *The School for Scandal*.

He soon found that he did not have enough material for a full-length play; indeed, in the play as we have it the two famous scandal-scenes advance the plot hardly at all. Sheridan combined the slander idea with another which had been in his mind for some time – that of the rich elderly bachelor in the city, who marries a country girl: Sir Peter and Lady Teazle. (This theme had been a favourite with Restoration dramatists.)

On 8 May 1977 the critic of *The London Chronicle* wrote:

> *The School for Scandal* is the production of Mr Sheridan, and is an additional proof of that gentleman's abilities as a dramatic writer. The object of the satire is two-fold: detraction and hypocracy, which are the prevailing vices of the times . . . The dialogue of the comedy is easy. It abounds with strokes of pointed satire, and a rich vein of humour pervades the whole, rendering it equally interesting and entertaining. Upon the whole, *The School for Scandal* justifies the very great and cordial reception it met with: it certainly is a good comedy, and we should not at all wonder if it becomes as great a favourite as *The Duenna*, to which it is infinitely superior in sense, satire, and moral . . .

This is one of those rare pieces of press criticism which recognizes the importance of a new play and estimates, correctly, its historical position. *The School for Scandal* very rapidly surpassed *The Duenna*, both in the frequency of performance and in box-office receipts, and it remains one of the two most often revived of all eighteenth-century plays in English, the other being *She Stoops to Conquer*.

Sheridan and his partners were soon able to buy out the remaining moiety on Drury Lane. Thomas Sheridan, observing the play's success with the weary eye of one who had seen more new plays fail than he might have cared to enumerate, declared that he could not understand why everyone thought it so funny. A rival dramatist, Richard Cumberland, attended the first night, with his children, in a prominent box. Every time his children laughed he pinched them and said, 'What are you laughing at?' When Sheridan was informed of this he remarked: 'It was very ungrateful of Mr Cumberland to have been displeased with his poor children for laughing at my comedy, for when I went the other night to see his tragedy, I laughed from beginning to end!' Sheridan later lampooned Cumberland as Sir Fretful Plagiary in *The Critic*.

The School for Scandal has a number of structural weaknesses, but in a good production these become submerged by the tide of mockery which carries the play along. One obvious fault is that the young lovers Charles and Maria, never meet on the stage until the final scene.

I Initial page of the fourteenth-century play of The Three Maries. This liturgical drama relates the story of the discovery of the empty tomb, and was intended for performance at Eastertide, probably at the Church of St John the Evangelist in Dublin. The action is interspersed with choral passages. This superb manuscript is preserved in Marsh's Library, Dublin.

VI

63

64

terias capitibus velatis quasi tres marie querentes xp̄m si-
mule portantes pixidem in manibus cū aromaticis quaꝝ prima ad ingressū chori vsque sepulcrū procedat ꝑ quasi lamen-
tan-
do di-
cat.

Heu pius pastor occiditur quem nulla culpa
effō ꝗ mosito metual-
lo nutrint sc̄ā ꝯiei
infe cit o mors lugen da. sist modo et dicat. Heu

nequam gens iudaica quam dira freudet vesana plebs
Deinde iij
maria cōn
ereciam da. sumu ꝯi. Heu verus doctor obijt qui vitā
ad huc paruulū procede-
do prima maria dicat
fūctis contulit o res plangen da. hoc in mo in do.

Deinde
ꝯinꝰ
Heu misere cur contingit videre mortem saluatoris. maria.

Deinde
tercia ꝯi
Heu consolacio nostra ut quid mortem sustinuit. ria. in-

Hūc se
comn
Heu redempcio nostra ut quid taliter agere voluint. gaut

et procedant
ad gradū cho
ri altari dicentes. Iam iam ecce ecce iam properimus ad

II The playwright William Congreve, as a pupil at Kilkenny College, about 1685. This portrait, which is still in the possession of the Congreve family, was painted by the English artist William Claret, who was probably in Ireland to undertake commissions in the great houses, including Kilkenny Castle, seat of the Dukes of Ormonde.

III Peg Woffington, the most celebrated Irish actress of the eighteenth century, and possibly of all time. Though she excelled at portraying high-born ladies, she in fact came from a very poor Dublin family. For many years, while in London, she was Garrick's mistress, as well as his leading lady. Portrait by John Lewis in the National Gallery of Ireland.

IV *Opposite* Staffordshire pottery figure of James Quin as Falstaff, one of his most popular roles. Such figures were sold in hundreds as souvenirs. Quin was the illegitimate son of a Dublin barrister; he joined the company at the Theatre Royal in Smock Alley in 1714, later moving to London, where he is reputed to have become the highest-paid actor of the day.

This point was put to Sheridan, who explained that the actress who was to play Maria was not accomplished in romantic roles and he had spared her the embarrassment of appearing in love-scenes. This was clearly nothing more than a hasty excuse in the face of valid criticism, for the writing of the play had covered such a lengthy period that he could not possibly have foreseen what actress would have been available at the time of casting. Charles Surface does not appear at all until the second half of the play, though his presence is constantly referred to. There is difficulty, for the audience, in comprehending which Mr Surface is being discussed, as both Charles and Joseph are described by their surnames. At the end of the play nothing is made of the unmasking of Joseph: he simply leaves the stage. It is left to the director to contrive stage-business in which Joseph can be made to look ridiculous.

Dublin was to see *The School for Scandal* less than a month after the London opening. It was given at Crow Street, and *The Public Advertiser* reported that 'the first two nights were crowded, but on the third the throng assembled would have made three audiences'.

In 1779 Sheridan's satire on literary and dramatic charlatans, *The Critic*, was produced at Drury Lane with a splendid cast, many of the players mocking the bombastic tragic roles in which they had often seriously distinguished themselves, for *The Critic* contains a remarkable play-within-the-play, *The Spanish Armada*, a burlesque intended as topical, but, as time has shown, quite applicable to its subject in any age. Sheridan pillories the critic who writes his review based on backstage gossip before he has seen the play; the playwright who affects to pay no heed to criticism, treating it 'with calm indifference and philosophic contempt'; the actors who learn and rehearse roles which are patently absurd. The remarks made by the actors in the rehearsal scenes show a hilariously close observation of professional idiosyncracy.

Among Sheridan's adapted, uncompleted and collaborative works is a farce with music called *The Camp* which was performed at Drury Lane for nine nights in 1778. An invasion from France was expected at the time, but as the danger did not appear too great the camp at Coxheath became the scene of social rather than military battles. Officers' uniforms became all the rage as ladies' attire. In short, just the sort of fashionable inanity which Sheridan would have found an attractive butt for ridicule. The play is usually attributed to Sheridan's brother-in-law Thomas Tickell, who possibly provided the plot, but the dialogue of the central scenes is unmistakably by Sheridan. Here is Sir Harry Bouquet on the camp:

Why seriously, then, I think it is the worst-planned thing I ever beheld. For instance, all the tents are arranged in a straight line! Now, Lady Plume, can anything be worse than a straight line? – and is there not a horrible uniformity in their infinite vista of canvas? No curve, no break, and an *endless* avenue of marquees: abominable!

Sheridan arranges his sentences in very precise segments, building towards a smile at the comma, a titter at the semi-colon, and a resounding laugh at the full stop. James Boaden, biographer of the actress Mrs Jordan, analyses the kind of delivery that is required: 'When you read *The School for Scandal* or *The Critic* you discover the "tune" to which, like a composer, he had set every line. Accordingly, a natural actress like Mrs Jordan was all abroad in this antithetic and pointed speech . . .' A throw-away style of delivery is required: a striving for literalness can mar the whole rhythm; the most mocking remarks achieve their effect by the inconsequential way in which they are spoken.

V *Opposite, above* Charles Macklin, born McLaughlin, was the most famous Irish actor of the eighteenth century, and the only serious rival to Garrick on the London stage. He was constantly at variance with managements over money and billing. He excelled as Shylock (the painting by Zoffany is in the Tate Gallery, London) and also in the comic parts which he wrote for himself in *The Man of the World* and *Love à-la-Mode*.

VI *Below* The screen scene from Richard Brinsley Sheridan's comedy, *The School for Scandal*, at its first production in Drury Lane in 1777. By this time Sheridan was manager of the theatre, and had installed several of his relatives, including his father Thomas Sheridan, in positions there. None of the theatrical members of the family ever returned to perform in Dublin after this period. The painting, by James Roberts, is in the Garrick Club, London.

Sheridan's wit has been mistakenly likened to that of Oscar Wilde. The two dramatists share nothing more than an Irish family background and upbringing, followed by a career abroad. Though they both satirize the English upper-middle-classes, their verbal techniques are totally different. The wit in Wilde's dialogue is based on paradox: the audience is required to make a mental adjustment. Sheridan's technique is descriptive: the audience is asked to *see* something in an unusual light. Most of the lines which occasion laughter in his later plays are descriptive of some person, place or action, usually offstage. The allusion is almost invariably visual, and the audience is asked to imagine what has been described.

– Shall you be at Lady Clackit's? I'm told the Brahmin will be there, and the new French philosopher.
– No, it will be much pleasanter at Lady Brittle's conversazione: the cow with two heads will be there.

The absurdity of these fashionable ladies 'collecting' foreign celebrities of doubtful authenticity is compounded by the picture of the cow with two heads.

– A pretty woman studying looks and endeavouring to recollect an ogle – like Lady Blank, who has learned to play her eyelids like Venetian blinds.

Sheridan planned to write a comedy on the subject of affectation, and its abandonment is very much to be regretted. His notes show that the characters were to represent, in their most preposterous forms, affectation of Modesty, of Accomplishments, of Love of Letters, of Love of Music and Love of Profligacy. A kind of farcical morality-play seems to have been in his mind.

The period during which Sheridan wrote all his comedies extends to no more than five years. In this there is an exact parallel with Wilde, though Sheridan's

63 William Farren as Sir Peter Teazle in *The School for Scandal*. In the first production in Drury Lane he played Careless only later taking on the more famous role.

In the Queens name I charge you all to drop your swords and daggers

70

Theatre-Royal.

Mr. MONTGOMERY, in accepting the Management of the Theatre-Royal, views with diffidence his Abilities for conducting so important a charge; but he trusts to the unbiassed Judgment of a Dublin Audience, and relying on the Generosity of his Countrymen, he pledges himself to use every Exertion in his Power to merit their Approbation and Protection.

This present Evening, (THURSDAY) Dec. 10th,

HIS MAJESTY'S SERVANTS WILL PERFORM SHERIDAN'S COMEDY OF THE

School for Scandal.

Sir Peter Teazle, - - - Mr. FULLAM.
Sir Oliver Surface, - - Mr. YOUNGER.   Charles Surface, - - Mr. MONTGOMERY.
Joseph Surface, - - - Mr. THOMPSON.   Mr. Crabtree, - - - Mr. WILLIAMS.
Sir Benjamin Backbite, - Mr. MACARTHY, (from the Theatre-Royal, Drury-La ne. his third Appearance here.)
Sir Toby Bumper, (with a Song) Mr. WARD.
Careless, - - - Mr. HARVEY, (his second Appearance here.)
Snake, - - - - Mr. POWEL.   Moses, - - - - - Mr. JOHNSON.
Rowley, - - - - Mr. ROWSWELL.   Trip, - - - - - Mr. LAMBERT.
Gentlemen, Mr. FITZHARRIS, Mr. SUTCLIFFE.
John, - - - - - Mr. STANLEY.   Thomas, - - - - Mr. GOOD.
William, - - - Mr. REID.
Lady Teazle, - - - Miss WALSTEIN.
Lady Sneerwell, - - Miss CURTIS. (her third Appearance here.)
Mrs. Candour, - - - Miss L. KELLY.   Maria, - - - - - Miss ROCK,
Maid, - - - - Mrs. MITCHELL.
Ladies at Card-Tables, Miss SULLIVAN, Miss MAHON, Mrs. SMITH, Miss E. MAHON, and Mrs. T. SMITH.

End of the Comedy the Band will Perform

AN OVERTURE,

Composed by Mr. Wm. O'ROURKE.

TO CONCLUDE WITH THE FARCE OF

The Devil to Pay.

Sir John Loverule, - - - - Mr. WARD   Coachman, - - - - Mr. REID
Jobson, - - - - - Mr. WILLIAMS.   Cook, - - - - - Mr. STANLEY.
Butler, - - - - Mr. CURTIS, Sen.   Conjuror, - - - - Mr. ROWSWELL.
Servants, Messrs. SUTCLIFFE, DOWNES, TURNER, BRENNAN, and DIGNUM.
Nell, - - - - - Miss WALSTEIN,   Lady Loverule, - - Miss L. KELLY.
Lettice, - - - - Mrs. JOHNSON,   Lucy, - - - - - Mrs. BROAD.
Servants, Miss SULLIVAN, Miss MAHON, Mrs. SMYTH, Miss M. MAHON. Mrs. SMYTH, Mrs. MITCHELL, &c.

On FRIDAY, Sheridan's Tragedy of PIZARRO.
Rolla, - Mr. Montgomery.   Elvira, - Miss Walstein,   Cora, - Miss Whittaker.
With the Farce of the REVIEW.

On SATURDAY, the Opera of THE SIEGE OF BELGRADE.
The Seraskier, - - - - Mr. Horn.
Lilla, - - Miss Byrne. (from the Theatre-Royal, Drury-Lane, her third Appearance here these two years.)

The Public are respectfully informed, that Indisposition has detained Mrs. KENNEDY at Holyhead, but she will make her Appearance in a few Days.

☞ The Opera of THE HAUNTED TOWER, having been received with distinguished Approbation, will be shortly repeated.

In consequence of a recent custom of admitting Strangers behind the Scenes, greatly to the inconvenience of the Performers, the retardment of the Business, and dissatisfaction of the Audience, the Public are most respectfully informed, that for the future, NO PERSON WHATEVER will be admitted behind the Curtain, who is unconnected with the arrangements of the Theatre.

☞ It having been represented to the Proprietors, that Fault is found with the present state of the SEATS in the PIT, the Public are respectfully informed, that it was adopted from the Usage of the London Theatres, to prevent the accumulation of Dust; but if this Arrangement be not agreeable, any Change will be made to prove the Desire of the Proprietors, to render the Pit, and every other part of the Theatre, as Comfortable and Commodious as possible.

NOLAN, Printer, 3, Suffolk-Street.

period of comic creativity occurred at the beginning of his working-life, Wilde's at the end. Nothing that Sheridan wrote for the stage after the age of twenty-eight is of any originality: *Pizarro* was very popular, but is merely an adaptation. The second half of his life was taken up chiefly with politics – he became Member of Parliament for Stafford – though he continued with the management of Drury Lane, and saw that theatre through several disastrous seasons, and two fires.

The difficulties of finding subscribers for the rebuilding of Drury Lane after the fire of 1809 are said to have undermined Sheridan's health. Constant recourse to the bottle did not help. His family life deteriorated accordingly. Yet when Elizabeth died he was said to be inconsolable. His second marriage, to a Miss Ogle (ironically, the name of an offstage character in *The School for Scandal*), did not improve the situation greatly. His distresses increased every year, and the sum arising from the sale of his remaining theatrical property was soon exhausted. He was arrested for debt. Whitbread, the brewer – who was to rebuild Drury Lane – arranged his release, but writs and executions followed in quick succession, and bailiffs took possession of his house, removing the furniture. He was in fact arrested while in bed of, as it turned out, his final illness – and would have been removed to prison had not the doctor threatened the officer with the responsibility which he might thus incur. Sheridan died on 7 July 1816, in penury.

'Whatever Sheridan has done or has chosen to do,' wrote Lord Holland, 'has been *par excellence*, always the best of its kind. He has written the best comedy (*The School for Scandal*), the best opera (*The Duenna*), the best farce (*The Critic* – it is only too good for an after-piece), and the best address (*Monologue on Garrick*), and to crown all, delivered the very best oration (the famous Begums of Oudh speech) ever conceived or heard in this country.'

65–6 *Left* Poster for a Dublin revival of *The School for Scandal* at the Theatre Royal in Crow Street in 1818, with an advance notice of Sheridan's still-popular tragedy *Pizarro. Right* Aiden Grennell as Sir Benjamin Backbite, and Fergus Cogley as Crabtree, in a revival of *The School for Scandal* by Longford Productions at the Gate Theatre, Dublin, in 1956.

64 *Opposite* Political cartoon of 1843 showing Daniel O'Connell at the height of his campaign for the repeal of the Act of Union, depicted as Whiskerandos in *The Spanish Armada* – the play-within-the-play in *The Critic*.

8
Truly national

The theatre in the provinces,
the 'National Theatre', John O'Keefe

While Richard Brinsley Sheridan was enjoying the early fruits of success as a playwright and manager in his adopted London, Ireland was entering a period of prosperity and self-fulfillment unequalled during its seven hundred years under British rule. In 1782 many of the restrictions imposed on the Irish parliament, which had found a noble and eloquent leader in Henry Grattan, were removed.

It is not surprising that the resulting increase in social intercourse, as well as the improvements in communications, should create a demand for entertainments and theatres, and the second half of the eighteenth century saw the establishment of new concert-halls and playhouses throughout the country. Handsome assembly-rooms, often on the first floor of the Town Hall or Market House, were built by public subscription, even in quite small towns like New Ross, Westport, Mount-mellick and Roscommon; many of these survive, though only the old Assembly
67 Rooms in the Wexford Cornmarket have been preserved in anything like their original dignity.

Theatres were built in some towns of less than ten thousand people. The first theatre in Newry was opened in 1769 by the actor-manager James Parker, who

67 The Assembly Rooms, also known as the Old Town Hall, Wexford.

made it a regular stopping-place for companies travelling between Dublin and Belfast, who up to then had been obliged to make use of inconvenient halls. In 1773 an eccentric clergyman, Courtney Melmoth, who had relinquished the pulpit in favour of the pen and buskin, opened Drogheda's first theatre, on the same principle.

Belfast, at the time of Grattan's Parliament, had only twenty thousand inhabitants – but it was the fastest-growing town in Ireland, the centre of the linen-industry and of shipbuilding yards which were to become the largest in the world. It was also the liveliest centre politically, the climax of high-minded patriotism being reached when Wolfe Tone and others founded the Belfast Society of United Irishmen in 1791. When Tone visited Belfast on that occasion there was a comfortable playhouse off Rosemary Street, and subscriptions were being raised for the building of another, in Arthur Square, by several leading citizens such as Henry Joy, the publisher of the *Belfast News-Letter* Samuel McTier, and Dr Andrew Halliday – the latter remarking that 'Religion and luxury with us go hand in hand, no ordinary partnership. We are building a new meeting-house and a new theatre, bane and antidote together!'

The earliest theatre of which there is record in Belfast was known as 'the Vaults', situated near the River Lagan, probably in a converted warehouse as in Cork. It was certainly operating in the early 1730s, when it was the venue for the Smock Alley players, but locally promoted productions would also have been given between seasons by the groups of strolling players run by James Parker, Richard Knipe, Michael Atkins and Thomas Ryder. In 1770 Ryder converted a building in Mill Gate as a small theatre, for which the Dublin playwright John O'Keefe, who was an actor with the company, provided some pantomimes, such as *The Giant's Causeway; or, Harlequin in Derry*. These were adaptations of entertainments seen elsewhere, with local allusions and specially designed scenery depicting picturesque local views. The more serious repertoire differed not at all from that offered in Dublin.

In 1773 a permanent company was established at Mill Gate by Michael Atkins, drawing its actors from several touring companies, as well as from Smock Alley. *She Stoops to Conquer* was presented there only six months after its London debut, and a now-famous edition of the text was published by James Magee 'at the Bible and Crown in Bridge Street'. One of Atkins' actors, Myrton Hamilton, following a disagreement which resulted in Atkins moving to Cork where Ryder's troupe was then performing, took over the Mill Gate theatre, but abandoned it subsequently for superior premises which he converted to theatrical use, in Ann Street. The company was advertised as 'The Belfast Comedians', though most of its members were drawn from elsewhere. The ancient family of O'Neill from Co. Antrim provided the most influential patronage for this venture.

After two successful years in management Hamilton returned to Smock Alley as an actor, and Atkins once more took up his duties of running the Ann Street theatre. Within a very few years the house became inadequate for the needs of the rising population, and Atkins set himself to erect yet another – this time off Rosemary Street, opposite Roger Mulholland's Presbyterian church (which still stands as one of the most elegant buildings in 'the Athens of the North'). This new theatre was favourably compared to those of Dublin, and, after many representations – supported by the O'Neills – Atkins succeeded in persuading Sarah Siddons to play in Belfast for ten nights in 1785.

The Rosemary Street theatre was well patronized by members and supporters of the Volunteers, the nationwide movement dedicated to removing the English

She Stoops to CONQUER:

OR,

The Miftakes of a Night.

A

COMEDY.

AS IT IS ACTED AT THE

THEATRE-ROYAL

IN

COVENT-GARDEN.

WRITTEN BY

Doctor GOLDSMITH

✗✗✗✗
✗

BELFAST:

Printed by JAMES MAGEE, at the Bible and Crown in BRIDGE-STREET.

M,DCC,LXXIII.

68 Title page of the Belfast edition of *She Stoops to Conquer*, printed only a few months after the first London production, in 1773.

government's policies of political and economic suppression, which found its most enthusiastic support in Belfast. In 1791 – the year in which Wolfe Tone visited the city and contributed to the patriotic fervour – Atkins announced his intention of building his larger theatre in Arthur Square. When it opened two years later, the disturbances caused by the Government's decision to disband the Volunteers led to frequent cancellation of performances, and no performances at all were given during the winter of 1793–4.

The following September the company reassembled with the Limerick actor Andrew Cherry as its guest star. In 1797 it was forced to close again on account of the agitation that preceded the Rising of 1798. Then all performances were suspended, until 1799. It was only after the Act of Union of 1800 that social stability was restored – a stability which continued well into the twentieth century, as far as Belfast was concerned. The Theatre in Arthur Square was remodelled several times, finally as a cinema in the 1930s – a fate which ultimately overtook all, except one, of the great theatres of Belfast.

Cork never experienced the political and military turmoil to anything like the extent known (and still known today) in Belfast. Theatres came and went, but closures were a result of management difficulties rather than civil unrest. Indeed, during the 1798 Rising the Commander-in-Chief of the Cork garrison, Major-General Lake, arranged that the curfew be postponed until midnight during the theatrical season – no doubt as much to accommodate the officers and their wives as to placate the citizens.

As has been seen, Cork was provided with a theatre of sorts in 1713 when Ashbury established a venue for the Smock Alley players off North Main Street. Cork at this period was more than twice the size of Belfast; when Belfast's first theatre was opening, Cork's second, the Theatre Royal, in what was originally Dunscomb's Marsh but came to be known as Playhouse Lane, was in the process of being designed by Edward Lovatt Pearce. Tantalisingly, no record exists of whether the plan actually carried out was Pearce's or not: most likely it was, since no other architect is mentioned, and since Pearce had just furnished the designs for Aungier Street. The new Cork theatre was inaugurated by the Smock Alley players, and occupied by them from time to time; during Thomas Sheridan's regime at Smock Alley the company travelled to Cork for an extended season every summer. Touring companies and other scratch groups, however, provided most of the fare.

In 1759 Spranger Barry, then manager at Crow Street, Dublin, raised a sub-scription in Cork towards the building of a new and much more sumptuous play-house in George's Street (now Parnell Street) which he was able to open on 21 July 1760. He produced *Othello, Macbeth, Romeo and Juliet, Antony and Cleopatra*, tragedies by Rowe, Lee and Otway, as well as comedies by Gay, Steele, Vanbrugh and others, with Ann Dancer as his leading lady. The regular presentation of plays by such excellent authors was something quite different from the haphazard and often trivial selection which had been the normal course in Cork up to that date. The people of Cork, however, were ever noted for a worthy preference for their own amateur players, as against the incursions of professionals from the capital (although the professional companies often contained Cork-born artists). An early manifestation of this provincial attitude occurred when Spranger Barry neglected to make a courtesy call on the Mayor of Cork prior to the opening of his season; the members of the Corporation immediately sensed an insult and resolved that 'Mr Mayor ought to prevent their acting until they apply for his permission and publish same in their bills.' As it turned out, the Mayor and Corporation had no legal right to prevent any performances whatsoever, and were powerless to act, but the feeling of rancour remained, and Barry and his players were never popular in Cork, in spite of the admitted excellence of their productions.

Barry soon left the Theatre Royal, George's Street, under the care of his son Thomas. When Thomas died at the age of twenty-five, Henry Mossop of Smock Alley took over the management of both the Cork theatre and Crow Street, Barry having returned to the richer and more appreciative Covent Garden and Drury Lane. In 1770, due to pressing financial problems, Mossop had to resign his management to Tottenham Heaphy, who was associated with a number of theatrical ventures, mainly in Limerick.

Some original plays were presented (as well as the usual mixture of Shakespeare with Restoration and established eighteenth-century classics), including *The Siege of the Castle of Aesculapius* by an anonymous local author. Richard Brinsley Sheridan's *St Patrick's Day* obtained its first Irish production in Cork in 1776. Two smaller theatres had short lives – the Henry Street Theatre and the Gentlemen's Theatre. The Theatre Royal in George's Street continued to flourish well into the nineteenth century.

69 The touring actor Andrew Cherry.

The life of the eighteenth-century touring artist was extremely hard. It took three days to travel by post-chaise from Dublin to Belfast, a journey accomplished by train in the Victorian era in under three hours. Those who could afford to own a horse often preferred to ride and risk being late for engagements. Andrew Cherry (1762–1812) recalled that his first professional engagement with a touring company at Naas under a Mr Martin earned him tenpence-halfpenny – the only money he earned that year! When he was unable to pay for his lodgings in Athlone the landlady impounded his wardrobe, including the few costumes which he wore on the stage and which were, so to speak, the tools of his trade. A kindly local lady, seeing him moping at an inn, lent him her husband's cloak and allowed him to sleep on a bundle of hay; during the night he could not sleep for hunger and descended the stairs, terrified that the creaking boards would waken the household and he would be taken for a thief; all he found in the kitchen was some stale bread which he was loth to eat as he supposed it to be the only means of sustenance for the following day.

Cherry's career is typical of the time, and shows how closely knit the profession was, and how actors moved with frequency from one company to another. His parents wished him to enter the priesthood, as he was 'good at his books', but he was more interested in reading the latest plays than his catechism. He left Limerick for Dublin and became apprenticed to a bookseller in Dame Street. He then took part in some amateur productions, distinguishing himself as Addison's *Cato*. After his disastrous experiences in Martin's touring company he joined Knipe's troupe, and later was with Atkins in Belfast and elsewhere. When Knipe died Cherry married his daughter, and they continued to tour together. In 1787, when Thomas Ryder was engaged by Covent Garden from Smock Alley, Cherry was sent for as his replacement, and for six years was the leading comic actor in Dublin. He later progressed to London by means of seasons in Bath and Manchester, and a tour of Wales. In 1802 he was taking leading parts at Drury Lane. He wrote several unremarkable comedies, which were performed in England as well as at home.

Cherry and actors like him were also familiar with the theatres of the smaller cities of Londonderry, Galway, Waterford and Kilkenny, which received touring companies. Londonderry's earliest theatrical fare came direct from Dublin, when the Exchange in the Diamond was used by the visiting performers; later, Michael

THEATRE, LONDONDERRY.

By Permission of the Worshipful GEORGE HILL., Esq., Mayor

UNDER THE PATRONAGE
OF THE
INHABITANTS OF LONDONDERRY,
AND NO OTHER PLACE IN IRELAND.

" Amicus certus in re incerta cernitur."

FOR THE BENEFIT OF
Mr. O'CALLAGHAN
AND NOBODY ELSE.
On THURSDAY Evening, SEPTEMBER 26, 1833,

When will be performed the popular and highly interesting Drama of

MARY STUART;
QUEEN OF SCOTS.

Lord George Douglas, - - - - - - - - - Mr. ROBSON.
Roland Grœme, Mr. DYOTT. .. Lord Lindsay, Mr. PIERCE EGAN. .. Lord Ruthven, Mr. WADDY.
Sir Robert Melville, Mr. M'GOWAN.—Dryfesdale, Mr. THOMPSON.

Sandy, - - - - Mr. O'CALLAGHAN.

Mary Stuart, ... Mrs. CAMPBELL.
Lady Douglas, Mrs. ROBSON. .. Catherine Seyton, Miss A. KELLY. .. Mattie, Miss KELLY.

In the course of the Evening

MISS M. FORDE

Will Sing *Believe me if all those endearing young charms—Kate Kear-ney,* and *I've been roaming.*

A DANCE BY MASTER D'ACOSTA.

The whole to conclude with O'Keefe's much admired Musical Opera of the

POOR SOLDIER.

Captain Fitzroy, Mr. DYOTT.—Patrick, Miss KELLY.—Dermott, Mr. M'GOWAN.—Father Luke, Mr. WADDY.
Bagatelle, Mr. PIERCE EGAN.

Darby, - - - - Mr. O'CALLAGHAN.

Norah, Miss FORDE, who will introduce several much admired National Airs.
Kathleen, ... Miss A. KELLY.

Tickets to be had of Mr. O'CALLAGHAN at Mr. WADDY's, Shipquay, and of PIERCE EGAN, at the Theatre, and at the Italian Saloon.
The Doors to be opened at SEVEN O'CLOCK, and the Performance will commence at HALF-PAST SEVEN.
Boxes, 3s.; Upper Boxes, 2s.; Gallery, 1s.—Out-door Checks not transferable.

NOTICE.— On FRIDAY the celebrated Comedy of The WILL and The DEVIL and the LADY, for the Benefit of Miss KELLY and Miss A. KELLY.
And on SATURDAY, for the Benefit of Mr. ROBSON, great Novelty will be produced both in the PLAY and ENTERTAINMENTS.
N.B.— The Theatre will also be closed in a few days after the above Benefits take place.

70–1 The Exchange, Londonderry, where plays were performed until the permanent theatre was built in 1789, and (*right*) a playbill of its successor, 'Theatre, Londonderry', announcing O'Keefe's *Poor Soldier*.

Atkins brought his Belfast players, and the connection with Belfast grew more constant as that city progressed in prosperity. A temporary theatre was built outside the walls at the foot of Shipquay Street in 1786, and three years later Atkins erected 'an elegant and commodious' theatre in Artillery Lane, at the back of the cathedral: it was modestly described on the playbills as 'Theatre, Londonderry'.

There was surprisingly little theatrical activity in Galway in relation to the size and importance of the city – perhaps a reminder that the Gaelic literary tradition, which lingered in the west longer than elsewhere, was inimical to the drama. Plays were occasionally presented by visiting troupes, at least from 1739, but the location of the hall or halls is not known. In 1783 a philanthropic landlord, Richard Martin, built a small theatre in Kirwan's Lane. The Martins were theatre enthusiasts, and liked to take part in amateur theatricals themselves; local pride was such that Mrs Martin was once seriously described as 'excelling Mrs Siddons'! The Martins obtained the services of Robert Owenson to organize their first season, a season in which Wolfe Tone played two parts, while staying as a house-guest. In 1792 the talented and attractive Mrs Martin disappeared from Galway with an English gentleman, and her husband sold his interest in Kirwan's Lane, which remained in use as a theatre for only a further three years.

Waterford's theatrical standing during the eighteenth century was more substantial. A theatre had been built at the Blackfriars in 1737 and remained in use until 1784, when an enlightened Corporation included a theatre in its new City Hall on the Mall. The architect was John Roberts, a Waterford man not known as the author of any building outside the Waterford neighbourhood. He also built the Chamber of Commerce and the Cathedral of the Holy Trinity, and completely remodelled Christ Church Cathedral adjacent to the City Hall which, with Wyatt's Bishop's Place, forms a truly splendid architectural group. The Theatre Royal (as it came to be called) was remodelled internally during the nineteenth century, but it remains today as the only continuously operated theatre in Ireland dating from the eighteenth century.

Kilkenny, just thirty miles to the north, a city with a theatrical tradition going back to the fifteenth century, never possessed as fine a theatre as Waterford. The Court House and the Tholsel were used for performances by visiting players, and it was not until 1794 that a real playhouse was erected. This was situated on the Parade opposite the Castle pleasure-gardens on a piece of land donated by the Earl of Ormonde. The ubiquitous Robert Owenson was its chief instigator; he and his company had previously played on a number of occasions at the Court House and believed there was a potential audience for a properly appointed playhouse.

The opening performance at the Kilkenny Theatre was Sheridan's *The Rivals*, and the remainder of the repertoire kept to the exceedingly high standard of authorship common to theatres throughout Ireland. Kilkenny's population did not prove to be as interested as Owenson had hoped, and the venture lasted only for three seasons. The Corporation, so prodigal of its financial support to the early religious drama, did not come forward to assist the secular. An amateur company

72 The Town Hall (now the City Hall) Waterford, which contains the Theatre Royal. The interior is lighted by several superb Waterford chandeliers.

under the private patronage of Richard Power took over the theatre in 1802, after it had been derelict for five years; and for the following seventeen, created an annual season which greatly enhanced the social scene in the city and county.

Robert Owenson (*né* MacEoin, 1744–1812) was the most interesting, through in financial terms largely unsuccessful, actor-manager of the period. He was a native Irish-speaker from the Barony of Tirawley, reared in great poverty far from the world of footlights and plush. He obtained the hedge-school education – which would have meant that he learned Greek and Latin through the medium of Irish, literally on the side of the road, formal education for Roman Catholic children being proscribed. It is probable that while in service with a local landlord he learned to speak English, and observed at close quarters the amateur theatricals in which his employers indulged.

Somehow he became attached to a troupe of strolling players, and in London made himself known to Goldsmith (born in the next county) who in turn introduced him to Garrick. He had a good singing voice, and was given Irish parts. Goldsmith also introduced him to Dr Johnson, and he was subsequently admitted to the Club. Thus, through Boswell's *Life of Samuel Johnson* we know something of Owenson's sojourn in England. He married a Miss Mill of Shrewsbury in 1744 and returned to Ireland two years later, reversing the usual process by which Irish actors first received their training at Smock Alley, thence moving to London.

In 1788 Owenson was a member of the company which played at the Cork Theatre Royal. He appeared in Bickerstaffe's comic opera *The Recruiting Sergeant*, and also as O'Flaherty in Cumberland's *The West Indian* and O'Carroll in Reed's *The Register Office*. In Thomas Sheridan's *The Brave Irishman* he was naturally cast as Captain O'Blunder. At his own benefit in Cork he sang several Irish airs and presented his act as 'Phelim O'Flanagan', a comic character of his own invention. These somewhat 'stage-Irish' appearances concealed a genuine love for the Gaelic tradition from which he had sprung; and when the moment came – following a disagreement at Crow Street which caused him to hire the Fishamble Street Theatre with some of his colleagues – Owenson put forward a plan for the establishment of a company in which not only the writers, actors and musicians would be Irish, but the subjects of the plays and even the choice of incidental music would be (as his daughter, Lady Morgan, later wrote) 'truly national'.

73

Lady Morgan's memory, unfortunately, cannot be relied upon. Theatre historians up to the present have taken her word for it, and have perpetuated her error in stating that the first production was Robert Jephson's play *The Carmelite*. Jephson did not write a play of that title, but the English dramatist Cumberland did; and the third production was a revival by another English dramatist, Otway, his famous *Venice Preserved*, as the newspapers of the time show. Perhaps it was Owenson's intention to produce Irish work only. *The Carmelite* was, indeed, supported by John O'Keefe's comic opera *The Shamrock*, with music arranged from the airs of Carolan; and Macklin's popular comedy *The True-born Irishman* was also given.

Lady Morgan described her father's National Theatre:

The audience was as national as the performance; and the pit was filled with the red coats of the corps to which my father belonged;* and the boxes exhibited a show of beauty and fashion, such as Ireland above all countries can produce. . . . Everybody took boxes, but few paid for them. Orders were given in profusion when, lo! in the midst of the apparent success of this rival to the great Royalties,† Government granted an exclusive patent for the performance of the legitimate drama to – Mr Daly! . . .

* The Volunteers.
† Smock Alley and Crow Street.

Richard Daly, the current lessee of Crow Street, had successfully petitioned for a theatrical monopoly in Dublin (a monopoly which Thomas Sheridan had twice sought without success), with the result that not only was Owenson made to stop producing at Fishamble Street, but Smock Alley itself had to close. Lady Morgan continues:

> . . . In a capital so dramatic as Dublin, the event made a great sensation, which how-ever, soon subsided, but not before my father's friends had devised legal grounds to sue for remuneration for his losses . . .

Owenson was guaranteed an income of £300 for ten years, and he also accepted the deputy managership of Crow Street for the time being; but the National Theatre scheme perished in theatre politics, and he was unable to revive it in any of the theatres in which he subsequently worked throughout the country. His only publication of any substance is a long poem, *Theatrical Tears*, in the manner of Charles Churchill's *Rosciad*. Lady Morgan became a famous novelist, the author of *The Wild Irish Girl* which became a sensation in polite English society. She wrote one play, a comic opera called *The First Attempt*, which was performed at Crow Street in 1807.

By the time Owenson was trying to organize his National Theatre, Macklin was in his nineties, Jephson (if he did indeed write anything for Owenson) in his fifties, and O'Keefe in his forties. It cannot be claimed, therefore, that Owenson en-couraged young Irish playwrights: but as the period of preparation for his Fish-amble Street venture was very short, he could hardly have been expected to

73 Robert Owenson's daughter, the future Lady Morgan, as the 'Wild Irish Girl' of her own novel.

74 Fishamble Street Music Hall as it appeared at the time of Robert Owenson's National Theatre. The building has been demolished.

75 John O'Keefe, by
Thomas Lawranson, 1786.

commission new work. The Irish Literary Theatre of a hundred years later proceeded as a result of much discussion; furthermore, its originators, Lady Gregory, W. B. Yeats and Edward Martyn, were people of means who had no cause to consider that unless a play were produced the following week, their dependants would starve.

Were it not for the unrivalled supremacy of Goldsmith and Sheridan, John O'Keefe (1747–1833) would be considered the foremost Irish playwright of the period. He was much admired in his day. His *Recollections*, published in 1826, show a good-humoured, hardworking and extremely modest man. He wrote over two dozen comedies and farces, and about fifty comic operas, pantomimes and interludes, many of them lost. Hazlitt was right when he said 'there is no labour or contrivance in his scenes, but the drollery of his subject seems to strike irresistibly upon his fancy, and runs away with his discretion, as it does with ours . . .', but one cannot agree with Hazlitt's comparison of O'Keefe to Molière, for O'Keefe's comedies lack serious intent, and are never based on the social upheaval caused by a dominating central figure.

O'Keefe has been derided by some literary critics for the extensive amount of theatrical hack-work which he undertook, but it has to be remembered that this was part of professional life and no one, least of all O'Keefe himself, would have set any store by trifles like *The Irish Mimic*, or *Blunder at Brighton*, or *Merry Sherwood*, which were intended to do no more than amuse as afterpiece or curtain-raiser. Those who sneer at O'Keefe for this kind of production forget to sneer at Sheridan for *Robinson Crusoe* or *Cape St Vincent*.

John O'Keefe was born in Dublin. He was sent to Mr West's academy to study art, but his interest in the theatre overcame his undoubted talent for drawing, and he was admitted to the Smock Alley company by Mossop. From about 1765 until 1777 he led the itinerant life of the actor, appearing in Dublin and provincial towns. He married the daughter of Tottenham Heaphy, manager of the theatre in Limerick. During this period he wrote six farces which were produced in Dublin, Cork, Belfast, Londonderry, Waterford, and no doubt other venues on the circuit as well. His plagiaristic use of Goldsmith's Tony Lumpkin won applause: he sent the script of *Tony Lumpkin in Town* anonymously to Coleman at the Haymarket Theatre in London – it was accepted, produced, and revived many times all over the British Isles. O'Keefe made at least two visits to London, where he eventually settled; and from 1778 all his plays, even those which were very Irish in character like *The Wicklow Gold Mines* (1796), received their initial presentations at either the Haymarket or Drury Lane before finding their way back to Ireland.

O'Keefe returned briefly to Dublin in 1779 to write the comic opera *The Son in Law* which was produced at the Haymarket later the same year. Another comic opera *The Dead Alive* came out at the same theatre in June 1781, followed in September by *The Agreeable Surprise*. The plot of this charming piece devolves upon the unknown parentage of two orphans, and the misconstructions which arise when they fall in love; the work succeeds on account of its witty songs and the highly original character of the butler, Lingo, who prides himself on his knowledge of Latin – it is really the lowest schoolboy form of the language – which he uses to hilarious effect, unaware of the ludicrous spectacle he is creating.

The Poor Soldier (Covent Garden, 1785) is a revised version of *The Shamrock*, which had been written for Crow Street eight years earlier. It is easy to see why Owenson chose this for revival at his National Theatre, for it abounds in patriotic Irish feeling, and the songs are set to traditional Irish tunes; for the London production these were arranged for orchestra by William Shield. The scene is a cottage in the grounds of the Duke of Leinster, at Carton, Co. Kildare; there is a variety of amusing characters – Father Luke, a priest in search of advancement; Captain Fitzroy, a handsome scion of the military profession, who is in love with Norah, a country girl, but in the end gallantly stands aside in favour of Patrick, the 'poor soldier' of the title, who has returned from the campaign in America; Kathlane, a rustic maiden; Dermot, an equally rustic and romantic young man; Bagatelle, a French valet; and Darby, a comical rogue in the mould of Foigard in *The Beaux' Stratagem. The Poor Soldier* was re-published thirteen times, until 1850.

O'Keefe's best play, *Wild Oats; or, The Strolling Gentleman*, first produced in 1791, draws on his own experiences as an actor and allows for his prediliction for introducing Quakers as whimsical characters. It was revived by the Royal Shakespeare Company in London at the Aldwych Theatre in 1976 and subsequently transferred to the Piccadilly, enjoying a total run of almost two years. Francis King, critic of the *Daily Telegraph*, said that *Wild Oats* was one of the half-dozen first-rate comedies to be written between Farquhar and Wilde; and Bernard Levin of the *Sunday Times* wrote:

> . . . I swear it is as good as all but the very best of Congreve and Sheridan . . . Certainly he has nothing to learn from even the best of earlier or later *farceurs* for intricacy of plot, humour of dialogue or charm of characters. And he has something, at any rate to judge by this play, which the Feydeaus and their like, and indeed the Restoration dramatists and the Ben Traverses and *their* like, largely lack: a great humane gusto, a sense of harmony and decency and optimism, an ability to leave an audience weak with laughter yet realising that if they had done no more than smile they would still be weak from happiness . . .

Finally, Michael Billington of *The Guardian* noted that O'Keefe, 'like all the best writers of English comedy, was born in Ireland'.

76 The 1976 revival of O'Keefe's *Wild Oats* by the Royal Shakespeare Company, London.

9

Scenes that are brightest

1802–1863

Kilkenny Private Theatre,
more new Dublin theatres, Sheridan Knowles,
the lyric theatre

The nineteenth century opened with the passing of the Act of Union which abolished the Irish Parliament. Thereafter, the Irish Members sat at Westminster, and most of the influential families moved to London as a result. The era of optimism and expansion of Grattan and Tone was past, and Ireland was once again in a subservient position. A feeling of pessimism began to pervade all aspects of Irish life, increasing every decade until the disastrous famine-years of the 1840s.

Especially galling to people of spirit, as far as the Irish theatre was concerned, was the growing reliance upon London to provide the plays and the actors. Dublin, Belfast and Cork became 'dates' – though 'number one' dates – on the English touring circuit, and the theatrical fare was chosen much more with the audiences of Manchester or Bradford in view.

Some of the small provincial theatres which had provided dramatic entertainment of a reasonably high quality – certainly the choice of plays was exemplary – with Irish actors, adding zest to the social life of the community, disappeared altogether. One, however, did not disappear (at least for another twenty years), and this was the small theatre on the Parade in Kilkenny, which was taken over by an amateur group organized by Richard Power of Kilfane, a country estate near Thomastown.

The Kilkenny Private Theatre's season took place in October, and, according to contemporary press reports, the number of nobility and gentry attracted to the city was quite prodigious. The inaugural performances in 1802 were given at Kilfane, but thereafter the theatre was used, and in 1805 the interior was re-modelled by the Kilkenny architect William Robertson. Reviewers of the period constantly applaud the selection of Irish authors, while conceding that Shakespeare should take precedence over all. After Shakespeare, then, the most frequently performed playwright was Sheridan; the other Irish-born authors were O'Keefe, Bickerstaffe, Goldsmith, Farquhar, Southerne and Murphy, in that order. No original works were presented; nor did this activity yield up a tyro dramatist from among the members of the lively and liberal-minded families who took part.

Professional players were sometimes engaged to strengthen the local talent, among them the singer and poet Tom Moore, Bessie Dyke (who later became his wife), and the London actress Elizabeth O'Neill, who would not accept her fee, so overcome was she in her admiration for the charitable nature of the proceedings, and by the nostalgia which assailed her on returning to the land of her birth.

77 Pony races at Crow Street in the early nineteenth century. When in normal use, the theatre forestage extended to the curved boxes on the lowest tier.

Richard Power took most of the leading roles himself, playing as many as eleven parts in one short season. The Kilkenny Private Theatre came to an abrupt end at the height of its popularity in 1819, possibly because the sustained effort had become too much for its founders. As with so many amateur undertakings, no provision had been made for the succession.

The Crow Street theatre in Dublin closed in 1820 after sixty-two years of operation, though for reasons very different from those applicable to Kilkenny. During the Rising of 1798 performances did not take place owing to the curfew, and Robert Emmet's Rising in 1803 had a similar effect, with disastrous results for the company's economy. So desperate did the position become, that the management felt obliged to try all kinds of stage-novelties, including pony races round a wooden track built out over the auditorium – but this did not attract the crowds, because, as might have been expected, pony racing could be better enjoyed out of doors.

Frederick Jones, Crow Street's manager since the resignation of Richard Daly in 1798, was unpopular among his associates and was blamed, probably with justification, for the theatre's ill-fortunes. An example of his want of what today would be called a sense of public relations occurred one evening in 1814, when a musical-play *The Forest of Bandy* was announced for performance before the Lord Lieutenant, the Duke of Dorset. When the curtain rose the audience immediately realized from their first view of the scenery that the play which was about to be unfolded was not the one advertised, but another musical, called *The Miller and his Men*. Booing and hissing ensued, and the Duke and Duchess hastily made their exit, fearing a riot. Their very action caused a riot, instigated by those who felt the office of Lord Lieutenant had been insulted: and the fabric of the building was severely damaged.

It transpired that the owner of the dog which played an essential part in *The Forest of Bandy* had been refused a perpetual house-ticket and had removed his dog, necessitating a quick change of programme. The affair was blown up to an inordinate degree, and eventually Jones had to resign. After several further changes of management, some of them involving legal proceedings, the patent of the theatre was not renewed when it became due in 1819, and Crow Street closed the following year. It was indeed a symptom of the times that the new patent should be awarded to a successful London manager, Henry Harris. He immediately set about the construction of a new theatre, while maintaining performances temporarily in the Rotunda concert-hall. Within the amazingly short space of one year Dublin's new Theatre Royal in Hawkins Street was ready for occupation. This theatre was burned down in 1880, and replaced after a temporary building known as the Leinster Hall proved unsuitable.

While the Theatre Royal was regarded as the 'number one' venue in Dublin, the Adelphi in Brunswick Street was a close rival from 1823; it was renamed the Queen's soon after Victoria's accession. The nineteenth century also saw the building of half-a-dozen other large theatres in Dublin – among them the Tivoli, La Scala (which became the Capitol), the Gaiety, and the Palace (previously known as Dan Lowrey's, and now called the Olympia); only the Gaiety and the Olympia survive. An increase in the numbers of theatres from the 1820s did not mean an increase in drama, for they all housed opera, operetta, music-hall variety and other types of spectacle. The taste of the public altered as often as the names of the controlling companies or managers, and it is not possible to state that any one house maintained any particular policy towards its presentations over a sustained period.

Certainly the appearance of several opulent new theatres in Dublin cannot be interpreted as being due to a resurgence of creative activity: in fact the opposite is true. Playwrights like James Sheridan Knowles, J. S. Coyne and James Kenney were well regarded in England as well as Ireland; actors like Tyrone Power and Barry Sullivan entranced the populace of American as well as British cities; and, in the lyric theatre, composers like Balfe and Wallace enjoyed enormous popularity, even on the Continent; yet of an outstanding local company comparable to Smock Alley (in the past) or the Abbey (in the future) there was no sign. Ireland was now truly part of the United Kingdom and, by extension, of the Empire beyond the Seas; but far from engendering an international outlook this new status simply brought forth a spirit of dowdy provincialism.

78 The brief career of the actor William Betty (1791–1874) in some way epitomizes the cult of the meritricious which was to continue into the Victorian era. Betty was born in Belfast and at a very early age astonished his relatives and teachers with his histrionic ability. When he was ten he was exhibited (that seems to be the only word) by his father as a prodigy, touring extensively in Ireland and Scotland before reaching Drury Lane in 1804. It is perfectly true to state that in major Shakespearian roles he took the town by storm, and Charles Kemble and Mrs Siddons were forced, quite seriously, to look to their laurels. Pitt even adjourned the House of Commons to enable its members to see Master Betty playing Hamlet. His picture was sold on thousands of broadsheets and calendars, and the term Bettymania was coined to describe the public furore created by the presence of this fascinating Irish boy in the capital. But Master Betty grew up; as an adolescent he no longer pleased; he was cruelly booed off the stage when he came on to play Richard III. His reign had been a nine-day-wonder, like that of a performing bear or some novel piece of stage machinery. The rest of his life was spent in obscurity.

VII James Sheridan Knowles, a first cousin of Richard Brinsley Sheridan, was born in Cork in 1784. His plays are now almost totally forgotten, but his tragedies were immensely popular in their time, and lauded by reputable critics, including Lamb and Hazlitt. This coloured print, with appliqué spangles, is a portrait of him as William Tell in his play of the same name.

The leading Irish dramatist – he certainly would not have used so lowly a term as 'playwright' – of the early nineteenth century was James Sheridan Knowles (1784–1862), a first cousin once removed of Richard Brinsley Sheridan. He was born in Cork. His mother died when he was sixteen, and he left home shortly after his father's second marriage because of his dislike for his stepmother.

London. A. PARK. 47. Leonard St. Finsbury.   Nº 85.

MR. SHERIDEN KNOWLES AS WILLIAM TELL.

VIII *Opposite, above* The Athenaeum, later styled the Opera House, at Lavitt's Quay, was the principal theatre of the city of Cork from the mid-nineteenth century until 1955 when it was accidentally destroyed by fire. It was replaced by a new building, also called the Opera House, on the same site in 1965. The successive theatres have played host to some of the world's most celebrated actors, dancers and singers.

IX *Below* Triple portrait of Tyrone Power as Conor O'Gorman in *The Groves of Blarney* by Mrs S. C. Hall, one of a series of rustic Irish plays in which Power excelled, touring all over the British Isles and the United States. The painting, by N. J. Crowley, is in the Tyrone Guthrie Centre at Annaghmakerrig, Co. Monaghan.

X Poster for the Victoria Hall, Belfast, one of the many Variety houses which flourished from the mid-nineteenth century until the first Great War. A few lingered on to the mid-twentieth century, including the Alhambra, the Royal Hippodrome and the Empire in Belfast, the Tivoli, Queen's and Capitol in Dublin, and the Palace in Cork. Some of the larger theatres, such as Dan Lowery's Music Hall (now the Olympia) in Dublin were famous for vaudeville.

THE SHAUGHRAUN

Conn

St Bridget's Abbey

The Escape of Robert Ffolliott.

Hogan's Shanty

"Drop those Knives!"

QUEEN'S THEATRE.

TWICE NIGHTLY

6.45 & 9

MATINEE
SATURDAY at 2.30.

David Allen & Sons Ltd Belfast

He joined the Wiltshire Regiment, and then studied medicine at Aberdeen. At some stage he must have given up medical practice, for his name appears as an actor on the Dublin, Wexford and Waterford playbills around 1809, and in the following year Edmund Kean acted in a play which Knowles wrote for him called *Leo; or, The Gipsy* at the Waterford Theatre Royal.*

In 1811 Knowles wrote *Brian Boroihme; or, The Maid of Erin*, which relates how Brian Boru's daughter was rescued from the Danish invaders by a dashing young prince named O'Donohue. It was first performed in Belfast, and subsequently at Covent Garden. *Caius Gracchus* (1815) also received its premier in Belfast, where Knowles was teaching English at the Royal Belfast Academical Institution. He then moved to Glasgow, where Kean suggested a Roman tragedy on the subject of Virginius. Kean must have made a ploy of suggesting this story to writers, for he appeared in a play of the same name, which is not by Knowles, at Drury Lane – but Knowles' version was produced in Glasgow by another management, and came to the notice of William Charles Macready,† then in the early years of a brilliant career.

Macready recognized *Virginius* as a showy vehicle for his own talents, and presented it at Covent Garden in 1820, with Charles Kemble as Icilius and Helen Faucit as Servia – an exceptionally distinguished cast. Knowles then rewrote *Caius Gracchus* for Macready, who produced it in 1823. The collaboration further resulted in *William Tell* (1825), which may perhaps be best described as a Swiss drama of grave moment, chiefly concerned with archery. In later years Knowles himself played the part of William Tell, and was the subject of a popular coloured print with gold-spangled appliqué work.

Knowles' dramas were intended to be 'Shakespearian', but in reality they hardly even achieve a feeling of pastiche. The sentiments are thin, the characters are wooden, the verse is blank and the verbiage is ponderous. (Lord Lytton, who noted Knowles' lack of talent, commented in a letter to Macready: 'I say, when I want a door to be shut, "Shut the door". Knowles would say, as I think he has somewhere, "Let the room be airless".') How, then, was it that William Hazlitt could have described him as 'the foremost tragic writer of the age'? – unless he was being subtly ironic, knowing that there were no tragic writers of importance about.

Charles Lamb was also Knowles' admirer. Knowles did know how to handle a situation, so perhaps his plays are good examples of situation-tragedies; but it is more likely that the critics (and the public) were dazzled by the show of spectacle on the stage, the pageantry, the lavish changes of scenery. *Alfred the Great* was produced at Drury Lane in 1831 after his first attempt at a comedy, *The Beggar's Daughter of Bethnal Green*, had failed. Undeterred, he tried another comedy, *The Hunchback*; this was taken on by Charles Kemble at Covent Garden, with Knowles in a supporting part – it was very well received, and when it reached Glasgow Knowles was treated as a local hero. His next play *The Love Chase* (1837) is a fine comedy, not unworthy of a kinsman of Richard Brinsley Sheridan, and public taste was not so wanting as to relegate it to obscurity, for it survived on the stage much longer than his 'serious' works.

Knowles returned to the stage as an actor in his later years, appearing in Shakespeare as well as in his own plays, in Ireland, England and America. In 1840 he was in Cork, and was supported in *Hamlet* and *Macbeth* by the young Barry Sullivan. In 1862 a public banquet was given in his honour in his native city – for Cork people are always pleased when one of their sons achieves eminence abroad. Knowles died shortly thereafter.

XI Playbill for *The Shaughran* by Dion Boucicault, the third in his Irish trilogy of melodramas. It opened at Wallack's Theatre, New York, in 1874, with the author as the loveable rogue or vagabond signified by the title. The background was in the Fenian uprising of 1865. The play was just as popular in England as in Ireland and the United States, and when special performances were given in aid of Fenian prisoners in British jails, the British public was still prepared to pay high prices for tickets.

VII

* Kean often performed in Waterford, where his son, the actor Charles Kean, was born in 1811.

† Macready was the son of William Macready, an Irish actor-manager who came to England in the late eighteenth century.

78 William Henry West Betty, child prodigy from Belfast, as Hamlet.

Two other prolific and popular Irish playwrights whose names were well known all over the British Isles were James Kenney (1780–1849) and Joseph Sterling Coyne (1803–38). Kenney wrote everything from tragedy to burletta – over fifty pieces in all. *Raising the Wind* (1803), a farce, *Ella Rosenberg* (1807), which was set to music by Michael Kelly, and *Sweethearts and Wives* (1823), a comic opera which ran for fifty-one performances at the Haymarket Theatre, London, were among those which continued to be billed as afterpieces until the end of the century.

Coyne wrote as many works, none of a high order, but all typical of the popular theatre of the time. His early farces were first produced at the Theatre Royal in Dublin, but after 1836 he was well enough known across the Channel to be able to command London productions first.

Two Irish composers contributed to the spectacular rise of the lyric theatre of their day – Michael William Balfe (1808–70) and William Vincent Wallace (1812–65). Both were fêted and honoured by opera companies, city corporations and governments, and their work was considered during their lifetimes to be of the highest international importance.

79   Balfe was born in Pitt Street (now Balfe Street), Dublin. His great grandfather had been a member of the Fishamble Street Music Hall orchestra which had given the inaugural performance of Handel's *Messiah*; his grandfather had been in the Crow Street theatre orchestra, and his father was a teacher of piano and violin. At the age of seven Balfe composed and arranged a 'polacca' for a military band, and at eight he appeared as soloist at a concert in the Royal Exchange. His father died when he was fifteen, and he persuaded the English musician Charles Edward Horn to take him to London, give him music lessons, and take a percentage of any fees he might earn.

This arrangement seems to have worked well for both parties, for within a year Balfe was a member of the Drury Lane orchestra and was showing remarkable competence as an arranger. At seventeen he discovered that he could sing, and he was taken up by Count Mazarra, who had lost his own son, and given tuition as well as luxurious accommodation in Rome. He also studied in Milan and Paris. He was engaged for three years at the Théâtre des Italiens where he sang Figaro and Don Giovanni. He was next appointed *primo baritone* at Palermo. While at Palermo he composed his first opera, *I Rivali de se Stessi*, which is said to have saved the company from collapse.

Balfe returned to London in 1833. Most of his operas received their first presentations there – *The Siege of Rochelle* (1835), *The Maid of Artois* (1836), *Joan of Arc* (1837), *Falstaff* (1838), *The Bohemian Girl* (1843), *The Enchantress* (1845), *The Bondman* (1846), *The Sicilian Bride* (1852), *The Rose of Castile* (1857), *Satanella* (1858), *The Puritan's Daughter* (1861) and *The Armourer of Nantes* (1863). *Les Puits d'Amour* (1843) and *L'Etoile de Seville* (1845) were first produced in Paris.

The Bohemian Girl was taken by the librettist Alfred Bunn from Cervantes, and so successful was the work that the gipsy costumes influenced the dress of London ladies for the season; the opera ran initially for a hundred performances and was produced in Germany as *Die Zigeunerin*, in France as *La Bohèmienne*, and in Italy as *La Zingara*.

Everywhere Balfe went he was met with acclamation; this may well have been partly due to his warmth of personality. His music was praised as being 'original and free from imitation of the style of any particular school'. He certainly possessed a gift for melody and for full romantic orchestration. While *L'Etoile* was running in Paris, Balfe was appointed musical director at Her Majesty's Theatre in preference to Spohr and Meyerbeer who were also contenders. Prince Albert sent fifty copies of the score of *The Rose of Castile* to his friends in Germany.

79 Michael William Balfe

80 A scene from Balfe's opera *The Puritan's Daughter*, first performed in London in 1861.

In 1838 Balfe returned to Ireland to visit his family, and coincidentally received an invitation to join the opera company at the Dublin Theatre Royal as a singer. He had been absent for sixteen years. At a civic reception he was presented with a gold snuff box (a curious gift for a singer!) but the public was disappointed that none of his own operas was presented among those which he chose to sing. He subsequently toured Ireland, and in Limerick the orchestra had to sit under umbrellas as the roof of the theatre was leaking. Balfe said it was the first and only *al fresco* performance he had given in his life, and promised to insert the following lines in future performances of *Diadeste*:

> *Diadeste, charming maid,*
> *Sing beneath th'umbrella's shade . . .*

Interior inundation or not, the tour was very profitable.

Many of Balfe's operas were performed up to the mid-twentieth century. Sir Thomas Beecham revived *The Bohemian Girl* at Covent Garden in 1951, and *The Rose of Castile* was the opera chosen by Dr Tom Walshe to inaugurate the Wexford Festival in 1951. A bust was placed in the National Gallery of Ireland in 1878; and the following year a memorial window was unveiled in St Patrick's Cathedral, Dublin.

81 The wayward traits and unsettled career of William Vincent Wallace probably contributed towards his receiving less acclaim during his lifetime than was enjoyed by Balfe. Certainly there is little to choose between them as far as their compositions are concerned, and Wallace's *Maritana* is more often revived than Balfe's *Bohemian Girl*.

Wallace was born in Waterford, the son of a bandmaster from Co. Mayo, in the theatrical lodging-house beside the Theatre Royal where Charles Kean had been born the previous year. In 1827 the family moved to Dublin where Wallace's father joined the Adelphi Theatre orchestra. At the age of eighteen he went as organist to Thurles Cathedral, in Co. Tipperary; the appointment carried with it the duty of teaching pupils of the adjacent Ursuline Convent, and Wallace fell in love with one of them, Isabella Kelly, whom he married the following year. One suspects that this may not have been looked upon with favour by the local religious authorities, for Wallace returned to Dublin shortly after. The 'O Salutaris' which he composed for the Thurles Cathedral choir was issued later as 'Hear me, gentle Maritana'.

Wallace became Deputy Leader of the Theatre Royal orchestra, but wearying of Dublin theatrical life, and fearing consumption (it is not known which force was the greater) he, his wife, and his wife's sister left for Australia in 1836. Various stories are related concerning his career there; one account states that upon arrival he abandoned Isabella and went off with his sister-in-law. He gave a concert in Sydney at the request of the Governor, Sir Richard Burke (who was Irish), and was paid in kind with a hundred sheep. He unsuccessfully tried to run a music school and bookshop, was hailed as the 'Australian Paganini', and when he decamped for Peru he was said to have had debts amounting to £2,000. He also visited Chile, Argentina, India and New Zealand. Berlioz, in *Les Soirées de l'Orchestre*, says that Wallace related stories of whaling in the South Seas.

By 1844 Wallace was playing his own compositions in Germany and Holland, and in 1845 in England, where Edward Fitzball showed him the manuscript of what was to become *Maritana*. The opera was produced at Drury Lane the same year, and ran for fifty consecutive performances. It was subsequently presented in most of the larger European houses.

Wallace's second opera, *Matilda of Hungary* (1847), failed at Drury Lane. A commission from the Paris Opera was abandoned when, again for reasons of health, he went on a voyage to Brazil, surviving an explosion in a steamboat on his way to New York, where in 1850 he married the pianist Helene Stoepel. (A lawyer advised him that his marriage to Miss Kelly was illegal, as he had been confirmed in the Church of Ireland, she was a Roman Catholic, and he had been under twenty-one at the time!)

In 1860, again to a libretto by Fitzball, he wrote *Lurline*, which made £50,000 for Covent Garden. *The Amber Witch* (1861) was musically an advance; *Love's Triumph* (1862) is said to have failed due to a poor production and playing; *The Desert Flower* (1863) ran for only two weeks.

A handsome plaque on a house in The Mall in Waterford commemorates Wallace's birth. Unfortunately, it has been erected on the wrong house.

81–4 William Vincent Wallace, and (*top, right*) the front page of one of his most popular arias. *Below, right* Mrs Honey as Lurline in Wallace's opera of the same name. *Below, left* The Theatre Royal, Dublin, built in 1821 in Hawkins Street to replace the old Theatre Royal in Crow Street. The new theatre was burned down in 1880.

10
The stage Irishman

1827–1890

Tyrone Power, Dion Boucicault,
Barry Sullivan and others

The mid-nineteenth century is usually cited as the period which introduced that much-maligned figure, the Stage Irishman; but this is simply because certain characters in Boucicault's Irish trilogy of plays – Myles na Coppaleen in *The Colleen Bawn*, Shaun the Post in *Arrah-na-Pogue*, and Conn in *The Shaughraun* – as well as characters in the novels of Carleton, Lever and Lover – are much more firmly embedded in the public memory than those of earlier writers.

The first Irishman deliberately used as a character in a play was probably Maurice Gibbon Fitzgibbon in George Peele's *The Battle of Alcazar* (1594); but as Fitzgibbon was Archbishop of Cashel, he is somewhat outside the common 'stage Irish' genre, which presupposes persons of less exalted rank. Shakespeare's Macmorris in *Henry V* (1598) is therefore the earliest known Irishman in the line of ignorant but well-intentioned rustics. Writers of the Irish school naturally introduced Irish characters: Farquhar's Roebuck and Foigard; Thomas Sheridan's O'Blunder; Richard Brinsley Sheridan's O'Trigger, O'Connor and O'Dawb; Macklin's O'Brallaghan and Mrs O'Dogherty; O'Keefe's Dermot and Darby and a host of others – these were favourites with audiences, and considered by actors to be 'plum parts'. Some English playwrights followed suit, making the Hibernian character the eccentric: Howard's Teague in *The Committee* (1665), Colman's Captain O'Cutter in *The Jealous Wife* (1761), Garrick's Sir Patrick O'Neale in *The Irish Widow* (1770) and Cumberland's Major O'Flaherty in *The West Indian* (1771) are outstanding examples.

Irishmen on the stage prior to the foundation of the Irish Literary Theatre of 1898 tend to fall into one or other of two categories – one, the lazy, crafty, and (in all probability) inebriated buffoon who nonetheless has the gift of good humour and a nimble way with words: in short, the ingratiating rogue; the other the braggart (also partial to a 'dhrop of the besht') who is likely to be a soldier or ex-soldier, boasting of having seen a great deal of the world when he has probably been no further from his own country than some English barracks or camp.

These stereotypes have a much longer pedigree than might at first appear: the former is an Irish naturalization of the parasite-slave, and the latter an adaptation of the *miles gloriosus* of classical comedy. There are many overlapping variations of the two types, depending upon the social class of the character depicted, and upon the extent of the author's knowledge (or otherwise) of genuine Irish speech and traits. Both Tyrone Power (1797–1841) and Dion Boucicault (1822–90) extended the range of the Stage Irishman through their performances in other authors' plays, and by means of their own writing: but it was the growth of middle-class audiences in the larger cities, and the accessibility of America as an outlet for plays and players, which resulted in their work reaching a vast public and thus, historically speaking, leaving an impression that the Stage Irishman was a nineteenth-century invention.

William Grattan Tyrone Power was born at Kilmacthomas, Co. Waterford. One assumes he was the son of the Marquess of Waterford, or at least of a member of that family; some sources state that he was 'of noble birth', others that his mother was 'taken care of' financially, as his father, whose name is not given, died in America when Tyrone was barely one year old. In any event his mother took him to Cardiff, where she had relatives, surviving a shipwreck off the Welsh coast on the way. He grew up in the household of a printer, and through supplying playbills to the local theatres became involved in theatrical life.

It would not be true to say that he 'ran away' with a company of strolling players – such a description would be more in keeping with some romantic incident in one of his own plays – but his decision to join a touring company at the age of fourteen certainly caused his mother much heartache. He led a fairly unsuccessful, picaresque (and indeed perhaps bohemian) life until he was nineteen, when he married a Miss Gilbert on the Isle of Wight. He continued playing small parts until the frustration due to want of professional recognition persuaded the young couple to emigrate to South Africa.

Power does not seem to have done well there either, for he was back in London in 1821. By the age of thirty he was still filling minor roles – often Irish ones – at Covent Garden; and it took the traditional stroke of fortune to set him at short notice before an admiring public in a highly suitable part. It happened that the leading Irish actor Charles Conor died suddenly while appearing at the Adelphi Theatre as O'Shaughnessy in William Macready's comedy *The Bank Note*; in the emergency, Power was pressed into the part. He was an immediate success (more successful, it was said, than Conor), and within a year he was able to command over £100 per week at the principal theatres of London and Dublin.

Tyrone Power was handsome in a rather delicate way; he had blue eyes, brown hair, and a light complexion. Contemporary portraits suggest a certain prettiness, 86 which was offset on stage by a dashing manner. He infused his portrayals with the same good spirits and exuberant humour which were a mark of his own character. For the next fifteen years he exploited his personality through the parts he played, writing several leading roles for himself in Irish comedies. Audiences went more to enjoy his familiar brand of character-acting than to see the play: his writing was a mere vehicle for his own talent, and while the plays which have come down to posterity have some theatrical merit, they have no literary value at all.

Power may be seen as an almost typical Victorian actor-manager – but with the difference that his lack of versatility prevented him from undertaking the variety of classical and contemporary roles which were a feature of the careers of his great English contemporaries Edmund Kean, William Charles Macready and, indeed, his countryman Dion Boucicault. Power's plays are slight affairs – with the kind of titles which made serious-minded Irishmen of a later era wince with embarrassment: *O'Flannigan and the Fairies*, *Paddy Carey the Boy from Clogheen*, and *The Irish Attorney; or, Galway Practice in 1770*. He also wrote a musical comedy, *Married Lovers*.

In 1837 Samuel Lover dramatized his own novel *Rory O'More*, with Power in the part of the romantic folk-hero of 1798. Another member of this Irish circle in London was the former Anna Maria Fielding, now Mrs S. C. Hall, who, with her

85–6 Tyrone Power, by d'Orsay, 1839. The 'last appearance' of Tyrone Power at the Theatre Royal, Dublin, in his own comedy *The Irish Attorney*, was his last appearance of the 1840 season, and also the last of his life in Ireland, for he died in a shipwreck in the following year.

IX

husband was engaged on that extravagantly comprehensive work *Ireland, its Scenery and Character*.

Early in 1838 Mrs Hall published *Lights and Shades of Irish Life*, which contained the story *The Groves of Blarney*. The character of Conor O'Gorman in this tale obviously appealed to Tyrone Power, for he and Mrs Hall collaborated on a stage-adaptation. The combination of Mrs Hall's cosy rusticity, the presentation of dramatic scenes (such as where Conor leaps a mountain chasm with a child in his arms), and Power's wayward warmth and bonhomie in the title role, completely captivated the London audience, and the play ran for a whole season at the Adelphi, followed shortly by visits to other British cities, to Ireland, and to America. The Irish artist Nicholas Joseph Crowley, who had recently settled in London, painted Tyrone Power as Conor O'Gorman in three characteristic poses.

St Patrick's Eve; or, The Orders of the Day stands outside the lighthearted vein of the rest of Power's writing. It is set in Prussia during the reign of Frederick II. It would amount to nothing more than a typical commercial drama of the period, were it not for the fact that a certain Major O'Dogherty – who is definitely not a Prussian – has a central role which diverts the doomed couple Gustavus and Catherine from their dangerous predicament and also diverts the theatre audience with amusing stories of his youth. Major O'Dogherty is in the *miles gloriosus* mould, though a dignified and witty example of it. The character perhaps demonstrates how Power, with approaching middle-age, moved from the parasite-slave type of charming young scoundrel to something better suited to his more mature

96

years. Major O'Dogherty's antics are verbal rather than physical, and expose a wealth of Irish country lore which Power must have obtained from his mother.

Tyrone Power toured the United States on four occasions, and wrote a lively account of visits to New York, Philadelphia, Boston, Newport, Providence, Baltimore and Washington in *Impressions of America* (1836). This, with its companion-volume which describes the Mississippi and the southern cities, provides a fascinating view of social and theatrical life between the early period of independence and the Civil War. In America, where the accents of rural Irish immigrants had coarsened in the cities, he was praised for presenting the 'true Irish brogue'. His success, and that of his company, was phenomenal, and he invested much of his American profits in the purchase of land in Texas and New York, as well as £3,000 in the United States Bank. He went to America to attend to property matters at the end of 1840. On 11 March 1841 he left New York on the steamship *President*, bound for Liverpool, as he was due to open a play of his own with (as matters turned out) the ironic title of *Born to Good Luck; or, The Irishman's Fortune*, at the Haymarket Theatre, London, on 12 April. He never again saw his beloved London public, or his family, for the *President* foundered in a gale off Cape Cod. It is said that the only copy of a new play by Mrs Hall, *Who's Who*, perished with him. One of Tyrone Power's great-grandsons was the American film actor of the same name; another was Tyrone Guthrie, a leading director of the twentieth-century theatre.

The most important Irish playwright of the mid-nineteenth century – indeed the only one whose works are still regularly performed – was Dionysius Lardner Boucicault. His life bridges the years between Sheridan and Shaw, and while his early dramatic style is not unlike that of Sheridan, his influence on Shaw was structural rather than stylistic. As the master of melodrama, he was the most prolific playwright of his age on either side of the Atlantic: he claimed to have written 250 plays, and if the adaptations and farces which he quite literally 'dashed off' for provincial managements and which were rarely printed are taken into account, the claim probably has substance. His biographer Richard Fawkes lists 142 works which are known to have come from his hand.

The obvious retort is that 'quantity is not quality'. Boucicault spent his life in a frenzied attempt to make money (he succeeded – many times) and to obtain the kind of 'position' which money could buy in the Victorian era. He also yearned after literary success, which eluded him mainly because of his constant anxiety to get the next play written and produced. He wrote seven first-rate melodramas, paragons of their kind – the Irish trilogy already mentioned, *The Octoroon* (after Mayne Reid), *The Corsican Brothers* (after Dumas), *The Poor of New York*, and *Jessie Brown*, as well as two excellent comedies of manners, *London Assurance* and *Old Heads and Young Hearts*, which stand not far below those of Farquhar and Goldsmith.

He was born at what was then 28 Middle Gardiner Street, Dublin, on 27 December 1820. The Boucicault (or Bourcicault) family were Huguenots who had been in the wine-trade in Ireland for four generations. Samuel Smith Bourcicault married Anne Darley, daughter of a respectable Co. Wicklow family, in 1814. Her father was the first Professor of English at Queen's (now University) College, Cork; her uncle, George Darley, was revered for his rather dull poetry and for a verse play about Thomas à Beckett which was produced in 1840; another uncle had a play called *Plighted Troth* performed in 1842; neither uncle recognized Dion's talent, being themselves of the school of literary gentry who looked coldly upon the professional proletariat.

87 Dion Boucicault, by Spy

The Darleys were not at all pleased when it became known that the father of Anne's youngest offspring Dion was the Dublin engineer and metaphysician Dr Dionysius Lardner. The 'situation' to some extent parallels that of Bernard Shaw's mother and the musician Vandaleur Lee – even the middle-class Protestant milieu is similar. Dr Lardner supported the young Dion until he was in his late teens, when the boy's profligacy estranged the father, and his allowance was discontinued.

Boucicault was sent to school in London and spent his early years, like Yeats, between the two capitals. When he was sixteen he played the part of Rollo in Sheridan's *Pizarro* in a school production. This experience convinced him that he should make his career in the theatre. Charles Lambe Kenney, son of the Irish playwright James Kenney, was an influential schoolfriend, and the Kenneys introduced Boucicault to their circle of playwrights and actors, but this first connection with theatrical life was severed when Mrs Boucicault decided that they should return to Dublin (her affair with Dr Lardner being ended) and so Boucicault finished his education under the eye of his disapproving relatives. Lardner, however, brought him back to London and found him a job as an engineering apprentice; but young Dion had no liking for his father's profession, took the name of Lee Moreton, and joined a company of players in Cheltenham, where one of his first parts was Rory O'More in Lover's play of that name.

His first farce to be performed professionally was *Lodgings to Let* (Bristol, 1839) in which he played the part of Tim Donoghue, 'an Irish emigrant, and a Genius of the first rate' – the play, the part, and the circumstances recalling Tyrone Power.

Unlike Power, Boucicault did not have to wait long for public recognition. After several uninteresting provincial engagements and a short period at a drama school where he was financed by his mother's cousin, Arthur Lee Guinness, of the firm of brewers, he took to full-time writing. *A Lover by Proxy* and *Woman* were not produced immediately (at the end of the century the former was to furnish much of the plot for Oscar Wilde's *The Importance of Being Earnest*), but a five-act comedy was accepted for production by Charles Mathews and his wife Madame Vestris who were managing the Covent Garden company. After much deliberation and considerable rewriting during rehearsal, it was named *London Assurance*, and opened in March 1841 with Mathews as Dazzle and Madame Vestris as Grace Harkaway.

London Assurance; or, Out Of Town (1841) takes place in England and Ireland. It is in the tradition of eighteenth-century comedy and might have been considered old-fashioned were it not for the fact that the 'box set', in which stage interiors were circumscribed by 'walls' and actors entered through real doors rather than from the wings, was a novelty which was only beginning to catch on and which Mathews made a major feature of his production, using real furniture, carpets and pictures. Yet it must have been the sheer buoyancy of the comedy, and the gay ebullience of the principal characters – an old-fashioned trait as well – which endeared the play to its public. Ronald Eyre, who directed a splendid revival for the Royal Shakespeare Company in London in 1970, describes it as 'a play of four love affairs: the love affair of Grace and Charles, the conventional meeting of the prettiest; the love-affair of Pert and Jenks, the conventional love affair of the most businesslike; the love affair of Mr Spanker and Lady Gay, the astounding meeting of the least likely; and the love affair of Sir Harcourt Courtley and his mirror'.

Boucicault's reputation was made. Queen Victoria attended a performance and was sufficiently amused to send round a gracious message. He obtained £300 for his work, but very soon spent the money on lavish entertaining. His next plays were not so popular, and they failed even to approach the standard of writing of *London Assurance*. It looked for a time as if he was going to be a 'one play author'. When he complained of his earnings the theatrical manager Benjamin Webster pointed out that first-class French comedies could be obtained for a translator's fee of only £25 – 'Why should I give you £300 or £500 for your comedy, of the success of which I cannot feel so assured?'

There was logic in the observation, and Boucicault turned to translations – he even went to live in Paris for a period – but the incident set him on the road to fighting the system of the single fee which did not take account of a long successful run. He proposed to the Dramatic Authors' Society that a royalty of ten per cent would be advantageous, but his idea was not taken up, and it was not until 1856 when he was at the height of his fame in America that he and other writers succeeded in having an amendment to an earlier Act carried by Congress giving the author 'the sole right to print and publish the said composition, the sole right also to act, perform or represent the same, or cause it to be acted, performed or represented, on any stage or public place', and making managers who pirated the works of other living writers – as Boucicault himself had done in Paris – liable for substantial damages. Boucicault used the amendment three years later when he successfully sued a Boston management for performing his play *Violet* without permission or payment.

Translations and adaptations were Boucicault's main source of income, and by the time he was twenty-six he had had thirty works performed in the West End. Of these, only *London Assurance* and *Old Heads and Young Hearts* (1844) endure. Both plays have a distinctly Georgian flavour, and both had Charles Mathews and Madame Vestris in the leading roles. *Old Heads and Young Hearts* was very warmly received, and the serious reviewers noted that Boucicault's real talent as a writer showed when he attempted original material.

When he was twenty-nine he accepted a post at £700 a year as writer-in-residence to Charles Kean, who had taken the Princess Theatre in London mainly as a showcase for his Shakespearian productions. Kean realized that he would have to vary this fare from time to time, and Boucicault's prolific pen provided first a comedy, *Love in a Maze*, and then a drama, *Pauline* (both 1851). The following year he gave Kean one of the most popular plays of either man's career, *The Corsican Brothers*, based on Dumas' novel, in which Kean appeared as the twins – parts which Henry Irving was to relish later in the century. Queen Victoria went five times to see it, and this considerably increased the public interest. The first production achieved sixty-six performances, and was pirated by several other managements.

Boucicault was next asked to write an afterpiece for Charles and Ellen Kean's benefit. The result was *The Vampire*, in which Boucicault took the title-role himself – a return to acting which drew much applause. The Queen, who was again present, commissioned a portrait of him in the part.

Among the cast of *The Vampire* was the actress Agnes Kelly Robertson, with whom Boucicault was in love. His first wife Anne Guiot, a French noblewoman, had died mysteriously after (it was said) her foot had slipped on a glacier in the Alps. Agnes was Charles Kean's ward, and Kean disapproved of the liaison. Personal as well as professional animosities flared; Agnes resigned from the company, quickly followed by Boucicault. Both parties sailed for New York, on different ships. Agnes obtained an engagement in Montreal in Boucicault's play *The Young Actress*, and shortly afterwards returned to New York where they were

88 The Scottish actress Agnes Robertson, Boucicault's second wife, who played many of his heroines, including those in the Irish trilogy.

married. She had an immediate success in New York in the same play under her husband's management, and the couple visited the principal cities of the United States.

The Boucicaults remained in America for seven years, travelling up and down the country, and for a time establishing themselves in New Orleans. They enjoyed success and failure, gradually becoming the leading theatrical duo of the day. With *The Poor of New York* (1857), *Jessie Brown* (1858) and *The Octoroon* (1859), Boucicault achieved recognition as the foremost playwright.

The Poor of New York was later adapted to every city in which it was played: it became *The Poor of Dublin, The Poor of Liverpool,* and so forth. It was also known as *The Streets of London,* and it is under this title that it was revived in the West End in 1980. It is pure melodrama, with a spectacular *dénouement* in which a house is burned to the ground. The setting was contemporary, and in spite of the pyrotechnics the play can be justifiably described as a social document of the times. When Boucicault returned to England he sent out several companies to play on different touring circuits concurrently.

Jessie Brown; or, The Siege of Lucknow also appealed because of its contemporary setting, though in this case there was the added advantage of an exotic Indian location. The heroine (played by Agnes Robertson in New York) is a Scottish maiden who, during the famous siege of the previous year, when all hope of relief seemed lost, exclaimed:

> *Dinna ye hear it? Dinna ye hear it?*
> *The pipes of Havelock sound!*

announcing the distant approach of the Highland regiment, which ears less well attuned to traditional Scottish music could not distinguish. Boucicault played Nana Sahib, the Sepoy leader, whom he made to appear as an arch villain (history may well have proved him wrong).

The third of Boucicault's contemporary melodramas to achieve wide acclaim in America was set in Louisiana and concerned itself with the intensely topical question of Negro slavery. *The Octoroon* is said to have been the first play in which this theme had been seriously explored, and it is unlikely that any American writer would have dared to touch it. As it was, Boucicault skilfully contrived to favour neither the Northern nor the Southern side, yet a great deal of personal hostility was raised against him by pre-slavery sections of the press. Disagreements regarding the Boucicaults' financial share of the very large box-office takings caused them to break with William Stuart of the Winter Garden Theatre and to join Laura Keene, the first actress in American stage history to manage a theatre. The move proved vastly profitable for both Miss Keene and the Boucicaults.

The chance discovery on a second-hand bookstall in New York of Gerald Griffin's Irish novel *The Collegians* (first published in 1829) set Boucicault on a new and highly lucrative course. He adapted the story of Hardress Cregan's love for the peasant-girl Eily O'Connor as *The Colleen Bawn* (1860), moved its setting to the romantic Lakes of Killarney, introduced spectacular visual effects, and made the scene in which Myles dives into the water to save Eily (whom the wicked boatman Danny Mann had tried to drown) the central dramatic moment in the play. These may be the usual trappings of melodrama; but Boucicault's characters are very real people, unlike those in Griffin's novel; the dialogue is brisk and witty, and the plot is most expertly framed.

Audiences in the United States, Britain, Ireland (and later, in France), simply adored the comic rogue Myles na Coppaleen ('Myles of the Little Horse'), the

89–92 The auction scene (*top*) from Boucicault's American drama *The Octoroon* (1859), his one really controversial play, and centre, Belfast poster for a production by the resident company in 1871. *Below*, *right* Design for a poster advertising a stock American production of *The Octoroon*. *Below*, *left* Woodcut illustrating the spectacular fire-scene in *The Poor of New York*.

93 Miss Louisa Pyne sings 'The Cruiskeen Lawn' from Benedict's opera *The Lily of Killarney*, based on Boucicault's play *The Colleen Bawn*, in turn based on Gerald Griffin's novel *The Collegians*.

part which Boucicault wrote for himself. In it he epitomized everything which American and British audiences regarded as charmingly and hilariously Irish. Surprisingly, Irish audiences were no less enthusiastic, finding no harm in the parasite-slave interpretation of Hibernian character. The accusations of 'buffoonery' which were directed against the Irish plays of Boucicault half a century later are understandable, for those connected with the nationalist movement felt in duty bound to rid the stage of any taint of forelock-touching drollery in the Irish character; and, contemporaneously, there was a general move against melodrama in favour of the new Scandinavian realism. Time, however, has shown how accomplished Boucicault was in his best writing, and – ironically for the founders of the Abbey Theatre to whom the theatre of Boucicault was anathema – revivals of his Irish trilogy were among the most successful Abbey productions of the 1960s and 1970s.

It was the success of *The Colleen Bawn* in New York that decided the Boucicaults to return to London, where they opened on 10 September 1860 for 260 performances, the longest run ever known in the London theatre. Queen Victoria went three times, the third being her last visit to any theatre, for after Prince Albert's death she never again entered a place of public entertainment. In Dublin Boucicault was treated, like Balfe, as a national hero. The four-week run at the Theatre Royal in Hawkins Street realized approximately £4,000 for himself and Agnes.

In 1862 the German composer Julius Benedict turned *The Colleen Bawn* into an opera, as *The Lily of Killarney*. It held the stage for at least fifty years, and even longer in Ireland where it was popular with amateur operatic societies up to the Second World War. It is certainly due for revival.

Arrah-na-Pogue (1865), the second play in the Irish trilogy, was first produced in Dublin with Agnes Robertson as Arrah Meelish and the author as Shaun the Post. The action takes place at the time of the Rising of 1798 and contains two famous 'set-pieces' – the escape of Shaun from a tower in which he is held prisoner, and the court-room scene which Bernard Shaw used as the model for the third act of *The Devil's Disciple*. In London, it ran for 164 nights, which disappointed Boucicault somewhat, but which, as was pointed out to him, was an admirable achievement if he would not compare it to *The Colleen Bawn*.

The Shaughran (1874) had its premier at Wallack's Theatre in New York. The story is set during the Fenian uprising of less than a decade earlier, and seems to have been of Boucicault's own composition. He cast himself as Con the Shaughran (Seachrán = wanderer or vagabond), and this turned out to be his most brilliant role, though at fifty-five he was much too old for the character. Audiences accepted him with acclaim everywhere, and he was presented with a testimonial by the Irish citizens of New York, a gesture which would not have been made by that essentially touchy immigrant community had anything which might have been thought defamatory of the Irish character been detected in the writing or the performance.

It is believed that Boucicault's private earnings from *The Shaughran* amounted to $600 per night. When the play went on tour in England, special performances were given an aid of the Fenian prisoners in British jails. It is an extraordinary tribute to the broadmindedness of the British people that they should have supported a fund for the relief of those who, by British law, were convicted felons: but perhaps tickets for the ordinary performances were so hard to come by that there was no other means of seeing the play! In 1878 the Irish trilogy was presented in New York with Boucicault and Agnes Robertson in their series of famous parts.

Boucicault married for the third time in 1885, having been blatantly unfaithful to Agnes, who had no other course than to divorce him. His new wife was the young actress Louise Thorndike, whom he married while on a tour of Australia. This estranged him from his children. His son Dot remained in theatre management in Melbourne and Sydney, returning in 1901 to London where he produced all the plays at the Duke of York's Theatre up to 1915. His daughter Nina became a celebrated international actress, creating the role of Peter Pan in J. M. Barrie's play in 1904. Boucicault died in New York on 18 September 1890.

94 Cyril Cusack as Conn the Shaughran in the 1967 revival at the Abbey Theatre, Dublin, directed by Hugh Hunt and designed by Alan Barlow. The production was immensely successful – ironically, the National Theatre Society had been founded sixty-four years earlier partly to stamp out Irish drama of this kind.

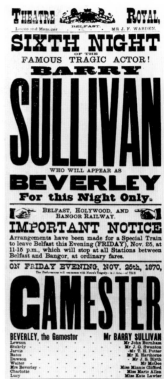

95–6 Barry Sullivan (*right*), and poster announcing his visit to Belfast in 1870.

97 Memorial statue at Glasnevin, Dublin.

Apart from Tyrone Power and Dion Boucicault – and they were writers as much as actors – the only Irishman of the mid-nineteenth century to gain international recognition as an actor of the first rank was Barry Sullivan (1821–91). He was almost an exact contemporary of Boucicault. He made his debut in Cork at the age of sixteen as Eustace in Bickerstaffe's *Love in a Village* – the play that had inspired Goldsmith. When Charles Kean visited Cork in the same year, Sullivan was cast as Rozencrantz in *Hamlet* and Seyton in *Macbeth*. In 1840 he played with Sheridan Knowles, possibly in one of Knowles' own dramas as well as in *Macbeth*.

From 1841 to 1847 Sullivan was acting in Scotland. In his first season at Liverpool he played Hamlet, Shylock and Othello, and by the time he reached London at the age of thirty-one he had a large number of important roles in his repertoire. A visit to America in 1858 earned him £8,000. He then visited Australia, where he remained for three years at the Theatre Royal in Melbourne in the capacity of actor-manager. Strangely enough, he did not appear in Dublin until he was nearly fifty, and here he received the traditional welcome accorded to the native son who has 'made good' overseas. He had the honour of playing Benedick to the Beatrice of Helen Faucit at the inauguration of the Shakespeare Memorial Theatre, Stratford-on-Avon, on 23 April 1879.

Barry Sullivan preferred Shakespearian tragedy to any other type of play. Though he appeared in many modern works, particularly in London, he was not at his happiest in them. As an actor of somewhat less stature than Charles Kean and William Charles Macready, he received greater acclaim in the United States than in England, possibly because the competition in Shakespeare was not so great there. He claimed to have played Richard III 2,500 times! His statue as Hamlet, by the sculptor Thomas Farrell, stands beside his grave in Glasnevin Cemetery, Dublin.

11
A delicate exotic fruit

1880–1895

Oscar Wilde

If critics fail to agree upon the supreme English-language comedy of the eighteenth century – considering equally the brilliance and longevity of *The Way of the World, The Beaux' Stratagem, She Stoops to Conquer* and *The School for Scandal* – there is unanimity in regard to the nineteenth century, for *The Importance of Being Earnest* has no serious rivals for the distinction.

Oscar Fingal O'Flahertie Wills Wilde was born in Dublin on 16 October 1854. When, one hundred years later, a subscription was raised in his native city by Lady Dunally and Micheál MacLiammóir to erect a marble plaque at 21 Westland Row commemorating the event, contributions were slow to materialize, and several harsh judgments concerning Wilde were expressed in the papers. On the day of the centenary celebration, when Lennox Robinson (Director of the Abbey Theatre) was unveiling the memorial, he received a tomato on the chest, thrown by a disapproving citizen. The small but vocal opposition to the project showed that over fifty years after Wilde's death, certain sections of the community still considered his name synonymous with moral outrage: the memory of the famous court proceedings which resulted in his imprisonment for homosexual offences being stronger than that of the superb comedies – as well as short stories, poems, and one astonishing novel – which he had given to the world.

98 Oscar Wilde's birthplace in Westland Row, Dublin.

The social milieu in which Oscar Wilde's parents moved, and the variety of activities which they pursued, exerted an undeniable influence upon his work and outlook. His father, William Wilde, was intensely interested in local history and folklore, and was at the centre of the Celtic Revival movement which resulted in much enthusiastic archaeological exploration, and the publication of countless bizarre theories on Irish pre-history and mythology; he named his house in Co. Galway 'Moytura' in the mistaken belief that the Battle of Moytura had taken place in the neighbourhood. His books on landscape and topography, *Lough Mask and Lough Corrib* and *The Beauties of the Boyne and Blackwater*, remain the most observant and charming guides to those areas. By profession an eye and ear specialist, he rose quickly to eminence, and was appointed surgeon to Queen Victoria and King Oscar of Sweden – hence his second son's given name.

In 1851 he married Jane Francesca Elgee of Wexford. Miss Elgee was a romantic Nationalist, her head crammed with the litany of Ireland's wrongs, which she hoped to put right by means of inflammatory verse. She was a contributor to the Young Ireland newspaper *The Nation* under the pseudonym 'Speranza'. In later years she undertook exhaustive research into Irish legends, and published collections of folk- and fairy-tales.

When the family moved to a large house in Merrion Square, Jane Francesca Wilde's salon became the chief meeting place of Dublin's 'artistic' coterie. She

99–100 Lady Wilde, Oscar Wilde's mother, *née* Jane Francesca Elgee, known to readers of *The Nation* as Speranza, and Oscar Wilde at the age of two.

had unconventional tastes in dress and interior decoration, which Oscar inherited. She dressed the boy in skirts up to the age of six, supposedly because of her disappointment at not having had a daughter. Biographers of Freudian disposition have attempted to claim that this was the reason for Oscar's sexual ambiguity. Others have laid stress upon a sentimental attachment to one of his schoolfellows at Portora Royal School, Enniskillen, where Oscar was a pupil from 1864 until his entry to Trinity College, Dublin, in 1871.

At Trinity he rapidly became known as a man of unusual sociability and charm. Quickwitted rather than profound, he nevertheless won the Berkely Gold Medal for Greek, and a foundation scholarship in classics. His principal mentor was the eccentric John Pentland Mahaffy, Professor of Ancient History, who was only thirty, and with whom Wilde later spent a momentous summer in Greece visiting the principal sites of classical Antiquity. Mahaffy's eccentricities evidently extended to the betrayal of former friendships, for when Wilde was sent to prison he primly declared, 'We no longer speak of Mr Oscar Wilde'.

In 1874 Wilde won a scholarship to Magdalen College, Oxford, where he immediately came under the influence of Ruskin and Pater. From the former he gained his enthusiasm for the art of the Italian Renaissance, and from the latter, quite clearly, his deliberately florid prose style, as exemplified in works like *The Happy Prince and Other Tales*. He visited northern Italy, and published poems, including his Newdigate Prize poem *Ravenna*, over a period in the *Irish Monthly*. Biographers have laid stress upon his aestheticism, his dedication to the precepts of Art for Art's Sake, his dabbling in the mystical elements of Roman Catholicism, his penchant for outrageous statements couched in the form of paradox. Yet his delight in outdoor pursuits, especially tennis, golf and – when on holiday in the west of Ireland – shooting is hardly recalled, for it does not accord with the accepted notion of the homosexual. Nor is the fact recalled that he worked extremely hard to obtain, and succeeded in obtaining, a double-first at Oxford, for this does not accord with the image of the indolent *flâneur*.

When he came down from the university in 1878 he was entirely lacking in 'prospects', and the income from the publication of poems and magazine-articles did not supplement his private means sufficiently to enable him and his friend the painter Frank Miles to remain in the opulent apartment which they had optimistically taken just off the Strand. They moved to Tite Street, Chelsea, which, as it turned out, was to be Wilde's home for the rest of his life.

In 1880 he wrote a play, *Vera; or, The Nihilists*, which he hoped to have produced at the Adelphi Theatre, but the production never took place. It was said that it might have offended the Prince of Wales (an inveterate theatregoer) as the royal family was related to the Tsar – the play being set in Russia. A more likely reason is that the prospective management realized in time that the play was dramatically weak. A few passages of heightened language may, with some stretch of the imagination, be taken as anticipating the prose style of *Salomé*, but there is little indication that the writer might one day be considered the most gifted dramatist of his age. Two years later, after Wilde had completed his phenomenally successful American lecture tour, *Vera* was produced in New York, but to a very poor critical response.

101 Wilde at the time of his American tour in 1882.

After his American tour in 1882 his tragedy *The Duchess of Padua* was printed privately, but also turned down for stage production. Its rejection by the American actress Mary Anderson was a cruel blow to Wilde's self-esteem, for he had described it as 'the masterpiece of my literary work, the *chef d'œuvre* of my youth'. In 1891 a Broadway production, under the title *Guido Ferranti*, with Minna Gale and Lawrence Barrett, ran for twenty-one performances and was later taken on tour by the same management with five other plays. Wilde wrote in wounded terms to his agent when he learned that it was being given fewer performances than the others, for he still believed it to be a work of 'value and importance'. Time, as well as contemporary opinion, has shown that it is no such thing. Set in sixteenth-century Padua, it has the revenge-theme typical of much early Elizabethan tragedy, but it is quite lacking in Elizabethan pyrotechnics in spite of the attempt at Shakespearian verse. *The Duchess of Padua* is a literary work, inspired by literature. Wilde had still to find his own true theatrical form.

In 1884 he married Constance Lloyd, daughter of a Dublin barrister, whose family home in Ely Place was within five minutes walk of the Wildes' in Merrion Square. They went to Paris, and then settled in London in Tite Street. The house was elaborately redecorated; a son was born; Oscar set himself to the urgent task of book-reviewing; and, in 1887, after the birth of his second son Vivian, to editing *Woman's World*.

His editorship, which he found irksome, flourished largely on account of his friendship with many of the leading artists and writers of the day; but there was a positive side-effect: application to formal routine and a regular timetable may well have induced what can only be described as a burst of creative activity, for over the next few years – that is, until the period of the writing of his five major plays in the early 'nineties – he published a very large number of short stories, poems and critical dissertations (often in the form of Socratic dialogue), as well as the novel *The Picture of Dorian Gray* which most critics found deplorably Satanic, if not utterly depraved; but Yeats and Pater wrote admiringly of it – and nobody now remembers the others.

If a period of history was ever embodied by one man, then Oscar Wilde certainly was the embodiment of the 'nineties. It was a time when artists in Europe as much as in the British Isles reacted most strongly against accepted social and artistic canons. The consciously-induced notion that the century was 'in decline' led to the cult of Decadence. The *fin-de-siècle* was at once the culmination and the finale for Wilde, as artist and social martyr. Between 1890 and 1900 all his most important works were composed and presented, while a sinister coda was being played, so to speak, in counterpoint: his arrest, trial, imprisonment and death.

102
103
Wilde's comedies, *Lady Windermere's Fan* (1892), *A Woman of No Importance* (1893) and *An Ideal Husband* (1895) are, theatrically speaking, very much of their time in structural and thematic terms. They are products of the taste for the 'well-made play' and closely resemble the later work of the English playwrights Henry Arthur Jones and Arthur Wing Pinero. Pinero's *The Second Mrs Tanqueray* (1895) shows influence in the opposite direction, for the first act is Wildean in its use of epigrammatic exchanges between the chief characters. Pinero, Jones and Wilde reacted against the Victorian predilection for melodramatic plots, but seen at the remove of almost a century it is obvious that they failed to rid themselves of all the vestiges of that genre. The theme of the 'woman with a past' is also part of the period currency.

In *Lady Windermere's Fan* (originally entitled *A Good Woman*) the 'woman with a past' is Mrs Erlynne, the mother of Lady Windermere. Lady Windermere

does not know that she is Mrs Erlynne's child, and it is upon the nature of this relationship that the plot of the play turns. The producer, George Alexander, wisely following the theatrical precept that one should never keep a secret from the audience (even if you keep it from the characters), tried to persuade the author that the mother-daughter relationship should be disclosed early in Act II, but Wilde was adamant that there should be a surprise *dénouement* in Act IV. After the opening performances he submitted to the change, and the press took satisfaction in declaring that the alteration was due to suggestions for improvement made by the critics. Wilde wrote a suitably *de haut en bas* reply, generously crediting Alexander with the idea 'long before I had the opportunity of studying the culture, courtesy and critical faculty displayed in such papers . . .'.

The play was a brilliant success with the London public – the attendance list for the opening night reads like a catalogue of the connoisseurs of art and letters of the day – but all the critics were unfavourably disposed. This view seems to have stemmed partly from their annoyance at Wilde's insouciance in taking his curtain call while smoking a cigarette, and partly from the disarmingly self-congratulatory tone of his curtain speech:

Ladies and gentlemen, I have enjoyed this evening *immensely*. The actors have given us a *charming* rendering of a *delightful* play, and your appreciation has been most intelligent. I congratulate you on the great success of your performance, which persuades me that you think *almost* as highly of the play as I do myself!

While the production of *Lady Windermere's Fan* was being prepared Wilde spent some time in Paris working on the text of a new play, *Salomé*. He composed in French, submitting the drafts to Adolphe Retté, Pierre Louys and Stuart Merrill, a Franco-American poet – all of whom helped to make linguistic correc-

102–3 First London productions: George Alexander and Lily Hanbury in *Lady Windermere's Fan* (1892); and Lewis Waller and Julia Neilson in *An Ideal Husband* (1895). Alexander and Waller were actor-managers, and produced these two plays respectively.

XII

tions without altering the shape or content of the work. It has been asserted that *Salomé* was commissioned by Sarah Bernhardt, but this is not so; Wilde met Bernhardt and presented her with a script: she was much impressed, and asked if she might play the title role. Wilde agreed on impulse, and accordingly she organized a French-speaking company to rehearse and open at the Palace Theatre in London. Neither author nor interpreter had reckoned with the possibility that the Lord Chamberlain (then the official British dramatic censor) might interfere, but interfere he did, by refusing to licence a performance under an Act designed to prevent the presentation of mystery plays of Roman Catholic ideology in the sixteenth century. The effective clause banned the portrayal of Biblical characters.

Sarah Bernhardt was incensed, largely on account of the loss of advance expenditure; and Wilde's rage was boundless. He declared, 'I will not consent to call myself a citizen of a country which shows such narrowness in its artistic judgement. I am not English. I am Irish – which is quite another thing!' As Wilde's son and biographer, Vyvyan Holland, has pointed out, it was a pity he did not carry out his threat of removing himself permanently to Paris and taking out French nationality – but at that moment he could not have foreseen his arrest under English law. Bernhardt eventually produced *Salomé* in Paris while Wilde was in prison. It was left to the Dublin Gate Theatre to give the first professional English language production, in 1928.

Wilde's next play, first known as *Mrs Arbuthnot*, was written, while Wilde and his family were staying at Cromer on the North Sea coast, specially for the actor Herbert Beerbohm Tree. Wilde claimed that he did not have Tree in mind for any particular part, but when it was presented, as *A Woman of No Importance*, Tree played Illingworth – the lead – as might have been expected. When they met to discuss Wilde's plans for the final act, Tree expressed some concern about the plot. 'Plots are tedious,' said Wilde. 'Anyone can invent them. Life is full of them. Indeed, one has to elbow one's way through them as they crowd about one's path. I took the plot for this play from *The Family Herald*, which took it – wisely, I feel – from my novel *The Picture of Dorian Gray*.'

Of course he had done nothing of the kind. The plot concerns Lord Illingworth, a dandy who believes that 'nothing succeeds like excess', and who has cast aside the woman who bore his son because he found her to be 'a woman of no importance'. The son, Gerald Arbuthnot, is unaware that Lord Illingworth is his father when he accepts the post of his private secretary. When Lord Illingworth makes an (undisclosed) improper suggestion to Gerald's fiancée Hester, Gerald threatens to kill him, and only then learns from the agonised Mrs Arbuthnot who Lord Illingworth actually is. An unsatisfactory final act ends with Mrs Arbuthnot striking Lord Illingworth, who departs (one assumes for ever), and her acceptance by Hester in spite of her tarnished past.

An Ideal Husband has a less strenuously contrived plot, and is altogether in a lighter vein. The story (taken from a play by Sardou) concerns blackmail and the selling of State secrets. This forms a solid base to the interplay of witty conversation. The most interesting character is Mrs Cheveley, 'a genius in the day-time, and a beauty at night'. Lord Goring, who may be taken as the typically debonair Wildean hero, possesses a latent seriousness which raises his position in the play far above that of the clever young men introduced mainly to scatter trivial remarks among the guests in Lady Chiltern's octagonal room in Grosvenor Square. However, if we look more closely, it becomes apparent that the many minor characters do have a function in helping to establish atmosphere and provide points of punctuation between the major scenes or confrontations.

104

Described somewhat tautologically as 'a new and original play of modern life', *An Ideal Husband* was produced by Lewis Waller and H. H. Morell at the Haymarket Theatre, London, with Charles Hawtrey as Lord Goring. The presence of that same Prince of Wales whom an earlier manager had sought not to offend brought added lustre to the first night in the eyes of the public, and even the critics were impressed by the Royal attention, and so did not find it possible to display their envy in print with such abandon: the author had clearly been 'accepted' in spite of his unconventional manner and appearance.

At this time George Bernard Shaw was theatre critic of *The Saturday Review* in London. He was, as always, astute:

> Mr Oscar Wilde's play at the Haymarket is a dangerous subject, because he has the property of making his critics dull. They laugh angrily at his epigrams. . . . They protest that the trick is obvious, and that such epigrams can be turned out by the score by anyone light-minded enough to condescend to such frivolity. As far as I can ascertain, I am the only person in London who cannot sit down and write an Oscar Wilde play at will. . . . In a certain sense Mr Wilde is to be our only thorough playwright. He plays with everything: with wit, with philosophy, with drama, with actors and audience, with the whole theatre . . .

While *An Ideal Husband* was in rehearsal Wilde was already working on the idea for his next play, *The Importance of Being Earnest*. Biographers of Wilde, and critics of his work, do not appear to have discerned that *The Importance of Being Earnest* is modelled on a farce by another Dubliner, Dion Boucicault, which was first produced in 1842. Wilde would hardly have bothered to seek inspiration by reading such a work by a dramatist then going very much out of fashion – but it is quite likely that he had seen the play on some casual visit to the theatre several years before, and he probably remembered the central situation, which everyone else would have forgotten.

104 Raymond Potter's drawing for *The Illustrated London News*, 1893, of the final moment in Act II of *A Woman of No Importance* stresses the melodramatic nature of the plot.

A Lover by Proxy concerns two effervescent young men, Lawless and Blushing-
ton, who live in town; and two delightful young ladies, Harriet and Kate, who live
in the country at Richmond: substitute Algernon and Jack (and Algernon's flat in
Half Moon Street), and Cecily and Gwendolen (at the Manor House, Woolton),
and the parallel is complete – except that Wilde made Gwendolen despise the
country. An aunt of forbidding demeanour, Miss Penelope Prude, clearly gave
Wilde the idea for *two* formidable females, Lady Bracknell and Miss Prism. Where
Boucicault's play strives after obvious effects, Wilde's has the appearance of
achieving them with a graceful ease; where the dialogue of one is quite flavourless,
the other recalls 'a delicate exotic fruit'; where Boucicault's characters could be
entertaining only if played by actors of poise and charm, Wilde's are implicitly
amusing, vital, and brimming with the energy of the naturally articulate.

Another sidelight on the genesis of *The Importance of Being Earnest* is given by
Hesketh Pearson in *Oscar Wilde* (1946). He mentions a theatrical tradition, un-
supported by any documentary evidence, that Wilde originally intended the play
to be set in the eighteenth century, no doubt in the same milieu as *The School for
Scandal*. It is fortunate that he abandoned the idea, for the result could only have
been pastiche, no matter how diverting.

The actual writing of the play took only three weeks. It is said that Wilde's
friend Robert Ross supplied the author with a list of his own witty sayings, which

Ross had recorded at dinner parties, and Wilde fitted them into the dialogue. There were originally four acts, but George Alexander wanted a shorter piece because he believed the public liked the main offering of the night to be preceded by a curtain-raiser. The four-act version was published in 1957, and it is clear that the editing process improved the work, though with the loss of a highly ingenious scene in which Algernon is arrested for debt, and the loss of an amusing minor character, Mr Gribsby, a lawyer's clerk. During rehearsals Wilde made a large number of small alterations, mainly in the sharpening of comic lines.

The Importance of Being Earnest opened to wild acclaim on 14 February 1895   105 at the St James's Theatre, while *An Ideal Husband* was still running at the Haymarket. Its plot is attractively simple, loaded though it is with improbable incident. The playgoer, attending a performance for the first time, does not need those frequent consultations of the printed programme which are so often necessary for comedies by writers like Congreve, where the series of intrigues and sub-plots can serve to confuse rather than illuminate. Wilde, in this play, makes no such demands: the patron sits back and allows the flow of repartee to carry him from situation to situation. Indeed, the play progresses entirely on the momentum created by its verbal precosity, and its structure is conditioned by the permutations of exchanges between the characters – of whom there are few. These characters gain their individuality from their own astonishing loquaciousness, their sense of language, their comprehension of the ultimate niceties of English speech. (Wilde's method seems to be contrary to that of other comic dramatists, who tend to create characters and situations and then give them expression.)

In *The Importance of Being Earnest* the form of expression conditions the character, and the seemingly inconsequential flow of dialogue – arranged as duets,

106 A 1982 revival of *The Importance of Being Earnest*, directed by Christopher Fitz-Simon and designed by Monica Frawley in black-and-white, at the Lyric Theatre, Belfast, with Liam Sweeney as Canon Chasuble, Margaret D'Arcy as Miss Prism and Kenneth Price as Jack.

107 Irish postage stamp, 1980, based on Toulouse-Lautrec's portrait of Wilde.

trios, quartets and full ensembles – imposes the dramatic structure. Interestingly, none of the stage musicals made from this play has been very successful; its structure may be that of operetta, in a sense, but Wilde's sentences are all-important – they cannot be chopped up as libretto, or subsumed by a score.

Some commentators, particularly in America, have remarked that Wilde perfectly conveys the speech-forms of the English upper classes, but this is far from the truth. No classes, in England or anywhere else, speak almost entirely in aphorisms. Indeed, the English aristocracy – if the record of debates in the House of Lords is anything to go by – are rather more ponderous, hesitant and lacking in wit than any other social group in that phlegmatic country. Wilde invented his own baroque form of dialogue: to this the actor must add *his* own observation of upper-class English *behaviour*. American interpreters are on weak ground here too, for they tend to sweeten, prettify and sentimentalize when they should be seeking crispness and lucidity, in an effort to obtain what they call 'period style'.

Wilde's epigrams are often quoted as the exhalations of a brilliant wit – and indeed this is what they are – but they lose something by being taken out of their theatrical context, whereas the maxims of La Rochefoucauld (for example) are meant to be considered for what they say without any dramatic inference. If, however, it is the case that Wilde 'inserted' epigrams into his dialogue, he did so with such consummate skill that the insertions do not – in his last play, at any rate – read that way; for one antithetical remark leads to another, and the flow of thought is guaranteed:

JACK: I am in love with Gwendolen. I have come up to town especially to propose to her.
ALGERNON: I thought you had come up for pleasure? . . . I call that business.
JACK: How utterly unromantic you are!
ALGERNON: I really don't see anything romantic in proposing. It is very romantic to be in love. But there is nothing romantic about a definite proposal. Why, you may be accepted. One usually is, I believe. Then the excitement is all over. The very essence of romance is uncertainty. If I ever get married I'll certainly try to forget the fact.
JACK: I have no doubt about that, dear Algy. The Divorce Court was specially invented for people whose memories are so constituted.
ALGERNON: Oh! there is no use speculating on that subject. Divorces are made in Heaven.

The director Tyrone Guthrie, in an interview on the subject of the Irish theatre in 1970, said '*The Importance of Being Earnest*, though it's full of nonsense, is also full of a great deal of profound and utterly charming sense. It is the greatest play of all time by an Irish dramatist.' In satirically exposing the *mores* of the English upper classes, and in making fun of the Englishman's serious regard for his own social institutions, Wilde follows the lead set by the earlier playwrights of the Irish school. As an outsider – in more senses than one – he is able to view the English national foibles with a fresh eye; and, like Goldsmith and Sheridan before him, he makes use of that most sacred of all English institutions – the language – to far better advantage than many Englishmen.

At the time of his trial Wilde's name was removed from the posters advertising the London productions of his plays, and also from the honours board at Portora Royal School – though it was later replaced there. The Hotel d'Alsace in Paris, where he died, was the first to honour him with a specially commissioned plaque. Dublin waited for more than fifty years before cautiously following suit. Dublin has a way of cutting its famous sons down to size.

12
The unspeakable Irishman

1892–1929

George Bernard Shaw

George Bernard Shaw (1856–1950) was his own greatest publicist. When he was XIV
not giving the world his views through the medium of the theatre, he was telling
the world about himself by means of speeches, articles, broadcasts and interviews.
There was little upon which he did not give an opinion, and he knew that his
opinion was worth the giving. His life, and his outlook on life, is so much an open
book that critics and biographers have had no difficulty whatsoever in finding and
repeating a thousand judgments and anecdotes, each one as apposite and amusing
as the last. There is no mystery: and perhaps that is why biographers have found
in certain other Irish writers – such as Swift or Wilde or Joyce – more fruitful
material for literary and psychological speculation.

Some biographers, finding no mystery, have sought to create one for themselves. Thus, there is a widely held view that Joseph Carr Shaw was not his father,
though Shaw, the most outspoken of men, who might even have revelled in the
idea of unconventional parentage, discounted the possibility.

He was born at number 3 (now 33) Synge Street, Dublin, two years after Oscar 108
Wilde, and only a few streets away. Their backgrounds, however, were quite 98
different: the Wildes were of the well-to-do professional class, with aristocratic
connections; the Shaws were mercilessly bourgeois, with aristocratic relations
who kept as far away from them as possible. The critic Arland Ussher has said
that 'in Shaw's boyhood there was in fact no recognized Irish middle-class, only
hordes of poor relations'; the Shaws were poor relations *par excellence*.

Joseph Carr Shaw had held a sinecure position in the Four Courts, which he
lost following changes in the legal administration. On the expiration of his post,
he received a sum of money which he invested in a small milling business; this
interested him not at all and he managed to run it inefficiently and unprofitably
until his death. He married Lucinda Elizabeth Gurley, who was seventeen years
his junior and who was by all accounts escaping from a distasteful family situation.
The Abbey Theatre playwright St John Ervine was later to describe her as having
'a cold unloving heart, a ferocious chin, and no sense of humour whatsoever'. She
certainly could have done with a sense of humour, for her husband was a secret
drinker, in spite of his amusing and spirited avowal that he was 'a lifelong and
bigoted teetotaller'. (His son, however, became such a one.)

The statement that Mrs Shaw had a 'cold unloving heart' is open to contradic-
tion. If she tended to ignore her husband, she had plenty of provocation. It is clear
that there was some kind of understanding – whether that word may be interpreted as 'love' is another question – between herself and the musician Vandaleur
Lee, who lived in an adjoining street. Whether Lee was Shaw's father or not we
are hardly likely to learn. The facts are that when Shaw was ten years old Lee

108 Bernard Shaw's birthplace in Synge Street, Dublin, then a shabby-genteel neighbourhood.

suggested that the whole family should share his newly acquired house and also his cottage on Torca Hill overlooking Dublin Bay. There was an excellent economic reason for taking up the offer, which the Shaws immediately did; and it may be supposed that Joseph Carr Shaw took advantage of the financial saving while turning a blind eye to his wife's relationship with Lee. She was an accomplished mezzo-soprano, and there was nothing strange in their spending hours of musical study together.

Shaw was sent to the Wesley Connexional School where he did not distinguish himself in any way. He said later that he was much more widely read than any of his associates, including the masters. A touch of intellectual snobbery may be discerned in the remark, yet he seems to have been an outgoing and cheerful schoolboy, with nothing aloof or reserved about him. He frequented the National Gallery of Ireland, which he said provided him with 'the only real education' he ever had in this country. He went to the theatre and became acquainted at first hand with the plays of Boucicault and the acting of Sullivan. He also went to concerts and the opera, probably on tickets supplied by his mother's friends in the music profession. He asserted that before he was fifteen he 'could sing or whistle from end to end leading works by Handel, Haydn, Mozart, Beethoven, Rossini, Bellini, Donizetti and Verdi'. All this had an inestimable value in preparing him for his work as critic during his twenties and thirties.

The idyllic summers spent at Vandaleur Lee's cottage came to an end in 1871 when Lee departed for London, followed (discreetly) by Mrs Shaw and her daughters. Shaw and his father moved into lodgings, and Shaw entered an estate-agency as office-boy. By the time he reached the age of nineteen he was doing well in the firm of Uniacke and Townshend, but on the death of his sister Agnes he joined his mother in London and lived with her there until his marriage. Contrary to many reports, Shaw contributed conscientiously to the upkeep of his mother's home, although his means at this period were always scanty.

During the twenty or so years which followed his arrival in London Shaw's prodigious physical and mental vigour supported him well in spite of his lack of money. Already a teetotaller, he became a vegetarian, and he subjected his body to rigorous exercise. He wrote endless articles, and five novels, none of which was published until he became better known for his other work. He joined the Zetetical Society (where he met Sidney Webb – the start of an enduring friendship), the Dialectical Society, Hyndman's Democratic Federation, the Land Reform League, the Economic Circle, and the Fellowship of the New Life – out of which he and the Webbs formed the Fabian Society. He joined the New Shakespeare Society, the Shelley Society, and the Browning Society. All this intellectual activity caused the raising of supercilious eyebrows: George Moore referred to him as 'the funny man in the boarding house'; Ezra Pound called him 'an intellectual cheese-mite'; and Henry James winced at the thought of the boundless energy of 'the unspeakable Irishman'.

He would, indeed, have been unbearable, were it not for his persistent good-humour and the practical kindness which he showed to those in less advantageous circumstances than himself. He continually sought advice and instruction: finding that he had all the faults of the nervous speaker, he took lessons in voice-production from an opera singer and, according to the drama critic C. B. Purdom, became 'one of the most fluent, cogent and attractive public speakers of his time'. Most of all, he studied in the library of the British Museum, where he read Karl Marx: 'From that hour I became a man with some business in the world.'

It is odd that he still had to discover that his real business was in the theatre; but he gradually approached playwriting by way of criticism. Shortly after his arrival in London Shaw took over from Vandaleur Lee as music critic of a weekly paper, *The Hornet*, and for two years Shaw delighted in expressing himself wittily on a subject about which he discovered he knew a great deal more than he himself had even realized. He made the acquaintance of William Archer, the leading British drama critic, who helped him to obtain a freelance position as book-reviewer for the *Pall Mall Gazette* from 1885 to 1888. From 1886 to 1889 he contributed art criticism to *The World*; and from 1888 to 1890 he was music critic for T. P. O'Connor's paper *The Star* under the pen-name Corno di Bassetto.

In 1890, having seen the London production of Ibsen's *A Doll's House*, and having defended Ibsen in face of the subsequent critical onslaught, he addressed the Fabian Society on the issue. His speech was expanded and published as *The Quintessence of Ibsenism*. This book is very much a forerunner of the type of writing he used in the prefaces to his own plays, taking up and discussing themes suggested by the subject but not necessarily relating directly to it.

It happened that some months after the publication of *The Quintessence of Ibsenism* a young Dutchman, J. T. Grein, came forward with money to 'give special performances of plays which have a literary and artistic rather than a commercial value'. The first production by the Independent Theatre was Ibsen's *Ghosts*, which was received with horror. Shaw quickly finished a play upon which he had unsuccessfully collaborated with William Archer seven years earlier, gave it the title *Widowers' Houses*, and Grein presented it for two nights in December 1892. Shaw described the theme as 'middleclass respectability fattening on the poverty of the slums'. As expected, it was not well received, Archer pointing out that Shaw was not really a playwright and Shaw partially agreeing; but he had

109

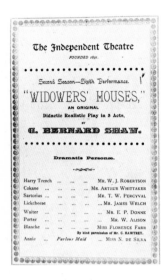

109 Original cast-list of *Widowers' Houses* with J. T. Grein's Independent Theatre company in London in 1892. Florence Farr who played Blanche was also associated with early productions of Yeats.

discovered the stage as an exhilarating means of propagating his ideas, and was in no way discouraged.

Shaw subsequently called *Widowers' Houses* his 'first and worst play'. Such it may be, for the plot is laboured and the main character Dr Harry Trench excites little curiosity or sympathy, but it demonstrates that from his earliest attempt he was using the device of presenting a moral dilemma for examination in the course of the stage action, and this was to be essential to his playwriting ever after. It also shows that he was already a master of pithy dialogue.

It is interesting to note that Oscar Wilde regarded *Widowers' Houses* as ranking with his own comedies of the period, and as part of the same 'Celtic School'. (The term used by critics today is 'Anglo-Irish School'.) Wilde wrote to Shaw in a way which suggests a feeling of 'welcome to the club' – and, surprisingly, he praises Shaw's realism: 'I like your superb confidence in the dramatic value of the mere facts of life. I admire the horrible flesh and blood of your creatures . . .' This is a very different view from the usual one adopted at the time in regard to Shaw's characters, most critics finding them to be no more than mouthpieces for ideas; but that is probably because they found his ideas distasteful and could not admit the fact.

Shaw's second play, *The Philanderer*, was written in 1893 but not performed for twelve years, by which time Harley Granville Barker and John E. Vedrenne had established a company at the Royal Court Theatre which sprang, via the Stage Society, from the ideals of the Independent Theatre. Shaw had his own doubts about the play, describing it to Ellen Terry as 'a combination of mechanical farce and realistic filth' – possibly he was hoping she would contradict him, which she did. Shaw was treating love and the idea of marriage as a game, much as a Restoration dramatist might have done – with the difference that characters in late seventeenth-century comedy would not have reflected upon the ethical considerations in the way that Shaw's did.

These first three plays were collected and published, with prefaces, as *Plays Unpleasant* in 1898. Shaw was determined that if the managements would not produce them, at least the public should be allowed to read them. The third in the trilogy was *Mrs Warren's Profession*, written in 1893 but not performed until 1902 in a one-night presentation by the Stage Society. It was produced, with difficulty, in the United States in 1905, but England was not ready for a major production until 1925, though it was produced by the Dublin Repertory Theatre in 1914.

Mrs Warren's Profession reveals Shaw as a master of stagecraft: this is his first 'well-made play', in which the characters have a genuine life of their own. He wrote it 'to draw attention to the truth that prostitution is caused, not by female depravity and male licentiousness, but simply by underpaying, undervaluing and maltreating women so shamefully that the poorer of them are forced to resort to prostitution to keep body and soul together . . .'.

The tone of the play is as far from depravity and licentiousness as one could possibly wish. The settings are eminently respectable, and the conversation cool and complacent. The play also has a perfectly moral conclusion, in which Mrs Warren's highly-educated and vivacious daughter Vivie, having learned that her comfortable upbringing and Oxford career have been paid for from immoral earnings, leaves to lead a different and independent life. Max Beerbohm, who was harsh in his review of the published text, changed his attitude when he saw the first performance two years later, and described it as 'an ennobling work'.

Plays Pleasant, published at the same time as *Plays Unpleasant*, contained *Arms and the Man*, *Candida*, and *You Never Can Tell*. *Arms and the Man* was written in haste for the actress Florence Farr when the Manchester tea-heiress Annie Horniman, who was providing financial support for serious plays at the Avenue Theatre, London, was looking for suitable new work. (Miss Horniman was later to support the Abbey Theatre for several years.) The play was immediately accepted, and Miss Farr created the part of Louka. It is as near a perfect comedy as has ever been written.

Arms and the Man ridicules the gallantry and false idealism of war. The main character is the anti-hero, a prosaic Swiss mercenary, Captain Bluntschli, who owns several hotels. Sergius, the dashing Bulgarian officer who sees himself as hero, is in fact a secondary figure in every respect. This reversal of conventional roles disturbed those critics who disliked anything they could describe as 'too clever by half'. Heroism is toppled, reality instated; the 'higher love' is shown to be worthless beside real feeling. *Arms and the Man* is described as an 'anti-romantic comedy', but it is full of theatrical romance – the setting with its picturesque view of the Bulgarian mountains, the concealing of the escaping mercenary in Raina's bedroom (which recalls Verdi's opera *Ernani*), the photograph inscribed by Raina 'to my chocolate cream soldier' – these create an atmosphere of great enjoyment, however disquieting the proceedings may prove to be for the main characters. Miss Horniman kept the play running for eleven weeks in spite of sparse attendances, and then gave it a six-month provincial tour.

Candida, which was received with as little enthusiasm later the same year, was described by Shaw as 'a mystery'. The Rev. James Mavor Morell, a clergyman as obsessed with socialism and socialist committee-work as Bernard Shaw, befriends a young and penniless poet, Marchbanks, who becomes a constant visitor to his home. One day Marchbanks informs Morell that he is in love with his wife Candida. Morell, over-reacting, demands that Candida should choose between them: Candida declares her love for 'the weaker of the two'. Morell is dumbfounded, believing the poet to be the weaker; but the poet realizes what Candida

110 Bernard Partridge, who played Sergius in the first production of *Arms and the Man* under the stage name of J. Bernard Gould, drew this sketch of Shaw at rehearsal.

111 Shaw on television: 1967 Radio Telefís Eireann production of *Candida*, directed by Christopher Fitz-Simon, with David Dodimead as Morell, Eithne Dunne as Candida, and Patrick McLarnon as Lexy.

means, and departs. In Ibsen's *A Doll's House*, in which Helmar, like Morell, is quite unaware that his wife has a mind and soul of her own, it is Nora who leaves; but Candida is a much more intelligent and resourceful woman, has known the truth all the time, and makes no such melodramatic gesture.

The play, which is an argument between rarefied sensibility and commonsense, is economical of dialogue, characters, and setting. It is undoubtedly Shaw's most delicately structured play, and also his most truly and warmly humorous. He seems on this occasion (as with *Heartbreak House* and *St Joan*) not to have been afraid of emotion, though he controls it very carefully.

You Never Can Tell, the third of the *Plays Pleasant*, was given a private performance in London at the end of 1899, and six matinées early the following year. Shaw was henceforth accepted as more than a cranky intellectual who could entertain by making use of the stage as a platform to air his own obtusely heretical views – views which always, in the end, turned out to be infuriatingly reasonable. Audiences began to realize, even if most of the critics did not, that an evening of Shaw was *fun*.

You Never Can Tell is a comedy about the irrationality of love: each character emerges as different from what he or she appears to be at the outset, and every situation develops unexpectedly. It is said to be Shaw's most often revived play. An Abbey Theatre production in 1978 appropriately visited the Shaw Theatre at Malvern, to much acclaim.

Shaw was forty-two in the year of publication of *Plays Pleasant and Unpleasant*. Had he written nothing further for the theatre, subsequent fame as a dramatist would still have been assured: but his stage masterpieces were yet to come.

It was through political connections (rather than theatrical) that Shaw met Charlotte Payne-Townshend, who had come from Ireland, and had told Sidney and Beatrice Webb that she would like to use her fortune to encourage a man of promising career – she meant a career which would benefit mankind in a social sense.*

Mrs Webb introduced her to Shaw; they met, and subsequently corresponded. When Miss Payne-Townshend visited him during an illness and saw the conditions in which he was living, she invited him to her house in the country to recuperate. It was typical of Shaw's thoughtfulness that he expressed fears for her social position (even though she was also forty-two and hardly likely to be thought of by her acquaintances in a scandalous fashion); so he agreed to accompany her if she married him; and *she* agreed to marry *him* if the marriage were never consummated. The ceremony took place in a registry office on 1 June 1898. From then until her death in 1943, they were rarely apart.

The comfortable surroundings in which Shaw found himself for the first time – Charlotte had an apartment in London and a house in Surrey – and the devoted attentions of a wife who was also a capable secretary, did not induce a relaxation of creative effort. Rather, an increase in political as well as theatrical activity ensued. Shaw also became absorbed in arrangements for the translation of his plays, and of productions in other countries, including the United States. *The Devil's Disciple*, as became its setting, had in fact received its first production in New York in 1897 (after the traditional American 'out of town' opening) and was his first play to enjoy box-office success.

One of the scenes in which the aristocratic and witty British General, Burgoyne, conducts a court martial (the play takes place during the American War of Independence) is based on the courtroom scene in Boucicault's *Arrah-na-Pogue*, with which Shaw was familiar from his theatregoing days in Dublin.

112

XV

* Mrs Shaw left part of her fortune as the Charlotte Shaw Bequest to found Fóras Eireann, a body which encourages cultural endeavour in rural Ireland.

XII Costume designs for Oscar Wilde's *Salomé* by Charles Ricketts. The play fell foul of the British censor, and was first produced in Paris (in French) by Sarah Bernhardt in 1896. It was not produced professionally in English until 1928 when Hilton Edwards and Micheál MacLiammóir gave it at the Peacock Theatre, Dublin. A number of Irish writers were deeply influenced by *Salomé*, and thus by European symbolist theatre.

XIII Avenue Theatre poster, London, 1894. Several Irish playwrights received support from the Manchester tea-heiress Annie Horniman, who produced new work which she believed to be worthwhile but which stood little chance of commercial success. She seems to have been mistaken in her encouragement for the Irish writer John Todhunter (1839–1910) whose plays were unsuccessful in every way, but support for Shaw and Yeats was astute and timely. She was later the chief benefactor of the Abbey Theatre.

XIV *Opposite* George Bernard Shaw was born in Dublin in 1856. During his lifetime his plays were constantly criticized for their 'soap-box' element, but time has shown how little the political and social issues of his day matter to the enjoyment and appreciation of his work in the theatre. The portrait is by his friend Augustus John.

XV *Right* Scene from *The Devil's Disciple*, George Bernard Shaw's play of the American War of Independence, as seen by the painter Dermod O'Brien. Lawyer Hawkins is played by M. J. Dolan and Christy Dudgeon by Barry Fitzgerald. The 1920 revival, like most Abbey productions of the period, was directed by Lennox Robinson.

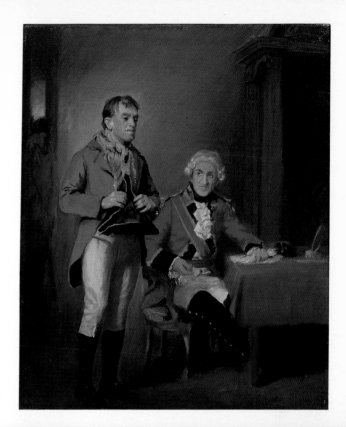

XVI *Below* Scene from *John Bull's Other Island* (originally entitled *Rule Britannia*) by George Bernard Shaw. This, with *O'Flaherty VC*, is Shaw's only play with an Irish theme and setting (except for one scene in *Back to Methuselah*). In the 1980 revival by the Irish Theatre Company, directed by Patrick Mason and designed by Monica Frawley, Peter Keegan was played by Cyril Cusack and Nora Reilly by Bernadette McKenna.

The play is described as 'a melodrama', but *The Devil's Disciple* could not be more different from the pale conventional dialogue proper to that genre; and in spite of the blameless heroine, the comic buffoon, the innocent orphan girl, the last-minute deliverance from the scaffold, and the happy ending, Shaw manages to laugh at the melodramatic form while using it as a structural base. He makes his hero and his villain one character: Dick Dudgeon, furthermore, acts from spontaneous feeling rather than from more obvious motives – such as desire to save the life of another man whom he believes to be more worthy than himself, or because he happens to be in love with that man's wife. Good deeds are thus performed as an *action gratuite*. The puritan ethic is punctured when Shaw makes Dick's mother, who has spent her life in virtuous self-denial, into a thoroughly disagreeable woman.

Shaw's other American play, *The Shewing-up of Blanco Posnet*, is also presented in melodramatic form. Its Wild West setting, and its collection of riotous and disreputable male characters, did not commend it to the British censor, who was also unimpressed by its feeling of religious exaltation, and so a licence was withheld. The first production was therefore given at the Abbey Theatre, Dublin, in 113 1909, after a lengthy tussle with officials of Dublin Castle who alleged that the Lord Chamberlain's writ extended to Ireland. The Lord Lieutenant threatened to remove the theatre's patent, but Lady Gregory and William Butler Yeats persisted with the production. Lady Gregory recorded in her journal:

> The play began, and till the end it was received in perfect silence. Perhaps the audience were waiting for the wicked bits to begin. Then, at the end, there was a tremendous burst of cheering and we knew we had won. Some stranger outside asked what was going on in the Theatre. 'They are defying the Lord Lieutenant,' was the answer; and when the crowd heard the cheering they took it up and it went far out through the streets . . .

The Abbey included the play in its American tour of 1911.

The Abbey was to have produced Shaw's first Irish play (provisionally entitled *Rule Britannia!*) in 1904, Yeats having discussed 'a play on the contrast between Irish and English character which sounds amusing' as early as 1901. The production had to be postponed because the play turned out to be 'beyond the theatre's resources', but fortunately Granville Barker had become interested and he and John E. Vedrenne produced *John Bull's Other Island* in London. It has been XVI suggested that the Abbey directors were uneasy about the realism with which Shaw treated certain aspects of the Irish character, but the Abbey directors of the period were not given to moral queasiness, and a glance at the composition of the company shows that it would have been impossible to cast the play adequately. The Vedrenne-Barker management brought it to Dublin in 1907 with Nigel Playfair as Broadbent, Harcourt Williams as Doyle, and William Poel as Keegan – a cast which could not have been remotely matched at the Abbey. *The Irish Times* critic remarked, 'The play is, in fact, a terrible indictment of Ireland, terrible on account of its directness and knowledge'; and the public flocked to see it.

The Abbey produced the play in 1916, drawing attention to the fact that it had been written at the company's instigation. From that date until 1931 it was revived every year there, usually with Barry Fitzgerald as Broadbent, F. J. McCormick as Doyle, and Fred O'Donovan as Keegan. It has been revived since then at the Abbey and the Gate in Dublin, and also by the Irish Theatre Company, which also brought the play to Britain in 1980. Critics noted that it seemed to grow fresher and more apposite with the years.

XVII The Grand Opera House, Belfast. Only three of the great nineteenth-century metropolitan theatres still exist in their original form in Ireland – the others are the Gaiety and the Olympia in Dublin. The Grand Opera House became a cinema in the 1950s, and this was followed by a period of closure. It was re-opened, with generous funding from the British Government, in 1980.

112 Cyril Cusack and
Desmond Perry in the
1978 revival of *You Never
Can Tell*, directed by
Patrick Mason at the
Abbey Theatre, Dublin,
and the Shaw Theatre,
Malvern.

As the immediate social or political concerns of any play by Shaw recede with the passage of time, the audience frees its mind from once-topical issues and concentrates on the universal implications. It can then be seen – and this the earlier critics almost always failed to appreciate – that the energy and interest in Shaw's verbal debates spring from the personalities of the characters to a much greater degree than they do from the subject-matter. The last act of *John Bull's Other Island*, a twenty-minute discussion between the three main characters, obtains its riveting theatrical effect because at an earlier stage the audience's attention has been engaged by the sheer force of three distinctive and articulate individuals reacting in certain ways to one another. When the final moments of the play arrive, the emotional impact is created not by the weight of philosophical argument but by the intensity and directness of the characters who make the argument.

Peter Keegan says, 'When you speak to me of English and Irish – you forget that I am a Catholic. My country is not Ireland or England, but the whole mighty realm of my Church. For me there are but two countries: Heaven and Hell; but two conditions of men: salvation and damnation.' Obviously, Shaw is putting an argument into Keegan's mouth, but he does it with such consistency and with such feeling for the man who speaks it, that the critic who baldly states that Shaw's characters are 'mere puppets' completely misunderstands the nature of the Shavian theatre. Time, however, has almost extinguished that one-fashionable critical view. *John Bull's Other Island* remains one of the three great plays of the Irish repertoire in the first half of the twentieth century – the others being *The Playboy of the Western World* and *Juno and the Paycock*.

114

Shaw gave one other play an Irish setting:* *O'Flaherty V.C.* (1915). It was also written at the instigation of the management of the Abbey Theatre, but on this occasion the political implications were genuinely too broad, as World War I was in progress, and many young Irishmen had been killed in the British army, fighting for 'the freedom of small nations'. It was not performed publicly till 1920 in New York.

* One act of *Back to Methuselah* takes place in Co. Clare in the year 3000; but the play can hardly be described as 'having an Irish setting'.

Private O'Flaherty has been decorated by the King for bravery. His prowess is judiciously promoted by the British army authorities in their recruitment campaign in Ireland, in which O'Flaherty is idealized as the brave young hero. His mother's attitude, which reflects that of a large proportion of the population, is that he should have been fighting *against* the British rather than for them. The central movement of the play is a long conversation, larded with entertaining paradox, between the peasant boy and the landlord of the estate upon which he was brought up, Sir Pearce Madigan – who, as it happens, is a general in the British army. This conversation again displays Shaw's mastery in presenting boundlessly energetic people whose exchanges of widely differing views, expressed with the utmost logic and reason, succeed because they are based on a foundation of genuine character.

The period from 1898 until World War I was Shaw's most productive in the theatre. Most of the lighter works had been written and produced, and *St Joan, Back to Methuselah* and *The Apple Cart* were yet to come. As well as *John Bull's Other Island, The Shewing-up of Blanco Posnet* and *O'Flaherty V.C.*, he wrote *Caesar and Cleopatra, Captain Brassbound's Conversion, Major Barbara, The Doctor's Dilemma, Misalliance, Androcles and the Lion, Pygmalion* and *Heartbreak House,* all of them superb comedies; *Fanny's First Play, Getting Married* and *Overruled* have not worn so well, but the total achievement is remarkable, and unsurpassed in the English language since Shakespeare.

The structure of *Man and Superman* (1905) is that of Victorian farce, the Shavian reversal being 'the love chase of the man by the woman'. Audiences were shocked (at least they came in great numbers, it would seem, for this purpose) at the notion of the woman taking the initiative in sexual matters; but it is easy to shock, and Shaw had something much less trivial in view: he set out to expound the idea of

113 The original production of *The Shewing-up of Blanco Posnet* at the Abbey Theatre, Dublin, in 1909. The principal parts were taken by Máire O'Neill (The Woman), Sara Allgood (Feemy), Arthur Sinclair (Elder Daniels) and Fred O'Donovan (Blanco).

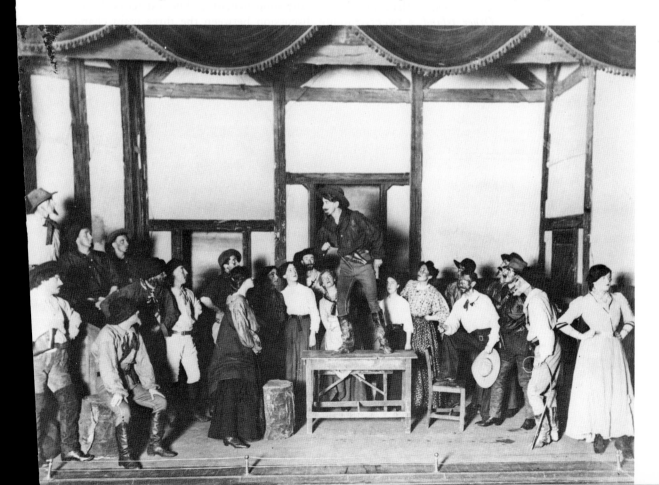

the Life Force, the force that relies on man and woman for achieving its ends, and that shows God's dependence upon Man to work out His divine purpose. Man must recognize himself as an instrument for the creation of something greater than himself – the creation of a better mankind.

In the Shavian 'vitality versus system' mode the eloquent and erudite (and, one cannot help feeling, slightly priggish) John Tanner represents the system, while Ann Whitefield represents vitality – the Life Force. Ann is beautiful, sexually attractive, and of a lively mind: not at all the rampant feminist or the promiscuously fecund Earth Mother, either of which a lesser dramatist might have made her. As Eric Bently has written, 'Tanner's intellectual pretensions sink to nothing before Ann's reality.'

The play, presented as a conventional *comédie de boulevarde* in fashionable and exotic settings from London to Granada, contains the famous 'Don Juan in Hell' scene, in which Tanner sees himself cast as Don Juan and Ann as Donna Anna (as in Mozart's opera). The dream is a discussion of the Life Force, in which this Don Juan tells of his 'passion for divine contemplation and creative activity' and explains why love has failed to interest him. The scene is often omitted, as the play is lengthy enough without it. It can be effectively produced as a one-act comedy; yet it is only in those productions in which it is retained that the splendid plan of *Man and Superman* can be properly observed and savoured.

Caesar and Cleopatra (1898), *Captain Brassbound's Conversion* (1899) and *Androcles and the Lion* (1912) are conceived with all the colour and pageantry which Egypt, Morocco and imperial Rome suggest. As they require very large casts, and because sumptuous pictorial scenery is *de rigueur* (*Caesar and Cleopatra* was first produced by Max Reinhardt with tremendous pomp, in Berlin; *Captain Brassbound's Conversion* by the Stage Society with not enough, in London; and *Androcles* very splendidly, also in Berlin), they are rarely performed today. *Androcles* is based on a charming fable which Shaw transplanted to the era of the Christian persecutions, and in which he proposes that life is only worth living if man has something worth dying for: a Christian moral, one should think – but his

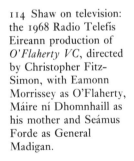

114 Shaw on television: the 1968 Radio Telefís Eireann production of *O'Flaherty VC*, directed by Christopher Fitz-Simon, with Eamonn Morrissey as O'Flaherty, Máire ní Dhomnhaill as his mother and Seámus Forde as General Madigan.

115 A scene from the 1951 revival of *Man and Superman* by Longford Productions at the Gate Theatre, Dublin, with Desmond Jordan, Iris Lawler and Dennis Edwards; designed by Alpho O'Reilly and directed by Dan O'Connell.

mildly satiric treatment of some of the Early Christians aroused the greatest possible ire among humourless Sunday-observers in England.

Major Barbara (1905) turns upon the personal moral dilemma of a young and idealistic major in the Salvation Army when faced with the choice of accepting large sums of money for charitable work from a distiller and a manufacturer of armaments, or allowing the work to discontinue. In *The Doctor's Dilemma* (1906) the eminent Harley Street practitioner Sir Colenso Ridgeon has to decide whether he should treat a talented painter of worthless character, or an old friend of no great achievement who is an admirable human being. The play is a satire on medical practice, and succeeds on that level, but the dramatic treatment is uneven, moving from farce to what is almost sentimental comedy. It requires extremely deft production and playing to make the elements coalesce.

Pygmalion (1912) is by now known more universally as *My Fair Lady* than in its original stage form. *My Fair Lady* contains many pleasing tunes, and its spectacular production was in the best tradition of the New York musical theatre; but its libretto is weak, and of course the real impetus comes from Shaw's scintillating characters and dialogue. If Shaw had been alive to agree to the adaptation, it is certain that he would have insisted upon writing the libretto himself. The vast income which this musical comedy brought into the Shaw estate benefited far beyond any expectations the three public institutions to which he left his fortune: the British Museum, the Royal Academy of Dramatic Art, and the National Gallery of Ireland – outside which his statue now stands.

The play is about human relations; on the superficial level it is about the possibility of altering a person's social standing through the study and application of phonetics, and in this way Henry Higgins manages to raise the Cockney flower-seller Eliza Doolittle from the gutter to a position of acceptability among people of the highest rank and birth. Higgins' interest is scientific, and when the experiment has been proved a success he has no further interest in Eliza, whose outlook has changed through widening horizons, and whose emotional responses have been heightened in the process. The conflict is between heart and head, and it is this which sustains the play through the fourth and fifth acts, which take place virtually after the main action has been completed.

Acts IV and V have been described as 'anti-climactic', and Shaw has also been accused of letting his audience down by allowing the scene in which Eliza is passed off as a duchess at an ambassadorial reception to occur offstage (or, rather, during the interval between Acts III and IV). However, such a scene would, dramatically speaking, be a repetition of the famous tea-party scene, and Shaw always felt the necessity for a disquisitory passage movement. In *Pygmalion* this takes the form of a working-out of the conflict between two highly charged personalities: Eliza has to liberate herself; and Higgins must, at all costs, retain his dominant position. The final act is an intense and intensely witty verbal battle between two people whose practical and spiritual futures depend upon the outcome. Here again, the interest is carried along by the argument which arises from the nature of the characters involved.

Shaw wrote *Heartbreak House* during World War I, but it was not produced until 1920. It is a sombre comedy, well suited to the times. He believed it to be his best play but was loth to discuss it: perhaps it was too near to his heart. He said it was 'worth fifty *Candidas*'. Its affinity with Chekhov is only superficial; Shaw did not then disclose that it 'began with an atmosphere', and in fact it touches on many subjects explored in both earlier and later works – politics, religion and education, as well as love. All of Shaw is here – including the paradox of a considerable amount of fun in the midst of much foreboding on the future of the human race. We are now entering the final phase of Shavian drama where a visionary all-seeing eye is cast upon man and his place in creation.

Micheál MacLiammóir, the actor and co-founder of the Dublin Gate Theatre, wrote, in response to a query concerning what he considered to be the 'greatest' play by an Irish dramatist, that *Back to Methuselah* is 'a very great play indeed – much greater than many of his best-known comedies. *Back to Methuselah* has a breadth, a scope, a brilliance of imagination, and a profoundly religious note . . .' Shaw called it 'a metabiological Pentateuch'; it is written in five parts, each of which is virtually a play in itself. When performed in full it is usually spread over at least three evenings.

The scenes are an Oasis in Mesopotamia (the Garden of Eden) in 400 BC; England, shortly after World War I; the official parlour of the President of the British Isles in AD 2170; Burrin (*sic*) Pier on the shore of Galway Bay in AD 3000; and a sunlit glade at the foot of a wooded hill – a distinctly Arcadian setting – in AD 31920 – 'As Far as Thought can Reach'.

There is almost no dramatic action, but the work is suffused with the light of intellect. The proposition seems to be that life is too brief for man to profit greatly from his experience: he must therefore increase his life-span by force of will. (Methuselah lived to be 969.) The notion of Creative Evolution is that since the universe creates itself from nothing, so man can make himself out of what he is. It is (to put it mildly) an optimistic concept and *Back to Methuselah* is a richly optimistic play. At its ending, Lilith, 'in whom father and mother are one', declares:

> Of life only there is no end; and though of its million starry mansions many are empty and many still unbuilt, and though its vast domain is as yet unbearably desert, my seed shall one day fill it and master its matter to its uttermost confines . . .

Back to Methuselah was first produced (by the Theatre Guild of New York) in 1922. Shaw's next important play is also his most celebrated: *St Joan*. It was produced by the Theatre Guild in 1923 with Winifred Lenihan and in London the following year with Sybil Thorndike. Joan ranks among the truly great roles

116 Siobhán McKenna as St Joan in her own Irish-language translation at the Taibhdhearc, Galway, in 1952.

of the Western theatre and offers leading actresses the kind of challenge which actors face with Hamlet or Tartuffe or Christy Mahon. Siobhán McKenna played 116 the part in Irish (in her own translation) at the Taibhdhearc in Galway in 1952 and later (in English) in Dublin, New York, London and several European cities. Her interpretation stressed the peasant background and made use of the rural Galway accent; the gradual transformation to a feeling of exultant spirituality as the play progressed realized a far more profound sense of tragedy than those performances where intimations of martyrdom are explicit from the beginning.

St Joan, of course, is not a tragedy in the Aristotelian sense. True, Joan is a victim of classic proportion, her death is inevitable and her fate is known to every member of the audience before the play begins, but the play does not possess that element of catharsis which is proper to tragedy. It is, rather, a drama of ideas, in which the protagonist dies in tragic circumstances. (The same might be said of *Hedda Gabler*.)

Yet there is real poignancy in the play, in spite of its crisp, unemotional and pithy dialogue. The audience identifies with Joan in a personal way, as it does with Eliza Doolittle, though perhaps to a more intense degree. It is, indeed, impossible not to become emotionally involved with this charming, uneducated peasant girl whose chief thoughts are for her family and farm in a remote corner of Domrémy, and who subsequently finds herself incapable of denying the inner voices which so inexplicably urge her to certain actions and into a compromising situation where instinct rather than experience is her only guide.

Joan was canonised in 1920, so her story was fresh in the public mind at the time Shaw wrote the play. He used Joan to show how human envy, hatred and malice align themselves against those who possess superior intellect or spirituality – in Joan's case, the latter. Both State and Church, in Shaw's play, combine to crush her goodness and purity, which are so inconvenient and embarrassing to them. Shaw described St Joan as 'one of the first Protestant martyrs' for he saw her as staking her conscience (however innocently) against the dogma of a corrupt and powerful established order.

The Epilogue, which takes place a quarter-century after Joan's martyrdom, was criticized as extending the play beyond its dramatic climax and introducing a feeling of levity inappropriate to a tragic theme. Such a view ignores the fact that the form of the play is not that of classical tragedy; and anyway it is inconceivable that Shaw would depict any character in a humourless fashion – a trait he shares with the majority of important playwrights of the Irish school. Max Beerbohm's remarks (made twenty-five years earlier) are very much to the point, however:

Mr Shaw has all the qualities which go to the writing of good farces. He may try, and try again, to be serious, but his nationality will always prevent him from succeeding in the attempt. When he writes seriously, he is always Paddy *malgré lui* . . . I hope in future Mr Shaw will be Paddy, and leave the rest to chance.

But Shaw did not leave anything to chance, and he continued to be Paddy, even to the extent of exaggerating his Irish brogue in his famous BBC broadcasts during the Second World War. With the exception of *The Apple Cart* (1929), his later plays are less remarkable – *St Joan* being a kind of summing-up in the way that Shakespeare's *The Tempest* is a summing-up. His stance on Irish affairs was unpopular in England, especially his condemnation of the execution of the leaders of the 1916 Rising and his support for Roger Casement; but he was courageous in his denunciation of anything he considered to be a barrier to the dignified evolution of the human spirit.

The contemporary critic Paul Durkan sees Shaw as 'a Tolstoyan figure who regarded his art as a means of reforming grave social ills: he took up avant-garde positions long before it was safe to do so: on war, on the rights of women, on cruelty to animals, on economics, on parents'. He refused public honours, except the Nobel Prize for Literature in 1923 and the Freedom of the City of Dublin in 1946. When he died four years later the lights were extinguished on Broadway – the heart of the commercial theatre which Shaw had fought so hard against and had later used so effectively to his own advantage: it was a paradoxical gesture which 'the unspeakable Irishman' would have relished.

13
An ancient idealism

1898–1939

The Irish Literary Theatre,
The National Theatre Society, Augusta Gregory,
Edward Martyn, William Butler Yeats and others

To many people throughout the world the term 'the Irish Theatre' signifies 'the Abbey Theatre' – the theatre which produced the most important work of Yeats, Synge and O'Casey and which introduced a style of presentation and of playing which was, and is, recognizably Irish. (The title 'Abbey Theatre' simply means the building in Abbey Street, Dublin, which has housed the National Theatre Society Ltd since 1904.) It is noteworthy that after three-quarters of a century the Abbey, in spite of some faltering along the way, remains the most vital force in the Irish theatre.

It is still commonly believed that the movement which culminated in the formation of the Irish Literary Theatre in 1898 and which in turn led to the National Theatre Society of 1902, was entirely rooted in Irish political and cultural history. Much of it was so, of course. The discoveries made by nineteenth-century scholars and antiquarians resulted in the translation and interpretation of the early sagas and the publication of a host of novels and poems set in a mythical heroic age, or, if not, in a romantic Irish landscape. There was also a growing interest in folklore and folk music – still a living tradition in a land which had been

117 Colophon of the National Theatre Society Ltd.

118 Interior of the old Abbey theatre, during a rehearsal.

119–20 *Left to right*
Augusta Gregory by John
Butler Yeats, William
Butler Yeats and Edward
Martyn by Sarah Purser.

scarcely touched by the industrial revolution. Allied to this was the revival of interest in the Irish language, at first through the research of amateur enthusiasts intent on unearthing quaint fireside tales, and then with much deeper nationalistic fervour by the members of the Gaelic League, which was founded by Douglas Hyde and Eóin MacNeil in 1893.

In 1898 Lady Gregory (1852–1932) met William Butler Yeats (1865–1939) in London, and recorded in her journal that 'He is very full of playwriting. . . . He, with the aid of a Miss Florence Farr, an actress who thinks more of a romantic than of a paying play, is keen about taking a little theatre somewhere in the suburbs to produce romantic drama, his own plays, Edward Martyn's, one of Bridges . . .'. The meeting had a sequel at the house of Count de Basterot on the shores of Galway Bay later the same year, when Edward Martyn (1859–1924) was also present. They discussed the possibility of an Irish theatre, and Lady Gregory wrote that 'things seemed to grow possible as we talked, and towards the end of the afternoon we had made our plans. We said we would collect money, or rather ask to have a certain sum of money guaranteed. We would then take a Dublin theatre and give a performance of Mr Martyn's *The Heather Field*, and one of Mr Yeats' own plays, *The Countess Cathleen* . . .'.

It is curious that these three representatives of what is loosely known as the 'Anglo-Irish ascendancy' should have been responsible for the foundation of a theatre which in due course would express the spirit of an Ireland quite different from that known to other members of their social class. Lady Gregory belonged to the Persse family which owned a large country estate called Roxborough in Co. Galway. She married Sir William Gregory, who had been Governor of Ceylon, and went to live at his home, Coole Park, some eight miles from Roxborough. After Sir William's death in 1892, and her subsequent meeting with Yeats, she started to learn Irish and collect folklore in the Clare-Galway district. The Martyns were wealthy Roman Catholic landlords who had been exempted from the Penal Laws of 1709 by special Act of Queen Anne; their country home, Tullira Castle, stood midway between Roxborough and Coole. Martyn was educated at Oxford, and on returning to Ireland became interested in the Irish language and folk music.

Yeats was born in Dublin, the elder son of the portrait painter John Butler Yeats. The family moved to London, but the young Yeats' school holidays were spent in Sligo with his grandparents, the Pollexfens, Protestant millers and ship-owners. When he was fifteen the family returned to Ireland, and he went to Dublin High School and subsequently to the Metropolitan School of Art. When he was about twenty-one he met John O'Leary, the Fenian leader, and Standish James O'Grady, author of many stirring Irish novels. He said, 'I turned my back on foreign themes, decided that the race was more important than the individual, and began "The Wanderings of Oisin"' – a consciously 'Celtic' poem.

A circular was issued, soliciting subscriptions for the new theatre – but it was more than a begging letter, it was a manifesto:

> We propose to have performed in the spring of every year certain Celtic and Irish plays, which whatever be their degree of excellence, will be written with a high ambition, and so to build up a Celtic and Irish school of dramatic literature. We hope to find in Ireland an uncorrupted and imaginative audience, trained to listen by its passion for oratory, and believe that our desire to bring upon the stage the deeper thoughts and emotions of Ireland will ensure for us a tolerant welcome, and that freedom of expression which is not found in the theatre in England, and without which no new movement in art or in literature can succeed. We will show that Ireland is not the home of buffoonery and easy sentiment, as it has been represented, but the home of an ancient idealism . . .

After considerable difficulty in finding a theatre – the Gaiety and the Theatre Royal had their long-term commitments to visiting dramatic and operatic companies from London, and the Queen's was totally given over to melodrama – the unprepossessing Antient Concert Rooms were hired for the week of 8 May 1899. There was a further difficulty presented by a pamphlet written by an enemy of Yeats, Frank Hugh O'Donnell, entitled *Souls for Gold*, which attacked his play's alleged absence of religious orthodoxy, before the opening night. The Roman Catholic archbishop of Dublin, Cardinal Logue, condemned the play's theme in a letter to the press, but (contrary to the legend which grew out of the affair) did not request that the play should be withdrawn. In time, the directors of the Abbey Theatre would become used to such incidents.

The title 'Irish Literary Theatre' had been suggested by Martyn, and it is a significant choice, for the Abbey was to be primarily a writers' theatre, rather than an actors' or a directors' theatre. Lady Gregory took charge of the organization of the productions, and the novelist George Moore (1852–1933) helped to seek a cast in London – it being found that there were no suitable actors available for Irish plays in Dublin! Moore, who up till this period had spent most of his working life in Paris and London, returned to Ireland with the cast.

Martyn's play *The Heather Field* is the first with an Irish setting to stem directly from Ibsen. Yeats' *The Countess Cathleen*, though set in a mythical Ireland, was taken from a French legend. But the European influence on the Irish Literary Theatre and subsequently upon the Irish theatre in general went much deeper than these tenuous links might suggest.

André Antoine's Théâtre Libre which opened in Paris in 1887 was the fore-runner of J. T. Grein's Independent Theatre in London which (as has been seen) was the first to produce the plays of Shaw. Other Irish writers whose early work was produced in London were George Moore with *The Strike at Arlingford* (1893), John Todhunter with *A Comedy of Sighs* (1894) and W. B. Yeats with *The Land of Heart's Desire* (also 1894, presented in a double-bill first with *A Comedy of Sighs* and then with *Arms and the Man*. London became a meeting-place for serious-minded Irish Writers, and also a place where, for practical reasons, their plays could be produced. But Paris, and the French language, were to become a

XIII, 123

deeper and much more pervasive influence than London, though quite how deep was probably not fully realized at the time.

XII It was in French that Oscar Wilde wrote *Salomé*, in many ways his most uncharacteristic play, in other ways his most important. Here we discover an inner Wilde expressing himself by means of heightened language and intensified imagery: a dark, tempestuous and sensual Wilde far removed (one might think) from his own creations in Lord and Lady Chiltern's drawing-room. The chief influences – apart from the James I version of the Bible, which goes far beyond mere story-source, providing a firm linguistic base – are the plays of the contemporary Belgian dramatist Maurice Maeterlinck, the poetry of Stéphane Mallarmé, and the painting of Gustave Moreau: in other words, the Symbolists; and, more particularly, Gustave Flaubert's story *Hérodiade*. If *The Importance of Being Earnest* is a great 'façade' play, *Salomé* looks behind the façade and shows us a drama of the interior which, by implication rather than by direct statement, tells us so much more about the soul of the artist, about theatrical performance and about life.

Salomé, ill-fated in its early productions, was so far in advance of its time as to be virtually unproduceable. Modern theatrical techniques render some of the difficulties less daunting. *Salomé* paved the way for the 'total theatre' of Yeats (albeit Yeats does not seem to refer to it as influential), with the use of poetry, music, masks, mime, dance and a fusion of visual effects whereby the scenery, costumes and lighting combine to express the spirit of the work rather than to depict any recognizable location or period.

The French association, in both the artistic and linguistic aspects, was not confined to Wilde and Yeats. John Millington Synge, who made up the third member of the Abbey triumvirate after Edward Martyn had lost interest, spent half of every year in Paris over a decade, obtained some of his material from early French drama, was deeply attracted by Rabelais and Villon, much influenced by Maeterlinck, and fluent enough with the language to write his working notes in it. There was also the curious case of George Moore's play *Diarmuid and Grania*, which he was to write in French; Lady Gregory was then to translate it into English so that Taidhg O'Donoghue could translate it into Irish: then Lady Gregory was to make an English version using O'Donoghue's Gaelicisms. From this pretentious project it is chastening to turn to the work of that other self-exiled Dubliner, Samuel Beckett, who writes in French and translates his own work into a very spare Irish English.

Thus the literary and theatrical strains which had their bearing on what was to become Ireland's national theatre came very much from outside Ireland. The jockeying for position between the followers of Ibsen and the realistic drama of everyday life, and the followers of Maeterlinck and the symbolic drama of the inner life, was a feature of the early years of the Abbey Theatre. If these influences came from Norway and Belgium via France, and if the intermediary state of sifting and scrutiny took place in England, it was in Ireland that the subject-matter was discovered: whether in the peasant cabins of Wicklow or the Aran Islands and the airless parlours of houses in small provincial towns (on the one hand), or on the mountaintops and in the palaces of Muirthemne or Emain Mhacha (on the other). Plays of the local and contemporary world jostled with plays that were otherworldly. It was a theatre of opposites: and it was a unique theatre, for the other emerging national dramatic movements of Europe or North America produced, at this period, nothing as rich, as varied, and – in spite of the heterogeneity of antecedent – as original.

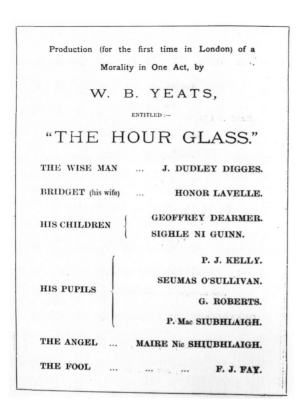

Production (for the first time in London) of a
Morality in One Act, by

W. B. YEATS,

ENTITLED :—

"THE HOUR GLASS."

THE WISE MAN ...	J. DUDLEY DIGGES.
BRIDGET (his wife) ...	HONOR LAVELLE.
HIS CHILDREN	GEOFFREY DEARMER.
	SIGHLE NI GUINN.
	P. J. KELLY.
	SEUMAS O'SULLIVAN.
HIS PUPILS	G. ROBERTS.
	P. Mac SIUBHLAIGH.
THE ANGEL ...	MAIRE Nic SHIUBHLAIGH.
THE FOOL	F. J. FAY.

The Irish Literary Theatre's second season coincided with the beginning of the twentieth century. Three productions were again staged by English actors, but this time presented in a real theatre, the Gaiety. Edward Martyn provided the funds to defray expenses, as he had done for the first season. The plays were *The Bending of the Bough* by George Moore and a double-bill consisting of *Maeve* by Edward Martyn and *The Last Feast of the Fianna* by the Ulster poet Alice Milligan. *The Bending of the Bough* was a rewritten version of an earlier work attempted by Martyn and then cast aside; it is set in a provincial town and is a poor imitation of the Ibsen of *An Enemy of the People*. *Maeve* has a curious blend of Ibsenish realism and storybook fantasy, awkwardly reflecting the two standpoints of the Irish dramatic movement itself.

The Last Feast of the Fianna was the first play to draw upon the Fenian mythological cycle for its subject-matter. The critic of the London *Daily Express* observed: 'If the aim of the Irish Literary Theatre is to create a national drama it is obvious that the development of Miss Milligan's method is the proper road to reach ultimate success . . .', but in fact her play does no more than relate an heroic tale, and there is no attempt to explore the new theatrical forms with which Yeats was already experimenting.

The Irish Literary Theatre's third season, in 1901, consisted of the Moore-Yeats *Diarmuid and Grainne*, and *Casadh an tSugáin** by Douglas Hyde. Frank Benson's company from London performed the former, and the Hyde comedy was given on two nights of the week's run at the Gaiety Theatre, as an afterpiece, by members of the Keating Branch of the Gaelic League, with the author in the leading role. This was the last occasion upon which English professional actors were imported, and the first ever upon which a play in the Irish language was produced on the stage of a professional theatre.

122–3 *Left* Cast list of the performance of Yeats' *The Hour Glass* presented by the Irish National Theatre Society in London in 1903, when its programme was received by the critics with acclaim. *Right* The epitome of folksy production: the English actresses Winifred Fraser and Dorothy Paget in the first production of Yeats' *The Land of Heart's Desire* at the Avenue Theatre, London, in 1894.

* *The Twisting of the Rope.*

124 Douglas Hyde by John Butler Yeats. Hyde was later to become the first President of Ireland.

Douglas Hyde (1860–1949), or 'An Craoibhín Aoibhainn' to use the pen-name which he characteristically took from an Irish song, was one of the most influential and inspiring figures of the Irish Literary Revival. The son of a Church of Ireland clergyman from the village of Frenchpark in Co. Roscommon, he grew up in very much the same kind of environment as Oliver Goldsmith a century and a half earlier. Unlike Goldsmith he won a number of prizes and distinctions at Trinity College, and after a brilliant academic career in Ireland and Canada he was appointed the first Professor of Modern Irish at University College, Dublin, a post which he retained until his retirement.

Douglas Hyde's influence on Irish literature was greater than his stature as a playwright. *Casadh an tSugáin* (1901), *An Tincéar agus an tSidheóg** (1902), *An Pósadh†* (1902) and others are based on folk tales. They are genial unpretentious comedies that seemed to herald the dawn of a school of playwriting in the Irish language. The dawn, however, did not break, for although there have been a number of fine plays in Irish over the years, and although there has been active State encouragement, all the most important Irish plays of the twentieth century have, like those in the preceding three centuries, been written in English.

The ridiculous situation whereby London had to supply actors for Dublin (a strange reversal of the eighteenth century) was altered when the poet and painter George Russell (1867–1935), better known by his *nom-de-plume* 'Æ', by chance met William and Frank Fay who ran the Ormond Dramatic Society. William Fay had been stirred by the Théâtre Libre experiment in Paris; he was also an accomplished comic actor. Frank Fay preferred poetic plays. The brothers had devised over a hundred productions of short plays and sketches and had performed professionally in small halls in Dublin and elsewhere. Æ introduced them to Yeats, and Yeats suggested that their talents might be put to a more worthy use in furthering the cause of the national drama. The Fays were immediately enthusiastic. It

* The Tinker and the Fairy.
† The Wedding.

125 Frank Fay, second from left, in the first production of Yeats *Cathleen ni Houlihan*. The actress Sara Allgood is declaiming the words 'They shall be remembered for ever'.

126 W. G. Fay

is probable that without their talents and their understanding of stagecraft the Abbey Theatre would never have come into being, for the writers did not appreciate the niceties of production-practice or theatre management.

The first of the productions in which the Fays became involved was a double-bill of *Deirdre*, a dull if well-intentioned tragedy by Æ based on the story of the Sons of Usnach in the Ulster Cycle, and *Cathleen ni Houlihan*, a patriotic prose drama by W. B. Yeats in which a Poor Old Woman (symbolizing Ireland) inspires insurgence at the time of the 1798 Rising. It contains the famous final lines:

PETER: Did you see an old woman going down the path?
PATRICK: I did not, but I saw a young girl, and she had the walk of a queen.

The plays were presented in St Theresa's Convent Hall in Dublin, and the Fays restyled their group the National Dramatic Society. The following year a committee was formed with W. B. Yeats as president, and the Irish National Theatre Society came into being, the Fays having produced five new plays in the meantime, including Yeats' *The Pot of Broth*, in a tiny unheated hall in Camden Street, Dublin.

In 1903 there were productions of *Twenty-Five*, the first of Lady Gregory's plays to be performed, and Yeats' *The Hour Glass* and *The King's Threshold*. These were given in the Molesworth Hall in the centre of Dublin, a venue normally favoured for Protestant missionary sales-of-work and evenings devoted to badminton. If the National Theatre Society was to develop, it needed more than writers and actors: it needed a theatre building. It is remarkable to think that two of the world's minor masterpieces, J. M. Synge's *In the Shadow of the Glen* and *Riders to the Sea* – Lennox Robinson called the latter 'the greatest one-act tragedy

127 Early – and by all appearances very static – production of Lady Gregory's *Spreading the News*. The Abbey Players of the period, though mainly amateur, possessed a highly professional sense of dedication and theatrical integrity.

139

in the modern theatre' – were first performed in these dismal surroundings. But a change was in store.

The Irish Literary Society in London invited the company to give two performances on Saturday, 1 May 1903. The players (most of whom had daytime jobs unconnected with the theatre) travelled on the previous night, gave their performances, and returned to Dublin on Sunday. It was only after they had arrived home and cuttings from London newspapers reached them that they began to realize that their visit had been the theatrical event of the year. Yeats' *The Hour Glass, Cathleen ni Houlihan* and *The Pot of Broth* were given, with Lady Gregory's *Twenty Five* and Fred Ryan's *The Laying of the Foundations* (the script of this play has been lost). None of them is a great play by any standard – strangely enough, Synge's *In The Shadow of the Glen* was not brought to London, for it would surely have made an even greater impact – but the style of writing and acting was totally new, and the themes unexpected by those to whom 'Irish' drama meant Boucicault. A. B. Walkley of *The Times* wrote:

> Stendhal said that the greatest pleasure he had ever got from the theatre was given him by the performance of some poor Italian strollers in a barn. The Queen's Gate Hall, if not exactly a barn, can boast none of the glories of the ordinary playhouse; and it was there that, only a day or two ago, a little band of Irishmen and women . . . gave some of us, who for our sins are constant frequenters of the regular playhouses, a few moments of calm delight quite outside the range of anything which those houses have to offer . . .

The doyen of the English critics, William Archer, wrote:

> In almost all of them there was a clear vein of talent, while the work they presented was all of it interesting, and all of it exquisitely and movingly beautiful . . .

Among those who saw the productions was Annie Horniman, who had financed the London productions of *Arms and the Man* and *The Land of Heart's Desire* at the Avenue Theatre; she had also designed costumes for Yeats' *The King's Threshold* in the Molesworth Hall. Miss Horniman offered to provide and equip a small theatre in Dublin and maintain it free of charge for a number of years. The derelict concert hall of the Mechanics' Institute in Abbey Street was acquired, along with an older bank building which for a time had served as the city morgue. The latter, fronting on to Marlborough Street, was converted as an entrance foyer and offices. It was believed that Miss Horniman spent £1,300 on the project, and in subsequent years she contributed the cost of purchasing adjacent buildings for use as a scene dock, dressing-rooms and the famous Green Room where Lady Gregory bountifully dispensed slices of Gort cake which she brought with her on her visits from Coole.

The Abbey Theatre opened its doors on 27 December 1904 with two short plays, *On Baile's Strand* by W. B. Yeats and *Spreading the News* by Lady Gregory. Both authors, significantly, had by this time 'come into their own' as playwrights: *On Baile's Strand* has been described by Professor James Flannery in *W. B. Yeats and the Idea of a Theatre* as 'the finest of Yeats' plays'; and *Spreading the News* is the most durable of Lady Gregory's rural comedies. Miss Horniman designed the costumes for the Yeats play, Frank Fay played Cuchulain in it, and William Fay directed both productions. There was a capacity audience, and Dublin in its usual provincial way applauded an Irish venture after it had been safely given the imprimatur across the channel.

Of the Abbey Theatre founders Lady Gregory and Yeats remained as mother- and father-figures until their deaths, with Lady Gregory the driving-force.

XVIII William Butler Yeats, by Seán O'Sullivan, one of the superb portraits in the Abbey Theatre collection, permanently on public exhibition in the theatre foyer. Yeats provided the chief inspiration for the national theatre movement, and remained a member of the Board of the National Theatre Society Ltd until his death in 1939.

122

XIX *Opposite* The actress Máire O'Neill. In 1902 the art critic and collector Hugh Lane (a nephew of Augusta Gregory) commissioned John Butler Yeats to paint a series of portraits of leading Irishmen and women of the day. Máire O'Neill played in many of the early Abbey productions, and was the original Pegeen in *The Playboy of the Western World*. She was engaged to the dramatist J. M. Synge when he died in 1909.

XX *Above* Stage design by Micheál MacLiammóir for *Mogu* by Padraic Colum at the Gate Theatre, Dublin, in 1931. MacLiammóir's style was heavily influenced by Bakst's designs for the Russian ballet, and by neo-Celtic art. Under Hilton Edwards' direction, productions at the Gate were the first in Ireland to give serious scope to the design elements of setting, costumes, and lighting.

XXI *Right* Costume design by Charles Ricketts for *The King's Threshold* by W. B. Yeats. While Yeats was undoubtedly the supreme poet of the English language during the first part of the twentieth century, his comprehension of dramatic structure was uncertain, and his stagecraft faulty. Yet he had a talent for finding appropriate designers, and his association with internationally recognized artists like Ricketts, Edmund Dulac and Edward Gordon Craig was fruitful.

XXII A scene from J. M. Synge's bleak comedy *The Well of the Saints*. In this 1981 revival, directed by Christopher Fitz-Simon, Eamon Kelly and Maura O'Sullivan played the blind beggars whose sight is miraculously restored, but who choose to return to their sightless condition when they see the villainy of the world.

XXIII *The Shadow of a Gunman* by Sean O'Casey. This play was O'Casey's first major success when produced at the Abbey in 1923. It is now considered as part of the great 'Dublin trilogy', the others being *Juno and the Paycock* and *The Plough and the Stars*. The 1980 revival was designed by Frank Conway and directed by Joe Dowling.

XXIV *The Star Turns Red* by Sean O'Casey (first produced in 1940). Many critics believe that O'Casey's later plays, with their dependence on allegory and symbolism, their socialist outlook, and their opportunities for technical effects, have not received sufficient attention from theatre companies. Tomás MacAnna, however, has successfully directed several of them, including this 1978 revival of *The Star Turns Red* at the Abbey.

As a member of the old colonial aristocracy Lady Gregory was able to smooth out many difficulties which arose between the theatre and the authorities at Dublin Castle – though her own views about Ireland were considered eccentric and wayward by the political establishment there. She wrote over thirty plays which were produced on the Abbey stage, as well as translations and adaptations from Molière and other French writers. Her 'wonder plays', taken from Irish folklore, are delightful, especially *The Dragon* (1919) and *The Golden Apple* (1920). It was from her translations of the early epics, published as *Cuchulain of Muirthemne* (1902) and *Gods and Fighting Men* (1904), that Yeats obtained most of the material for his plays on ancient Irish themes.

Yeats dominated every phase of the Abbey Theatre's development up to the time of his death – often irritatingly, as far as the other directors were concerned; but it was impossible to disregard his authority, for he was a literary figure of world importance, a Senator of the Irish Free State, and in 1923 the recipient of the Nobel Prize for Literature. His essays *The Irish Literary Theatre* (1900) and *The Irish Dramatic Movement* (1923) outline the objectives and achievements of what he regarded as his theatre.

There is little argument against the proposition that Yeats was the English language's greatest poet during the first half of the twentieth century, but his position as a playwright has been questioned from all quarters, and it is still difficult to ascertain whether his plays stand among the most significant of their time or whether they are theoretic effusions of restricted dramatic force. He believed that his plays should be performed in a small theatre, or a private house, before a gathering of friends or initiates. (It is possible that he declared this intention in canny realization of the fact that his work for the stage could hardly appeal to the masses.) That his self-consciously theatrical play *At The Hawk's Well* (1917), set in 'the Irish heroic age', should have been presented in Lady Cunard's drawing-room, is eminently risible; but that select audience, whether its members were aware of it or not, was participating in a certain kind of intimate theatrical event, in a prototype 'theatre in the round' – long before this type of presentation had become common currency.

Yeats' fifty years of working at the Abbey in one capacity or another did not, some critics believe, endow him with a sense of stagecraft, and Professor Robert Hogan has even suggested that he made use of dance because he was aware that, as his plays contained very little dramatic action, this ingredient would have to be supplied in some other way. T. R. Henn said that he lacked 'the true dramatist's incessant curiosity for character'.

All this may seem like classroom sophistry in the face of the practicalities of stage production, but Yeats' most successful works for the stage are his version of Sophocles' *King Oedipus* (1928) and *Oedipus at Colonus* (1924); and even if these theatrical *tours-de-force* are taken as mere translations (which they are not) it is clear that their dramatic viability arises from the fact that the structure and characters were ready provided. These two tragedies have never been so resoundingly rendered in English, nor yet with such economy of utterence – as when the Chorus in *King Oedipus* makes its remarkably austere final declaration:

> *Make way for Oedipus. All people said*
> *'That it is a fortunate man';*
> *And now what storms are beating on his head!*
> *Call no man fortunate that is not dead.*
> *The dead are free from pain.*

Yeats' early plays are poetic dramas, much influenced by Maeterlinck. They are full of mysterious figures glimpsed by moonlight – or rather, in a Celtic Twilight, a phrase coined by Yeats himself. Even the stage-directions have a vague crepuscular quality: *Outside there are dancing figures, and it may be a white bird, and many voices singing.* The ambiguity is deliberate, but later, when Yeats had cast aside the vestiges of the Celtic Revival, he was to become quite definite about his stage requirements. It is hard to discern how often (if ever) contemporary productions of his plays were satisfactorily presented in the visual sense, in spite of his collaboration with international designers such as Edward Gordon Craig, Charles Ricketts and Edmund Dulac. Photographs of early productions often look amateurish.

Lady Gregory collaborated on *Cathleen ni Houlihan* (1902) and *The Pot of Broth* (1904), both of which were written in bucolic prose. *The King's Threshold* (1905), though written in verse, is relatively representational. In *On Baile's Strand* (1904, but considerably altered in later versions) Yeats takes a portion of one of the sagas of the Ulster Cycle and gives it theatrical substance by the use of poetry, music, dance and visual effects. In the short course of the action the warrior-hero Cuchulain, whose great sorrow is that he has no offspring, submits to Conchubhar, the old High King of Ulster, consenting to the rule of Conchubhar's sons after the High King is dead. A Young Man with an army from across the sea invades the province; Cuchulain fights and slays him. The knowledge that this is his son, begat upon Aoife, a queen in Scotland, is withheld from him, though the audience is made aware by the Blind Man (an 'all-seeing' Chorus) that there is some terrible secret about to be divulged. After the fight Cuchulain learns that he has killed his only son. He accomplishes his fate by dying while fighting the waves of the sea, from whose depths he had originally sprung.

There are all the constituents of great tragedy here. But the tragic impact would be greater if the play were less brief. Most of Yeats' plays, indeed, take little more than forty minutes to perform, and this diminishes their dramatic stature, for both actors and audience require a certain period of time in which to build up a mutual empathy before a sharing of cathartic release can be possible.

Cuchulain is the central figure in four plays, the others being *The Green Helmet* (1910), *The Only Jealousy of Emer* (1919), and *The Death of Cuchulain* (1939). Taken together as 'the Cuchulain cycle' they demonstrate how Yeats' style continually altered over the years, and how eager he was to experiment. Cuchulain, the 'amorous violent man', is Yeats' exemplar of the tragic hero: he described him in a letter to Frank Fay as one who is 'living among young men, but has himself outlived the illusions of youth'. Cuchulain is very much a mask for whatever was passing through the author's mind at the time of composition, and actors playing the role in sequence have found that they have had to provide a kind of overall ethos themselves because the character does not develop consistently or logically through the canon.

The Only Jealousy of Emer delicately plumbs the deeply-felt but almost inexpressible tides of emotion which flow between husband and wife – in this play the dying Cuchulain and Emer; and the emotional undertow which separates a man from his mistress, here personified as Eithne Inguba. The play was written at a period when Yeats was himself undergoing an emotional crisis, and the personalities of his recent bride George (Georgina) Hyde-Lees, the revolutionary Maude Gonne (to whom he had several times proposed marriage), and Maude Gonne's daughter Iseult (who had rejected his love) are reflected in the female characters; the relationships expose 'intricacies of pain'. Yeats speculated at the time as to whether he had not in fact 'betrayed three people'.

132

130 The 1974 production by the Greek director Michael Cacoyannis of Yeats' version of Sophocles' *King Oedipus* at the Abbey Theatre and the Edinburgh Festival. Desmond Cave played Oedipus, and Angela Newman Jocasta.

The Only Jealousy of Emer is the first play which Yeats built upon the Japanese
Nō form of drama, using symbolic devices such as the folding and unfolding of the
cloth by masked musicians who set the location and introduce the characters,
making it possible also to dispense with expository dialogue. In *The Death of
Cuchulain*, the last play which he wrote, he introduced the distancing effect of
having an old man address the audience in a speech in which he refers to 'the old
epics and Mr Yeats' plays about them'.

Of the plays for dancers, *The Dreaming of the Bones* (1919) is perhaps the most
perfect. The Nō influence is entirely formal, for the action is set in 1916 in a
minutely described landscape in Co. Clare where a young Aran Islander, returning
from active service in the General Post Office during the Easter Rising, encounters
two mysterious figures who, unknown to him, are the shades of Dermot and
Dervorgilla, 'that most miserable, most accursed pair / Who sold their country
into slavery', precipitating the Anglo-Norman invasion. The play, which takes
barely half-an-hour to perform, is remarkably unified and concise, emotionally as
well as dramatically effective, making use of all the theatrical elements at the
author's disposal. Nowhere is Yeats' desire for a theatre which is 'remote, spiritual
and ideal' made manifest with more felicity and discretion; and nowhere does the
fulfilment of this desire make a play more inaccessible to an audience unfamiliar
with Irish legend, Irish medieval history, contemporary Irish events, and the
tradition of the Nō stage on to which these elements are grafted.

It is no wonder that in the same year Yeats wrote to Lady Gregory describing
his twenty years at the centre of the Irish dramatic movement as a time of 'dis-
couragement and defeat', for the writers who favoured plays which sprang from
the Scandinavian theatre of realism had won the hearts of Irish audiences. Part
of the reason may have been Yeats' failure to give appropriate expression to the
great Irish epics, in the way in which Sophocles and Euripides had given theatrical
expression to the Greek myths. If he had done for *Deirdre* (1907) what Sophocles
had done with *Antigone*, the history of the twentieth-century Irish theatre would
have been quite different.

The Celtic mythology has continued to elude Irish dramatists, and the great epics are still popularly known as children's tales, or as material for scholastic study.

A Full Moon in March (1935) has echoes of *Salomé*, especially in its 'dance of the Severed Head'. The density of ideas expressed or implied in its ten pages make study prior to witnessing a performance essential. The same may be said of *Calvary* (1920) and *The Resurrection* (1921); although the splendid choruses in the latter render it slightly more comprehensible to the normal theatre audience.

Purgatory (1939) relinquishes the chorus, the dance, and the Nō convention. It is a dark, sepulchral work, in which the two pieces of essential stage-scenery, a leafless tree and a ruined house, serve as external counterweight to the Old Man's internal drama of self-loathing and of resentment against his dead father and grief for his mother, whose shades pursue him until he performs the exorcistic act of killing his son (the Boy: there are only two characters). Sound effects – hoof-beats – perform an essential dramatic function. The parallels with Beckett's *Play* (excepting the physical action which Yeats allows) is marked, and one assumes that *Purgatory* has been influential.

Yeats wrote twenty-six plays. As he was primarily a poet it is natural that those which are written in verse or contain verse passages should spring more commandingly and upliftingly to life on the stage. He possessed immense creative integrity, and unusual courage for a successful literary man who, having gained a measure of excellence in one mode, continually pressed forward to seek new states of vision and to attempt new methods of expression. He died at Rocquebrune in the south of France on 28 January 1939. His body was reinterred in 1948 at Drumcliffe churchyard in Co. Sligo, where his grandfather had been rector.

132 Louis Rolston in the 1978 revival of Yeats' last play, *The Death of Cuchulain*, at the Lyric Theatre, Belfast.

14
Great literature
in a barbarous idiom

John Millington Synge and his followers

Lady Gregory, W. B. Yeats and J. M. Synge all concerned themselves with the aristocratic and with the peasant mind: there was nothing in between. It is impossible to think of any of them setting a play in a suburban drawing-room. Yeats, however, often seems somewhat aloof or patronizing when deliberately in 'contact with the soil'; Lady Gregory less so; whereas Synge concerned himself entirely with the soil and even placed earthy country dialect in the mouths of the highborn Deirdre and the sons of Usna.

In the literal sense, the characters in Synge's plays are very close to the soil, or else they are vagrants, constantly speaking of the earth, of roadsides and ditches. In the metaphorical sense, his works abound with reminders of death, decay, and the brevity of time – 'it is the timber of poetry that wears most surely, and there is no timber that has not strong roots among the clay and worms'. During the last ten years of his life, when all the works for which he is remembered were produced, he was slowly dying of Hodgkin's disease, and images of death infuse even the most warmly humorous passages in his writing.

134   John Millington Synge (1871–1909) was the figure for which the Irish Literary Renaissance had been waiting. He provided the Abbey Theatre with its master work, *The Playboy of the Western World*, still the greatest play to come out of Ireland in the twentieth century. His writing is a fusion of Gaelic and European traditions expressed in a language that is neither standard English nor Irish. He said: 'With the present generation the linguistic atmosphere of Ireland has become definitely English enough for the first time, to allow work to be done in English that is perfectly Irish in its essence, yet has sureness and purity of form.'

He came from a puritanical Protestant landed family in Co. Wicklow. His father, a younger son of the Big House, became a barrister, and died when Synge was only a year old. Mrs Synge raised her five children in a house in Orwell Road, Rathgar (a suburb of Dublin), where John, the youngest, lived until he was a student at Trinity College. Synge was something of a solitary. His great love was for nature – both in the scientific sense of collecting birds' eggs and butterflies, and in the spiritual sense of communion with the living environment; as a boy and as a young man he walked and cycled over great distances – 'in converse with the mountains, moors and fens' as he expressed it in an early poem.

During his rambles in these desolate places he talked with tinkers and drovers, became intimate with the ways of mountain farmers, and on one famous occasion, which in the relating brought him much scorn from literary critics, 'got more aid

than any learning would have given me from a chink in the floor of the old Wicklow house where I was staying, that let me hear what was being said by the servant girls in the kitchen'. He enjoyed a 'fine bit of talk', and the fine bit of talk found its way into his theatre.

At Trinity Synge attended the minimum number of lectures. He learned the Irish language – the first major Irish dramatist ever to do so – and immersed himself in the study of Irish antiquities. He also studied at the Royal Irish Academy of Music. He joined none of the student societies in either institution. When he left Trinity in 1892 he was allowed a pass degree. With a private income of £60 a year he faced the world – and the world meant Europe. He spent some time in Germany, ostensibly studying music, but he soon gave that up – discovering that he had no real talent. From 1894 he made his home-from-home in Paris, visiting Ireland every year for eleven years until the Abbey Theatre absorbed his energies.

He attended H. d'Arbois de Jubainville's lectures at the Sorbonne on 'La civilization irlandaise comparée avec celle d'Homer'. Later Synge was to review books by Jubainville on early Celtic literature, and he praised Jubainville's work in an article, 'La vielle Littérature Irlandaise', in L'Européen in 1902. He spent much of his time in Paris reviewing books and writing poetry, but he was not kept busy, and he found it very difficult to earn a few francs from newspaper articles. His original poems are slight, and only of passing interest in the light they throw on some of the ideas developed in his plays, but his prose translations from Villon contain the kind of real passion for life which one would expect of a man who was already in death's thrall.

On 21 December 1896 there occurred the meeting which was to have a crucial effect on the future of the Irish theatre. Synge wrote tersely in his diary: 'Fait la

133-4 *Left* Caricature by William Orpen of Hugh Lane (Lady Gregory's nephew, and creator of the Municipal Gallery of Modern Art in Dublin), J. M. Synge, W. B. Yeats and Lady Gregory, central figures in the Irish literary and artistic circle of about 1907. *Right* John Millington Synge by John Butler Yeats, one of the portraits described in W. B. Yeats' poem 'The Municipal Gallery Revisited'.

connaissance de W. B. Yeates' (*sic*). Yeats' description of the meeting is more enlightening:

> He had, however, nothing to show but one or two impressionistic essays, full of that kind of morbidity that has its root in too much brooding over methods of expression, and ways of looking upon life which come, not out of life but out of literature, images reflected from mirror to mirror. . . . I said, 'Give up Paris, you will never create anything by reading Racine, and Arthur Symons will always be a better critic of French literature. Go to the Arran Islands. Live there as if you were one of the people themselves; express a life that has never found expression.' I had just come from Arran and my imagination was full of those grey islands, where men must reap with knives because of the stones . . .

It was not until 1898 that Synge took Yeats' advice. This was the year of *The Countess Cathleen* and *The Heather Field* in Dublin; and Synge stayed with Lady Gregory at Coole, where he discussed playwriting with her, and with Yeats and Martyn. From then until 1902 he spent every summer on the Aran Islands. His remarkable journal of his sojourn there is full of explicit and implicit source-material for his plays: it was published as *The Aran Islands* in 1907, the year in which *The Playboy of the Western World* was first produced.

Synge's first play to be staged by the National Theatre Society was *In the Shadow of the Glen* at the Molesworth Hall, Dublin, on 8 October 1903. *The Irish Times* critic objected to what he felt was the author's intentional 'slur on Irish womanhood' – this being a reference to Nora Burke leaving her distrustful – and probably impotent – husband to engage in a fuller life. Arthur Griffith, editor of *The United Irishman* and a vociferous representative of prissy nationalism, wrote in a pious frenzy that the play derived its inspiration from 'the decadent cynicism that passes current in the Latin *Quartier*'.

Nora Burke is indeed something of the New Woman, in spite of the fact that she has probably never been out of the long glen in Co. Wicklow which symbolizes the isolation of the Irish mind; but *In the Shadow of the Glen* is the furthest thing imaginable from a preaching play. It is interesting to note, however, that the critics took so brief a first work by an unknown writer so seriously.

135   A year later *Riders to the Sea* was produced in the same hall. There is no record of any member of the first audience recognizing it for the masterpiece which it is. The play is so short it is difficult to establish a tragic atmosphere on the stage: radio productions have often been more successful. Into his minuscule tragedy Synge fused several of his experiences on Aran. Instances may be found in the text of his anthropological interest in the primitive yet immensely dignified way of life of the islanders, in local superstition and folklore and in the paradoxical orthodoxy of the Roman Catholic religion of the island people. The language is highly coloured, yet possess an extraordinarily sparse vocabulary. These are some of the parts which make up the whole, and the whole concerns the bitter struggle of the people against the harshness of nature, and ultimately of man's place in so malevolent a universe. Synge's play discloses an heroic acceptance.

XXII   Synge got the idea for *The Well of the Saints* (1905) from the fifteenth-century play *Le Moralité de l'Aveugle et du Boiteux*, changing the two protagonists to blind beggars. (Yeats took up the idea of the blind and the lame beggar for *The Cat and the Moon*. These grotesque vagrants point the way to Samuel Beckett.) *The Well of the Saints* also has affinities with Maeterlinck's *Les Aveugles* – the blindness of the main characters makes this obvious, but there are clear similarities in the deliberate remoteness of time and place in both plays.

135 The first production of *Riders to the Sea*, with Honor Lavelle, Sara Allgood and Emma Vernon, 1904. Probably the greatest short tragedy of the modern Western theatre, the play's very brevity makes stage presentation difficult, and it can perhaps be best appreciated on radio.

136 Máire Kean as Maurya in an Abbey Theatre revival of *Riders to the Sea*.

Synge's Martin and Mary Doul (*dall* = blind), in spite of the delight they take in hurling colourful abuse at one another, are happy after their fashion. They have created their own world, in which they can live with comparative confidence; they also have the imaginative inner vision of the sightless. When their sight is restored by the Saint, their conventional world is shattered: they see ugliness all around them, in the actions of the normal 'seeing' people, and in each other. They become, in their 'cured' state, lazy, peevish and objectionable. Only when their sight fades again do they regain their (relative) composure.

The Abbey players were afraid that the 'unpleasantness' of the characters would alienate the audience, and Willie Fay, who directed and also played Martin Doul, complained that the characters were 'bad-tempered'; but Synge was obdurate and would not make the hoped-for alterations. The response from the first audiences was non-committal, and several of the Dublin critics felt the characters were caricatures and that the language they spoke was a travesty of rural speech; but George Moore wrote an unsolicited letter to *The Irish Times*, hailing the play, and saying that 'Mr Synge has discovered great literature in a barbarous idiom, as gold is discovered in quartz . . .'.

The Well of the Saints is still considered to be a 'difficult' play. The balance between the poetic 'drama of the interior' and the overt realism of the characters and of the physical action, is easily upset. It is a favourite with directors and designers, for it invites interpretations. *The Tinker's Wedding* (published 1908) was written in 1902 but not performed at the Abbey because Yeats and Lady Gregory felt that the Dublin audience was not 'ready' for scenes such as the one in which the priest is tied up in a sack. A letter from Synge to his friend Stephen McKenna, written some years later, shows that in principle he agreed with their view, and it reveals that the play was based on an incident which had taken place in Co. Wicklow only a few years previously, so there might possibly have been a case for a libel action.

Since that time *The Tinker's Wedding* has been performed all over the world, but it cannot be claimed as one of the great plays of its time. It is Rabelaisian in spirit, packed with robust humour but lacking in dramatic force. The preface to the published edition contains two paragraphs which are central to Synge's view of the theatre, and of Ireland:

> Of the things which nourish the imagination humour is one of the most needful, and it is dangerous to limit or destroy it. Baudelaire calls laughter the greatest sign of the Satanic element in man; and where a country loses its humour, as some towns in Ireland are doing, there will be morbidity of mind, as Baudelaire's mind was morbid.
>
> In the greater part of Ireland, however, the whole people, from the tinkers to the clergy, have still a life, and view of life, that are rich and genial and humorous. I do not think that these country people, who have so much humour themselves, will mind being laughed at without malice, as the people in every country have been laughed at in their own comedies.

The difficulty, which Synge should have realized from the general reaction to *In the Shadow of the Glen* (and which would be much more vehemently asserted against *The Playboy of the Western World*) was that the 'country people' had *not* been laughed at to any great extent in their own comedies, because in Ireland a tradition of popular comedy like that of Molière or Goldoni had not existed; and because Irish-born writers had written largely for a non-Irish public. Synge's plays were produced or published at a time of intense nationalist ferment, and nationalist agitators were only too ready to find the Irish character or the Irish nation 'insulted', especially if the writer had a Protestant background. Questions of literary or dramatic merit were quite beside the point.

When Synge was writing *The Playboy of the Western World* his illness, a symptom of which was a glandular swelling of the neck, was progressing rapidly. In spite of his outdoor activities he had always been a prey to colds and fevers, and his constant references to his health in conversation and in letters were a source of irritation to Molly Allgood, the actress 'Máire O'Neill', with whom he was in love, and who became his fiancée in spite of Mrs Synge's mild opposition on XIX religious and economic grounds. Máire O'Neill joined the Abbey Theatre in 1906, her sister, Sara Allgood, being already a member of the company. Her first important part was Pegeen in *The Playboy*; she also created the role of Deirdre in

Synge's posthumously produced tragedy. Later, she played many leading parts in Shaw at the Abbey, and in Hollywood became well known as a character-actress. She married within a year of Synge's death, and called her children John, after Synge, and Pegeen, after the famous part she had created.

In *The Aran Islands* Synge says that 'the impulse to protect the criminal is universal in the west. It seems partly due to the association between justice and the hated English jurisdiction, but more directly to the primitive feeling of these people, who are never criminals yet always capable of crime, that a man will not do wrong unless he is under the influence of a passion which is as irresponsible as a storm of the sea.' This passage unintentionally anticipates and answers the Dublin critics of the day who found they could not believe the central situation in *The Playboy of the Western World*. Synge described the play as a comedy, but it is a comedy (as the actor Cyril Cusack has aptly remarked) 'interlaced with tragic feeling'. This is a characteristically Irish trait – and Russian too, perhaps.

The Playboy is more assured, more deftly realized, and more articulate than anything Synge had attempted before for the theatre. From the moment the play begins it races forward, urged on by the unravelling of Christy's story of parricide. Pegeen's interest in a man she has never seen before is ill-disguised: those she *has* seen are all too familiar in this desolate and inbred corner of Mayo. Shawn Keogh's pathetic fear of a rival, the Widow Quin's determination to get Christy for herself, and the mounting admiration which every recounting of his tale brings him, gains for Christy the self-esteem he so sadly lacked when living under the thumb of his father. By the end of the act he has developed to the extent of being able to say to himself, with a touch of modest pride, 'wasn't I the foolish fellow not to kill my father in the years gone by?'

The second act brings intimation of disaster. Shawn Keogh makes a bargain with the Widow Quin that she'll remove the danger by wedding Christy herself; Christy's father appears – 'the walking spirit of my murdered da!' – and reveals his story to the Widow, placing her in an ideal position for blackmail. Act Three starts with a comic or 'holding' interlude with the drunken Philly Cullen and Jimmy Farrell. Old Mahon makes an unfortunate reappearance, but the Widow convinces them he is a drunken madman. Christy returns, having won the races in the sports: he is now a hero. A passionate love-duet follows between himself and Pegeen. The tension explodes when, as expected, Old Mahon returns again. Christy appears to kill him for good and all this time: but his father is only stunned. The people turn against Christy, but he is no longer the snivelling boy: he has become a man. He rejects his father, Pegeen, and the fickle people of Mayo, and walks out into the world 'romancing through a romping lifetime from this hour to the dawning of the judgement day'. At the final curtain Pegeen realizes what she has lost, and gives her great cry of anguish and despair: 'Oh, my grief, I've lost him surely. I've lost the only Playboy of the Western World.'

The Playboy possesses a unique consistency. It contains elements that are in turn farcical, tragical, sentimental, melodramatic, romantic and wildly comic. T. R. Henn has said that it is, 'for all its apparent simplicity of plot, a delicately balanced system of ironies, ambivalences, both of words and situation'. Likewise, Nicholas Grene has written that 'the success of *The Playboy* is that the precisely achieved structure holds together the different modes of action in a complex and resonant whole'. Very little of this, it seems, was understood by the players, and even less by the audiences, in 1907.

Lady Gregory said of the script: 'We were almost bewildered by its abundance and fantasy, but we felt, and Mr Yeats said very plainly, that there was far too

137–40

much "bad language".' Willie Fay, who directed, was equally worried, and Synge agreed to the removal of several of what Lady Gregory described as 'violent oaths'; among these were phrases which have become so well known since that time that they are quoted unwittingly in Ireland in daily conversation.

It was rumoured that opposition was being organized, but no one anticipated how intense the opposition would be. On the opening night the first two acts passed without any objections being heard, but there was some muttering during the third act, and when the word 'shift' (meaning an undergarment) was spoken there was a hissing, which continued until the final curtain. *The Irish Times* critic thought the play a 'brilliant success' marred by 'indiscretions'. *The Freeman's Journal* found it to be 'a libel upon Irish peasant men, and worse still upon Irish peasant girlhood'. Police were present for the second performance. There was continuous uproar, through which the actors manfully kept speaking. On the third night Yeats organized a claque, and invited a larger contingent of police.

Several arrests were made. Enormous publicity resulted, and the house was packed for the fourth performance at which fifty policemen were present – the critic Andrew Malone recorded 'five hundred'! – and fines were imposed in the magistrate's court. When Arthur Griffith's paper (now called *Sinn Fein*) came out at the weekend, *The Playboy* was described as a 'vile and inhuman story told in the foulest language we have ever listened to from a public platform'. The Saturday-night audience was the first to listen attentively – Malone wrote that till then 'the play had never been heard in the theatre, it had only been heard *of* in the columns of newspapers and gossip in the streets'.

It is easy with the advantage of hindsight to conclude that 'the Playboy riots' were providential, and 'made' the Abbey Theatre, but the experience was shattering for members of the company; only Yeats was capable of turning the event to good use by means of speeches and articles – the period equivalent of television

137 Sara Allgood as Pegeen, Barry Fitzgerald as Michael James, and Arthur Shields as Christy, in an early revival of *The Playboy of the Western World*.

138 Sketch in a letter from Jack B. Yeats to J. M. Synge for Christy's jockey costume in Act III of *The Playboy of the Western World*.

139 *Right* Scene in Act II of *The Playboy of the Western World* where Christy (Niall Buggy) tells the Widow Quin (Siobhán McKenna) how he killed his father, from a 1976 revival in Dublin and Vienna.

140 *Below* Print by Jack B. Yeats captures the atmosphere of the off-stage race in *The Playboy of the Western World*. The author and artist travelled together in the west of Ireland when writing and illustrating magazine articles, and would have come across many such scenes.

AN ORATION BEFORE THE
PERFORMANCE.
AND
ITS
SEQUEL

A FOREIGN VISITOR
STOLIDY CONTEMPLATING
THE SCENE

OBJECTS TO THE
POLICE AND
FEELS PUT OUT
FOLLOWED
BY

AN INVITATION
OUTSIDE

and radio interviews. The rabble, whether organized or not, had been unable to stop a performance: but the play had hardly made its mark.

London, as usual, provided recognition. During the summer of 1908 *The Playboy* was presented at the Great Queen Street Theatre, where, as Lennox Robinson has written, 'it was immediately recognized as a masterpiece'. The company also played in Glasgow, Manchester, Birmingham, Cambridge and Oxford – probably the first Irish company to visit Oxford since the Smock Alley Players in 1677. Requests for copies of the script started arriving from other countries – *The Well of the Saints* had been produced at the Deutsches Theater, Berlin, and *In the Shadow of the Glen* at the Inchover, Prague, as early as 1906.

The Abbey brought Synge's work to the United States in 1911 – by which time the author was dead – and here the *Playboy's* opening was as painful as it had been in Ireland. It would have been easy to exclude *The Playboy* from the American repertoire, but Lady Gregory was determined not to yield to pressures, even though she did not particularly admire the play. The players, naively perhaps, expected a welcome from the Irish communities in Boston, Philadelphia and Chicago – but Irish-Americans were in no humour to see the land of their fathers portrayed in so uncompromising a light – they much preferred the uncritical whimsicalities of Boucicault. In Philadelphia the cast was arrested for producing 'immoral and indecent plays'. The Director of Public Safety (who, presumably, was not of Irish descent) was called as witness and said he had enjoyed *The Playboy of the Western World* very much. The case was dismissed.

Synge had died on 24 March 1909, after two unsuccessful operations, in a nursing-home in Mount Street, Dublin. He appreciated its view of the Dublin mountains, where he had roamed first as a child and later with Molly Allgood. *Deirdre of the Sorrows* was presented at the Abbey the following year, with Molly in the name part. Compared to Yeats' pristine verse-drama *Deirdre*, it is a warm and passionate play, full of rich melodious language. It has been produced at the Abbey and elsewhere many times, but often in too obvious a spirit of determination on the part of the director and actors to prove that it must be made to 'work' at all costs. Unfortunately, it does not 'work'. It is uniformly sombre, lacking in contrasts of mood, and lacking in the kind of rhetorical urgency which propels the Greek or Elizabethan tragedies to their point of explosion. *Deirdre of the Sorrows*, in contrast, seems to die away, though with a tenderness which cannot fail to cause a catch in the breath of the beholder. Yet one expects more. The subject, perhaps, needs a more 'heroic' or 'theatrical' utterance than Synge's western-Irish English, laden with the subtleties of its Gaelic lineage.

The first decade of the movement which had started as the Irish Literary Theatre ended with the departure of Frank and Willie Fay due to disagreements on management policy, the death of Synge, the successful battle with Dublin Castle over the presentation of *The Shewing-up of Blanco Posnet*, and the end of the period in which Annie Horniman subsidized the theatre's activities; but the movement had by now become an institution and there was no stopping. New players were to join the company – Fred O'Donovan, Arthur Sinclair, J. M. Kerrigan, Harry Hutchinson, Arthur Shields and (later) his brother 'Barry Fitzgerald', Maureen Delany and May Craig. Important new dramatists were appearing – Lennox Robinson and T. C. Murray in particular. For the moment, the Abbey continued very much as before; many new plays, now forgotten, were produced – they are well documented in the series of volumes of *The Modern Irish Drama*. A word, however, must be said about the supremacy of the 'folk' or 'peasant' play, for which the Abbey was already famous.

Many minor authors attempted to write in the style of Synge, and this school was parodied with great humour by the Belfast writer and director 'Gerald MacNamara' (*né* Harry Morrow, 1866–1938) who was a leading member of the Ulster Literary Theatre, a regional variant of the Irish Literary Theatre. The title of MacNamara's farce *The Mist that does be on the Bog* is in itself a wonderful caricature. Yet the folk play persisted, as a theatrical extension of the Gaelic storytelling tradition, and experienced a remarkable resurgence in the 1950s and 1960s with the first plays of John B. Keane. Of the earlier writers in this idiom, those whose work has survived relegation to the shelf of quaint fireside drama are Padráic Colum (1881–1972) and George Fitzmaurice (1878–1963).

Colum's *Broken Soil* (1903, later published as *The Fiddler's House*) was produced at the Molesworth Hall in the year before the opening of the Abbey Theatre. Colum was one of the first, as Andrew Malone has written, to break away from 'the narrow conventionalized concepts of the contemporary English theatre'. Latterday impatience with Abbey peasant plays has resulted in critics and public forgetting just how original his work was. *Broken Soil* concerns the fiddler Con Hourican, an instinctive artist and wanderer – Synge remarked that the artist in a poor Irish family tends to become a tramp.

The Land (1905) was immediately popular – a newspaper report of the time succinctly sums up the reasons for its success, and the lack of success of certain other productions: 'Mr Yeats has proved a little too abstruse, and Mr Synge a little too bizarre, to get fully down to the heart of the people. What distinguishes *The Land* and gives it a special value in the development of the Abbey Theatre in its spirit and subject. Mr Colum has caught up his play out of the mid-current of Irish life . . .'.

Colum deals with the plight of families and with the flight from the land, which is also a flight from a way of life. He was a member of the anti-Synge faction at the time of the *Playboy* controversy, but gave his play *Thomas Muskerry* to the Abbey after Synge was dead. He spent most of the remainder of his life lecturing in universities in the United States.

The plays of George Fitzmaurice (1878–1963) are undeniably 'folk', but this shy, reclusive writer cannot really be labelled as consciously belonging to any particular coterie or school. His plays are extremely individual, both in theme and expression. *The Pie-dish* (1908) and *The Magic Glasses* (1913) issue from a strange inner world which does not draw upon obvious folk-sources but upon the lives of curious rustic people who subsist upon their own fantastic imaginings. These, and several other plays which have not been produced at the Abbey Theatre but which have come to be admired by experimental producers, are written in the language of North Kerry, a delicately idiomatic English with a distinctive rhythm which can only be reproduced accurately by actors brought up in that district, or who are familiar with it. It is, therefore, 'regional' drama of a special sort, and difficult of access to outsiders – just as Synge's language makes his plays difficult of access to New Yorkers or Londoners.

Fitzmaurice's first play *The Country Dressmaker* was written before he tapped the rich idiosyncratic vein which makes the most part of his work so engaging; it became one of the Abbey staples. Lady Gregory and Yeats were uncharitably accused of failing to give him the encouragement he deserved, through envy of his talent. The fact is that Fitzmaurice lacked confidence to such an extent that he was often reluctant to allow his plays to be performed at all, and it is hard to accuse Lady Gregory and Yeats of professional jealousy when it can be demonstrated how assiduously they promoted the work of Synge, and later of O'Casey.

141 Cartoons from the *Evening Herald* showing reactions on and off-stage to the first production of *The Playboy of the Western World* at the Abbey Theatre.

XX

15
Parlour tragedy and kitchen comedy

1908–1955

Lennox Robinson, T. C. Murray, George Shiels, Paul Vincent Carroll, M. J. Molloy and others

142 Members of the cast of the first production of *The Far-off Hills* by Lennox Robinson, cartoon by Grace Plunkett. *Below* Eileen Crowe and F. J. McCormick. *Opposite* Maureen Deaney and P. J. Carolan.

From the death of Synge in 1909 until the destruction by fire of the Abbey premises in 1951 the outstanding Irish achievements in the theatre are the plays of Sean O'Casey (the more enduring of which were first produced at the Abbey), and the emergence of the Dublin Gate Theatre. During this half-century, Irish-born playwrights tended to remain in Ireland and to write primarily for an Irish audience: O'Casey, in his later years, is the notable exception. The latter part of the period is marked by the arrival of broadcasting and the creation of radio drama.

'We all did something,' said George Moore, 'but none did what he set out to do: Yeats founded a realistic theatre.' Soon after Synge's death the 'realists' had all but taken over the Irish drama. The two most important writers of this school, Lennox Robinson and T. C. Murray, came from Cork, and they, with some of their Munster adherents, were categorized as 'the Cork realists'; yet it is quite clear that at the time they did not see themselves as forming a school.

Esmé Stuart Lennox Robinson (1886–1958) was a 'man of the theatre' as well as a prolific playwright. He held several successive posts at the Abbey, including that of manager. He also became a member of the theatre's Board, and was its official historian, publishing *Ireland's Abbey Theatre* in 1951. A tall, gangling, shortsighted figure, he had a vague demeanour that concealed an astute and witty personality. He it was who, when confronted for the hundredth time with the criticism that 'the Abbey is not what it used to be', replied 'It never was!'. He directed over seventy productions there, among them original work by Lady Gregory, W. B. Yeats, Daniel Corkery, T. C. Murray, Lord Dunsany, St John Ervine, Brinsley MacNamara, Teresa Deevey, Rutherford Mayne, George Shiels, Sean O'Casey and himself.

Lennox Robinson wrote upwards of thirty plays. His first to be performed at the Abbey was *The Clancy Name* (1908), a gloomy one-act drama in which the upholding of a family's 'good' name is seen to be more important to Mrs Clancy than the life of her son. *The Dreamers* (1915) centres around Robert Emmet's rising of 1803; in it Robinson seems to be saying that the dream which man creates of the past, or of himself, is stronger than the reality.

In 1916 came *The Whiteheaded Boy*, his first major success. This expertly tailored comedy of small-town life concerns the sacrifices which are made by the Geoghegan family in order to send the wastrel son to university. *The Whiteheaded Boy* typifies Robinson's most enduring work, in which no profound thesis is put forward, but an intuitive feeling for character engages the audience's attention

and carries it along in a delightfully entertaining way. *The Far-off Hills* (1928) is another such 'evergreen' comedy, remembered when many of his more consciously serious plays are forgotten. *Drama at Inish* (1933), described as 'an exaggeration in three acts', is set in a small seaside town which is visited by a theatre company led by the extrovert Hector de la Mare. The authors whom Mr de la Mare presents in the local hall are those Russians and Scandinavians who influenced so much Irish dramatic writing of the same period. The townsfolk take the plays very much to heart; introspection and gloom become rife; dramatic suicides are contemplated, though never successfully carried out.

Two plays in Chekhovian mood, set on the dwindling estates of the Anglo-Irish ascendancy, *The Big House* (1926) and *Killycreggs in Twilight* (1937), seemed to be important statements at the time they were written. Both plays are fine period pieces: the term, unfortunately, implies that they would hardly command new productions, even in the present climate of Big House nostalgia. Among Lennox Robinson's other memorable plays are *Never the Time and the Place* (1924), *Ever the Twain* (1929), and *Church Street* (1934).

A far less prolific (and less versatile) playwright, but one whose work seems to be revived more often, is T. C. Murray (1873–1959). Murray was a schoolteacher from West Cork; most of his plays are set in that region, and their language is the rural English spoken there – a language much less ornate than that of Fitzmaurice's (or Keane's) North Kerry. His first play for the Abbey was *Birthright* (1910), a short family drama in one act. *Maurice Harte* followed in 1912; and though he wrote sixteen plays it is these, with *Autumn Fire* (1924) and *Michaelmas Eve* (1932), that maintain his high reputation.

Maurice Harte is a spoiled priest; Ellen in *Autumn Fire* has been disappointed in love, and watches her father become infatuated with a young girl of her own age; Moll in *Michaelmas Eve* sees the young man with whom she is in love marry for money and land. The plays of T. C. Murray are imbued with an overpowering feeling of frustration, but the author's innate sense of delicacy prevents him from

143 Lennox Robinson and friend, by Desmond O'Brien.

allowing his action to become turgid. He tends to let the situations and characters develop to a searing climax, when pent-up emotions are painfully released. Yet, as in much Irish drama, there is a stoic amusement to be gained in the most uncompromising situations.

Next to Sean O'Casey, the most popular playwright of the 1930s and 1940s – if the number of performances is accepted as the yardstick – was George Shiels (1881–1949). He came from Co. Antrim and returned there as a comparatively young man, following a railway accident in Canada which caused permanent disablement. Shiels is regarded as the master of the 'Ulster comedy', which, like the 'Ulster fry' relentlessly served up in boarding-houses in Belfast, has really nothing remarkably 'Ulster' about it. Most of Shiels' plays were first performed at the Abbey: had he remained faithful to Belfast, where his earliest work was produced, he might have started a school of playwriting and established the permanent professional company which that city so surprisingly lacked until World War II, when Harold Goldblatt and others founded the Ulster Group Theatre.

The Belfast theatre is worth noting again at this point, for the Ulster Literary Theatre had produced a number of fine plays in the early years of the century, often taking the Grand Opera House in Belfast for its more ambitious productions. Most of the actors were, however, amateur, and only able to offer their talents to a limited extent. Rutherford Mayne (*né* Samuel Waddell, 1878–1967) was its most impressive playwright, with *The Drone* (1910) and *Red Turf* (1911). (His most famous plays, *Peter*, 1930, and *Bridgehead*, 1934, were, like Shiels', first produced at the Abbey.) Such rural plays seemed to grow naturally out of the Ulster countryside.

During the late 1920s the British Broadcasting Corporation established its Northern Ireland Region. Due largely to the enterprise of Tyrone Guthrie (1900–71), its first producer, broadcast drama became a staple of the service. Guthrie's own radio plays *Squirrel's Cage* (1929) and *The Flowers are not for You to Pick* were influential in creating a special style for 'the theatre of the air'. Radio, too, became the only real source of income for many Ulster actors, and the Ulster Group Theatre was largely made up of freelance players who became known to one another and to the public via the BBC studios. R. H. McCandless, James Mageeon, James F. Tyrone, J. G. Devlin, Elizabeth Begley, Margaret D'Arcy and others, with the actor-playwright Joseph Tomelty (born 1911), appeared with Harold Goldblatt at the Group Theatre in the Ulster Hall building, a few yards from Broadcasting House. Tomelty, during the war years, wrote a marvellously witty and pungent radio serial about a Belfast family, *The McCooeys*, in which all these actors took part. The period 1939–45 is, significantly enough, regarded as the 'great' period of drama broadcasting in Northern Ireland.

145   George Shiels' best play, *The Passing Day* (1936), began as a radio drama, *His Last Day in Business*. Up to this time theatre audiences had been delighted with his series of well-wrought kitchen-comedies, of which the best are *Paul Twining* (1922), *Professor Tim* (1925) and *The New Gossoon* (1930). The idea of a more serious play from this most lighthearted of writers seemed improbable: but as it turned out there was plenty to laugh about in *The Passing Day*, in spite of its sombre theme, and in spite of the fact that there is not one character whose actions are motivated other than by self-interest.

The comedy is Molièresque: John Phibbs, the miserly small-town *commerçant*, who is about to make his Will, is in the line of family despots which includes Tartuffe, Argan and Harpagon. It is quite likely that Shiels never saw his play in this way; it is even less likely that he saw it, on another level, as a kind of modern morality in the Everyman mould. Phibbs, on what is to be his last day on earth, is visited by his doctor, his lawyer, the town gravedigger, and other characters all of whom could be given symbolic personifications such as Health, Worldly Goods, Death, and so forth. These possibilities seem to have escaped producers: the 1981 Abbey revival of *The Passing Day* treated the play as naturalistically as the earlier productions.

Shiels' bleak 'duet' *The Rugged Path* (1940) and *The Summit* (1941) contains a continuing story, and reveals a much deeper vein of disenchantment than anything lying below the surface of *The Passing Day*. The former broke the Abbey's record with a run of three months.

144

The years 1935 to 1938 were highly productive at the Abbey, with the English director Hugh Hunt and the designer Tanya Moiseiwitsch in charge of stage presentation. They included the first productions of Shiels' *The Passing Day*, *The Jailbird*, and *Quin's Secret*. Other fine new plays were *The Grand House in the City* by Brinsley MacNamara (né John Weldon, 1890–1963); *Boyd's Shop*, the quintessential Ulster comedy, by St John Ervine (1883–1971); *Katie Roche* by Teresa Deevy (1903–63); *Shadow and Substance* by Paul Vincent Carroll (1900–68); and adaptations of Frank O'Connor's prose fiction *In The Train* and *The Invincibles*, dramatized by the author and Hugh Hunt.

A playwright whose work was almost as 'popular' as George Shiels' was Louis Dalton (1900–51). He was also an actor and director, and ran his own company for many years. He occasionally directed for the Abbey, and managed the Abbey's second company of players when the National Theatre enjoyed a brief period of bringing its work to provincial centres in the early war years. His best comedies are *The Money Doesn't Matter* (1941) and *They Got What They Wanted* (1947).

Joseph Tomelty's comedy *Is The Priest at Home?* (1945) was widely acclaimed. If an Ulster school *is* to be discerned, Tomelty is surely Shiels' gentle and worthy successor. His comedies, as well as the drama *All Soul's Night* (1949), were equally

144 Curtain-call for the first production of *The Rugged Path* by George Shiels at the Abbey Theatre in 1940.

145 A scene from the 1981 revival of *The Passing Day* at the Abbey Theatre, directed by Tomás MacAnna and designed by Frank Conway, with Edward Golden as Samson, and Ray McAnally as John Fibbs.

popular at the Abbey and Ulster Group theatres, and, like the plays of Gerard Healy (1918–77), Bernard McCarthy (b. 1888), Walter Macken (1916–67) and others, were widely disseminated by the members of the amateur drama movement which became so strong during the war and post-war years. Many superb local groups sprang from this movement, among them the Sligo Drama Circle, the Lifford Players, the Tullamore Runners, the Listowel Players and the Tuam Theatre Guild. Annual competitions were established, with an all-Ireland drama festival taking place in Athlone.

In Dublin, as in Belfast a little earlier, the era of the 'wireless' was a significant one for the drama, especially after the formation of the Radio Eireann Players. Radio plays, of their nature, tend to become 'lost', principally because they are not often published, and because recordings are not generally available to the public. Padraic Fallon (1906–75) succeeded in giving the Celtic myths a viable dramatic form, bringing much more life and immediacy to them than ever Yeats or Moore had done. His deliberate appeal to the ear – a prerequisite both of story-telling and of the radio medium – is achieved chiefly through an easy-flowing verse form, a piling-up of radiant verbal imagery, and the use of an involved narrator or commentator. *Diarmuid and Gráinne* (1950), *The Vision of MacConglinne* (1953) and *The Wooing of Etáin* (1955) are outstanding works – one is tempted to say 'of theatre', and indeed in a broad sense they are just that. Other writers whose best dramatic work was written expressly for broadcasting are James Plunkett (b. 1920) and Micheál O hAodha (b. 1918).

During the fifteen or so years prior to the Abbey fire and the temporary exile of the company to the Queen's Theatre in Dublin, the two outstanding Irish plays were Carroll's *Shadow and Substance* (1937) and Molloy's *The King of Friday's Men* (1948). Paul Vincent Carroll was born in Co. Louth and spent most of his adult life in Glasgow where, with James Bridie, he helped found the Citizen's Theatre in 1943, writing several plays for it and for the BBC. His first Abbey play of note was *Things That Are Caesar's* (1932); in it he introduces the figure of the overbearing priest which was to feature in several of his plays and of which he was to make a superb character study in *Shadow and Substance*.

Carroll was naturally accused of anti-clericalism, but in fact his real target is the abuse of clerical power and responsibility, and the tyranny of misused authority. Canon Skerritt finds himself opposed to the village schoolteacher O'Flingsley, who has published a controversial book which the canon finds subversive enough to warrant dismissing the teacher from his post. The servant girl at the presbytery confides to O'Flingsley that she has seen a vision of her namesake, St Brigid. O'Flingsley advises her to consult the canon, who refuses to take her simple belief seriously. When local feeling against the teacher's book erupts, Brigid is accidentally killed in a local brawl, and both priest and teacher realize that they are mutually responsible for her death.

Carroll very subtly allows the audience to sympathize with the canon in his downfacing of certain hypocritical parishioners; he also presents the teacher as something of a hothead, so there is no obviously black-and-white conflict. *Shadow and Substance* won the New York Drama Critics Award for the best foreign play of its year – as did Carroll's next work, *The White Steed*, in which the leading character, Canon Matt Lavelle, an easy-going elderly priest, confined to a wheelchair, finds himself having to oppose the narrow morality of his young curate.

146 Shelah Richards.

Paul Vincent Carroll was inadvertently involved in a curious theatrical venture in Dublin during the war years. Press censorship was so rigid in Ireland, and the public was so cut off from external events, that when the actress and director Shelah Richards presented Carroll's play of Glasgow life, *The Strings, My Lord, Are False*, at the Olympia Theatre, Dublin, during the German bombing, the queues of people hoping to catch a glimpse of the reality of life and death in a participating country, stretched for several city-blocks. There is no official theatre-censorship in Ireland – in any case, it would have been difficult to find a convincing reason for banning this touching play – and so Shelah Richards was able to mount several productions of plays which would have been considered too 'controversial' for the Abbey during the period euphemistically known in neutral Ireland as 'the Emergency'.

M. J. Molloy (b. 1917) was born and brought up in a village in Co. Galway where life, during his childhood, was very much as it had been for a couple of hundred years. Some of his plays are 'historical' in the sense that they are set in a defined period of the past, but their feeling is unmistakably that of the present – in the sense of 'at the time of writing', in rural Ireland. He tends to show society at crucial moments of social change such as the break-up of the feudal order, or of the economic change that induces rural decay and depopulation.

Old Road (1943) and *The Visiting House* (1946) are realistic folk-plays. *The King of Friday's Men* (1948) has a much broader canvas. Set in the remote Barony of Tirawly in the eighteenth century, the plot concerns the obsession of the landlord Caesar French with the perpetuation of the ancient right to choose his own tally-woman (mistress) from the families of his tenants. Such privileges, however, are no longer acceptable to the lower orders, and fighting breaks out, resulting in the violent death of French. The chief character is Bartley Dowd, a famous shilelagh fighter, and a leader of the faction-fights which were a feature of the time. Una, the girl chosen by French, appeals to Bartley; convinced that she loves him, he takes up her cause against the landlord. The theme, of course, is the age-old one of the struggle against tyranny.

Ireland has changed so radically since *The King of Friday's Men* was written that the modern audience might find it implausible, for all the accuracy of its eighteenth-century background. Molloy's later plays are less humorous, as if the passing of a distinctive folk-culture were a subject too dispiriting for laughter.

16
Green crow and flying wasp

1922–1962

Sean O'Casey

147 Sean O'Casey by Robert Ballagh.

XXIII

The celebrations marking the centenary of the birth of Sean O'Casey (1880–1964) placed the dramatist in the position of a national hero – a position which would have surprised him very much. There was considerable State involvement in the commemorative proceedings. The Department of Posts and Telegraphs issued a postage stamp showing an indomitably irascible countenance.* Lectures and seminars were held. The Abbey Theatre gave expert revivals of *The Shadow of a Gunman*, *Juno and the Paycock* and *Red Roses for Me*, taking the first to the United States. Radio Telefis Eireann and the BBC collaborated on television versions of *Juno and the Paycock*, *The Silver Tassie* and *Red Roses for Me*. There was a well-intentioned thirteen-episode television dramatization of O'Casey's autobiographies, entitled *Sean*. RTE radio presented *Purple Dust*, *Within the Gates*, *The Bishop's Bonfire* and *Cock-a-Doodle Dandy*. The Lyric Players in Belfast gave *The Drums of Father Ned*. In Britain, *The Plough and the Stars* was produced by the National Theatre, *The Shadow of a Gunman* and *Juno and the Paycock* by the Royal Shakespeare Company. A large number of productions were given in other countries and in other languages.

Amid the public adulation and the ballyhoo several interesting points emerged. It was seen that O'Casey was the author of three masterpieces – *The Shadow of a Gunman*, *Juno and the Paycock*, and *The Plough and the Stars* – all of them flawed, in the manner of true masterpieces. It was also seen that his later plays had not yet been adequately assessed. He emerged as the Irish dramatist whose name seemed to encapsulate the Irish theatre in the mind of the whole world.

This last revelation is a curious one, for O'Casey's work is not at all typical of Irish dramatic writing either during his own lifetime or since his death. While it can easily be demonstrated that Synge influenced two whole generations of playwrights, O'Casey had few followers or imitators. His work is *sui generis*.

John Casey was his given name: he used the Irish version 'Sean O Cathasaigh' while actively involved with the Gaelic League, 'Casside' when speaking of himself in the third person in his autobiographies and 'Sean O'Casey' on his published plays. He was born into a militantly respectable lower-middle-class God-fearing Protestant family in Dorset Street, Dublin. A myth persists to the effect that he came from the same poor tenement background as the chief characters in his Dublin plays. It is no more true than that Richard Brinsley Sheridan (who had been born in the same street) came from a splendid town mansion like Sir Peter Teazle's.

O'Casey's father died in 1886, and this date marks the start of the family's decline into genteel poverty, and eventually want, but his mother made sure that his father's wish for Sean to be well-read and industrious was realized.

* Other playwrights represented on Irish postage stamps have been Goldsmith, Wilde, Shaw, Yeats and Synge.

During his long life O'Casey embraced many causes. His upbringing was fiercely Unionist; his membership of the Irish Republican Brotherhood may perhaps be explained as a natural reaction to this upbringing. In young manhood he became a member of the Gaelic League, and an ardent attender at the *soirées* held by that organization, at which jigs, reels and hornpipes were primly danced. He learned the Irish language – an eccentricity for any Dubliner, and a kind of betrayal for a Protestant one. In 1914 he became secretary of the left-wing Irish Citizen Army, and a devoted admirer of its leader, Jim Larkin. Like Shaw – whom, in later life, he came to know and to trust – he was profoundly affected by reading Karl Marx. The principles of socialism soon overtook his nationalist and religious ideals; he wrote: 'I never lost my faith, I found it. I found it when Jim Larkin came to Dublin and organized the unskilled workers.'

At fourteen he went to work as a store-assistant. He had many other jobs, from clerk to navvy. He appeared in plays by Shakespeare, Boucicault and others, which his brother produced first in their mother's living-room, and later with the manager of a fit-up company, Charles Dalton, in a converted stable. On one occasion O'Casey played Father Dolan in *The Shaughran* in the Mechanics' Theatre – the building which later became the Abbey. He admired Boucicault's stagecraft, and it is quite likely that Boucicault's deft manner of alternating scenes of tragedy and farce was influential – as it was for Shaw. By the time the Abbey accepted *The Shadow of a Gunman* in 1922 (for production the following March) he had already written three shorter plays. He was now forty-three: his greatest plays were all to be written over the next four years.

Lady Gregory understood that O'Casey's first attempts at playwriting were too polemical, and advised him to 'develop his peculiar gift for character-drawing'. *The Shadow of a Gunman* – originally entitled *On the Run* – is a series of character-sketches held together by a rather tenuous thread of plot which hardly develops until the final moments of the play. It is set in a room in a tenement-house on the north side of Dublin in 1920 during the period of vicious guerrilla fighting between Sinn Fein and the Black-and-Tans. The room is inhabited by a young proletarian poet, Donal Davoren (an idealized though purposely unflattering picture of O'Casey himself) and a pedlar, Seumas Shields. The other residents in the house assume that Davoren is a gunman in hiding, and he allows them to think so, especially, as he says to himself at the end of Act I:

> ... A gunman on the run! Be careful, Donal Davoren. But Minnie Powell is attracted to the idea, and I am attracted to Minnie. And what danger can there be in being the shadow of a gunman?

As in all O'Casey's major work, the men are seen as egotistical or cowardly or indolent, or a mixture of all three. It is the women who display the finer qualities. Minnie Powell, for the sake of Davoren, hides a bag of bombs which has been planted in his room, but the auxiliaries (the Black-and-Tans) discover the bag in her room, and Minnie is shot in a Sinn Fein ambush when being taken away on a lorry for questioning. Davoren and Shields are left, the one impotently bemoaning his state as 'poet and poltroon', the other stupidly uncomprehending of the enormity of the waste of human life.

The subsidiary characters in the play provide a skein of earthy humour expressed in rich Dublin vernacular. O'Casey had found his *métier*, his theatre, and his public. Most of the players were Dubliners who at once recognized and identified with the characters which this unconventional author presented to them. O'Casey 'made' many of these players, just as they 'made' O'Casey. The audience, bowled over by the topicality of the political content, and by the novelty of the local colour, took O'Casey to its heart. Yet the success of *The Shadow of a Gunman*, as time has shown, rests very little on such superficial considerations as topicality and novelty: there is an archetypal quality in the depiction of the central characters as imperfect human beings, and in the working-out of the theme of man's eternal undervaluing of the nobility and resilience of the human spirit.

148–9 *Juno and the Paycock* was accepted for production in 1924, and opened on 3 March. Juno Boyle is the once-handsome but now sadly careworn wife of 'Captain' Jack Boyle, the eponymous 'paycock', to whom work is anathema and who prefers drinking and gossiping with his good-for-nothing crony Joxer Daly. (Boyle and Joxer are, respectively, examples of the bibulous *miles gloriosus* and the parasite-slave types beloved of Boucicault.) The Boyles have two children – Mary, who is involved in a workers' strike, and Johnny, who has been wounded for his part in the current Civil War. The comic elements – such as the shiftless nature of the Boyle/Joxer relationship, and the ostentation of the party to which the Boyles invite their less-fortunate co-tenants when they believe they have come into a legacy, only serve to heighten the tragedy. The Boyles are reduced irrevocably into debt and penury; Mary is made pregnant and deserted by her lover as well as by her morally outraged father; Johnny is shot by his former comrades to avenge the betrayal of his neighbour Commandant Tancred; and Juno has to bear all the accumulation of distress because no one else is able or willing to do so.

O'Casey's main theme in this (his greatest) play is the unthinking vanity of the male in his incessant pursuit of aggrandisement. Juno, the mother-figure (as in the classical myth), is exalted by the dramatist as the ultimate source of good sense, courage and responsibility. Juno ultimately abandons the menfolk to care for her daughter and her unborn granddaughter. The divided family may be seen as a symbol for the divided Ireland of the Civil War – but this consideration is irrelevant to a rapt audience, captivated by the human tragedy:

> . . . What was the pain I suffered, Johnny, bringin' you into the world to carry you to your cradle, to the pains I'll suffer carryin' you out o' the world to bring you to your grave! Mother o' God, Mother o' God, have pity on us all! Blessed Virgin, where were you when me darlin' son was riddled with bullets? Sacred Heart o' Jesus, take away our hearts o' stone, and give us hearts o' flesh! Take away this murdherin' hate, an' give us Thine own eternal love!

The success of *Juno and the Paycock* enabled O'Casey to stop working as a manual labourer and devote himself, albeit precariously, to a writing career. He dedicated his next play, *The Plough and the Stars*, 'to the gay laugh of my mother at the gate of the grave'. This fanciful alliteration represents an aspect of his prose style which, when he writes in standard English – as in the autobiographies – can seem irritatingly coy and artificial; yet when he places the most convoluted constructions, circumlocutions and figures of speech into the mouths of his backstreet Dublin characters they appear altogether appropriate and natural. O'Casey was accused of inventing certain 'Dublinisms', and no doubt he did so in the sifting and selecting process which goes into the creation of dramatic dialogue. Some of his Dublin catch-phrases have now entered the language.

The Plough and the Stars (1926) is described as 'a tragedy', and like its two great predecessors contains some of the most boisterous comedy in the modern theatre. It is set during the months which culminated in the Easter Rising of 1916 – an event which after only ten years had already assumed an almost mythical place in

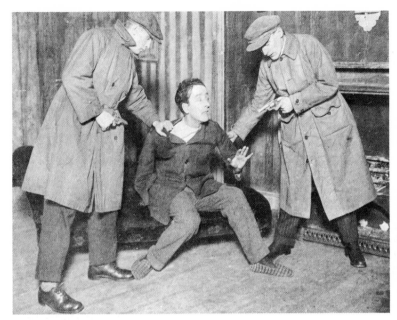

148–9 Scene from *Juno and the Paycock*, and Sara Allgood as Juno Boyle, the Royalty Theatre, London, November 1925.

the Irish folk-memory. Here again the lives of ordinary people are shown against a flaming background of extraordinary events.

The characters are for the most part residents in a slum tenement. Jack and Nora Clitheroe are expecting their first child; Nora tries to persuade him against accepting the post of Commandant in the Citizen Army; in this she fails, Jack is killed, and Nora, having lost her baby, becomes mentally deranged. The other residents are Mrs Gogan, a charwoman with a gift for the pithy phrase, and her consumptive daughter, Mollser; Bessie Burgess, a bibulous hymn-singing Protestant, who dies from a stray bullet when trying to shield Nora from the shooting; Peter Flynn, Nora's querulously patriotic uncle; the 'Covey', an ineffectual young man inspired by Communistic ideals; and Fluther Good, a loquacious wastrel in the Seumas Shields/Joxer Daly tradition. There are several subsidiary characters, including Rosie Redmond, a young prostitute; a 'speaker' whose street-oration recalls the words of Padraic Pearse; and two British non-commissioned officers.

The Plough and the Stars has a cinematic quality. Unity of place is abandoned, with scenes in the street and a pub as well as in two of the rooms of the tenement. Violent actions take place before the audience, instead of offstage as in the earlier plays. Yet the physical breadth does not diffuse the theme – the subversion of creative human relationships by (in this case) fanatical patriotism and what passes for the 'noble cause'. In *The Plough and the Stars* the truly brave are those who are unwittingly drawn into the holocaust, and perform humane actions through ordinary kindness or goodness of heart. The play's main flaw is a sentimentality amounting to mawkishness in an early scene between Jack and Nora.

Among the players who served Sean O'Casey so superbly in these plays, and whose names will ever be associated with the formation of the characters in them, were F. J. McCormick (who created Seumas Shields, Joxer Daly and Jack Clitheroe), Barry Fitzgerald (Jack Boyle and Fluther Good), Sara Allgood (Juno Boyle), Maureen Delany (Maisie Madigan and Bessie Burgess), May Craig (Mrs Grigson and Mrs Grogan), Eileen Crowe (Mary Boyle) and Shelah Richards (Nora Clitheroe).

150

151
150

150–1 *Left* Barry Fitzger-
ald as Fluther Good in
The Plough and the Stars.
Right The actor F. J.
McCormick is depicted in
eleven famous roles in
The Vacant Throne, a
painting by Cecil French
Salkeld in the Abbey
Theatre Collection.

Unfortunately, O'Casey had made himself unpopular by tactlessly criticizing
several members of the company – and especially the director M. J. Dolan – for a
production of Shaw's *Man and Superman.* He was barred from the theatre green-
room, and relations were poor when *The Plough and the Stars* went into rehearsal.
The Government nominees on the Board found that several speeches were
'objectionable', and the character of Rosie Redmond was thought to be far too
realistic. Yeats and Lady Gregory allowed some changes to be made in order to
placate members of the company as well as outside observers, but stated that they
would prefer the Government subsidy to be withdrawn rather than concede to
censorship from whatever quarter.

The play was a tremendous success with both the public and the critics, but
after some nights of scattered catcalling and hissing a planned demonstration took
place in the theatre, organized by those who felt that the men of 1916 had been
wilfully insulted. Yeats, recalling *The Playboy* riots, addressed the audience: 'You
have disgraced yourselves again!' he declaimed, in a now-famous speech which he
had earlier issued to the press. By the date of this disturbance a production of
Juno and the Paycock was running in London under the direction of J. B. Fagan: a
transfer to a larger theatre was planned, and O'Casey's presence was requested in
London for promotional purposes. Pique at the Abbey actors' unfriendliness – for
which he was entirely responsible – and annoyance at the reaction of a section of
the Irish audience which should have known better, caused O'Casey to accept the
invitation and travel to London. He wrote in *Inishfallen, Fare Thee Well* (1949)
that he had decided to leave Ireland forever – but this is not quite true, for he told
an English journalist at the time that he would be returning to work in Dublin,
and he retained his room there.

The subject of exile, whether heartbreakingly imposed or gleefully embraced,
is one which has infused Irish literature for centuries. Irish voices have spoken

from overseas since Early Christian times, and in our century Shaw, Joyce, O'Casey and Beckett have continued the tradition in their own peculiar fashions. (Joyce's only play, indeed, is entitled *Exiles*, though for figurative reasons.) O'Casey's was an angry exile: he felt let down by the country he loved – and, for all its faults, continued to love – and by the theatre to which he had given his best work. Undoubtedly there were faults on his side: among them arrogance and an ability to harbour rancour, and an outspokenness which, if decidedly honest, could be extremely hurtful to friends and well-wishers. The fact is that, in spite of the many critical arguments put forward in their favour, the plays which O'Casey wrote after he abandoned Ireland for ever (after the Abbey's rejection of *The Silver Tassie*) are quite clearly not as good as the Dublin trilogy.

The Silver Tassie (first produced by C. B. Cochran at the Apollo Theatre, London, in 1929) has moments of almost incredible intensity of feeling. Yeats should have recognized it as a 'not-quite-so-good' submission from Ireland's leading dramatist, and allowed it to be produced, partly for its own sake, and partly as an encouragement towards future work. O'Casey's anger and resentment resounded through the columns of the Irish and British press, and occupied his mind for the rest of his life. The Abbey produced the play in 1936, but this did not heal the wound. O'Casey described himself as 'a voluntary and settled exile from every creed, from every party, and from every literary clique in Ireland'.

The 'tassie' of the title is a silver cup won by Harry Heegan at football before he is permanently disabled in the Great War: it is the emblem of his promising career. When, in his wheelchair at the football-club dance, he destroys the trophy, he is symbolically expressing his utter disillusionment. The play is completely pessimistic in feeling. Its second act, set on a battlefield in northern France, exaggerates the mood of despair, and the author makes use of visual and literary techniques (which may be loosely described as 'expressionistic') to emphasize the mood. This scene is, stylistically speaking, out of key with the remainder of the play: but it is one of the most powerful in twentieth-century drama.

152

152 Act II of *The Silver Tassie* in Hugh Hunt's celebrated 1972 revival at the Abbey Theatre, designed by Alan Barlow.

In 1927 O'Casey married the Irish actress Eileen Carey. Their subsequent life together, chronicled in his florid prose, and more simply in her book *Sean*, touchingly demonstrates the power of supportive family love during long periods of financial difficulty. They had three children, Shivaun, Brehon and Niall. The latter's death in 1956 caused terrible anguish, which O'Casey manfully determined to overcome by setting himself to write a comedy, *The Drums of Father Ned*. This play was to have been performed at the Dublin Theatre Festival, but was abandoned because the festival authorities stupidly expected the Roman Catholic archbishop to celebrate a votive mass on the opening day, and this the archbishop refused to do. Ironically, these were just the kind of senseless procedures which O'Casey had satirized in his play, and they convinced him that Ireland had not changed one iota in thirty years.

153

O'Casey's biographer, the director Hugh Hunt, divides his 'later' plays – they are more numerous than the 'early' ones – into three categories: *Within the Gates* (1934), *The Star Turns Red* (1940) and *Oak Leaves and Lavender* (1947) are described as 'tragic moralities'; *Cock-a-Doodle Dandy* (1949), *The Bishop's Bonfire* (1955) and *The Drums of Father Ned* (written in 1958) are 'comic moralities'; while *Figuro in the Night* (1951), *The Moon Shines on Kylenamoe* (1962) and *Behind the Green Curtains* (1962) are 'fantasies'.

XXIV

European and American expressionism is the chief influence upon the tragic moralities. *Within the Gates* is set at a kind of Hyde Park Corner, where characters representing forces that O'Casey felt to be pernicious – such as religious power – attempt to subvert the quest of Janice, who is an embodiment of the Shavian life force. *The Star Turns Red* is a synthesized confrontation of Communism and Fascism. The Star of Bethlehem turns to a meaningful red when the common people triumph over the forces of reaction, and Christianity is, somewhat surprisingly, reconciled with Marxism. The opposing doctrines are too obviously portrayed, but the play, if produced with the kind of technical bravura which is an essential property of the expressionist theatre, can succeed very well before an audience, as it did in a memorable Abbey production directed by Tomás MacAnna in 1978.

Oak Leaves and Lavender, set principally during the Battle of Britain, is an amorphous piece in which a number of lines of thought become confused in the expression. The principal strand that emerges is a paean to the indomitable spirit of the British people – who probably stand for all men of goodwill.

Of the comic moralities, *Cock-a-Doodle Dandy* is by far the most assured. The enchanted rooster (played by an actor) represents freedom and enjoyment. The parish priest in an Irish country town, Father Domineer, treats this figure as the Devil incarnate. Those who follow the priest – they are, one supposes, typical citizens of De Valera's repressed Ireland – attempt to slay this cock, but end by displaying themselves as ridiculous bosthoons. *Cock-a-Doodle Dandy* attempts to equate Dionysian abandon with the Christian ethic of taking no thought for the morrow: a curious equation, and one which only O'Casey could have conjured up.

The Bishop's Bonfire, 'a play about the ferocious chastity of the Irish', as O'Casey described it, concerns an episcopal visit to a rural community where Councillor Reiligan has been created a papal count and where works of 'evil literature' are to be publicly burned. Reiligan is a despot who arranges a financially advantageous marriage to an elderly farmer for one daughter, and arranges for his other daughter to enter the religious life although she wishes to marry. Some embarrassingly sentimental dialogue, and an unnecessarily melodramatic conclusion, mar what might have been a good satirical comedy. When the play was produced in 1955 by

153 The 1980 revival of
The Drums of Father Ned
at the Lyric Theatre,
Belfast.

Cyril Cusack Productions, with Tyrone Guthrie directing, there were some protests from the first-night audience. These were thought to have been uttered by shocked pietists, but were later discovered to be merely from students voicing their disappointment in the play. *The Drums of Father Ned* is equally innocuous, and it is astonishing to recall the furore created by its non-appearance in 1958.

The three one-act 'fantasies' are not much more than curiosities. However the farces *The End of the Beginning* (1937) and *A Pound on Demand* (1947) show O'Casey writing in a vein of which he was a master, but which he usually kept for moments in his tragic plays when tension had to be dispelled.

A play which stands somewhat outside the categories of those already mentioned is *Red Roses for Me* (1946). It seems to connect, in an interesting way, the style of the Dublin trilogy with that of the later comedies. It is O'Casey's most overtly autobiographical play: Ayamonn Breydon is a quite sympathetic portrait of the young O'Casey, involved in amateur drama, trades unionism, and Protestant good works. The first two and the final acts are naturalistic, but the third is an extravagant mixture of song, dance and drama in which heroes of old are conjured and in which it is suggested that the salvation of Ireland (and the world) lies in the energizing spirit of the younger generation.

O'Casey is still the most often performed of the Irish dramatists in Ireland, and probably also abroad. The languages into which his plays have been translated are many; and certain plays which have not been so well thought of at home have been hailed as significant *teaterstucken* in translation. His mantle does not seem to have fallen on any one of the succeeding Irish playwrights, though Maura Laverty, Brendan Behan, James Plunkett, James KcKenna and Heno Magee probably would not have written in the way they did without O'Casey's example before them.

173

17
The brave new Ireland

After 1928

The Dublin Gate Theatre and Taibhdhearc na Gaillimhe

After the Act of Union of 1800 all eyes turned towards London; after the Treaty of 1921 it was somehow disloyal and unpatriotic to acknowledge the presence of London at all. Yet, in addition to the natural and necessary preoccupation with the revival of the Irish language and other almost forgotten manifestations of the distant past, Ireland did manage to retain some artistic connection with the world outside.

There was the Dublin Drama League, for instance, founded by Yeats and Robinson from within the Abbey, and others outside, to relieve the monotony of what was rather unkindly referred to as 'the native product'. All the plays given by the Drama League in its ten years of existence from 1918 to 1928 were by contemporary foreign authors (except two plays by Lord Dunsany and one by Shaw) including Eugene O'Neill, Jean Cocteau, Martinez de Sierra, the Quintero brothers, Luigi Pirandello and Gabriele d'Annunzio. The performances took place in the Abbey Theatre on Sundays and Mondays, often with members of the Abbey company strengthening the amateur casts. The fact that these authors attracted good attendances proves that there was a desire in Dublin – if not in any other part of the country – to experience the breeze blowing across the seas from America and from the European mainland.

Once the aims of the founding members of the Drama League had been achieved, there seemed little else to be done, and, unlike many amateur groups which go into a decline once the immediate objective has been attained, the Drama League sensibly discontinued its activities. A partial reason may also have been the appearance of the Dublin Gate Theatre Studio, whose founders Hilton Edwards (1903–82) and Micheál MacLiammóir (1899–1978) announced a professional and full-time programme rather similar to the League's amateur and part-time one.

Hilton Edwards' involvement in the Irish theatre began when Anew McMaster, the Irish actor-manager, had suddenly to replace a member of his company in a Shakespearian tour of the southern and western counties, and engaged at short notice the young Englishman who had acted in London at the Old Vic and with the Charles Doran Company, and who had ambitions as a director. He had also been associated with Peter Godfrey who had been mounting productions of plays like those the Dublin Drama League was producing at the Gate Theatre in London; and he was an admirer of Adolph Appia in stage lighting. Edwards joined McMaster in Enniscorthy in 1927, and there he met the Irish actor and designer Micheál MacLiammóir. Their partnership lasted until MacLiammóir's death in 1978.

154–5

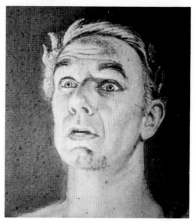

Micheál MacLiammóir was born in Cork. His family emigrated to London when he was a child, and lived constantly on the brink of poverty. His first professional stage-appearance was at the age of ten in a children's play at His Majesty's Theatre. He toured England as a child actor, and played Oliver Twist with Beerbohm Tree. During his adolescence he went to the Slade School of Art, becoming in due course a professional designer and illustrator, at the same time learning the Irish language at the London branch of the Gaelic League. He developed a romantic attachment to Ireland, its history, myth, legend and language, and began to make nostalgic visits to relatives to absorb the atmosphere of the new State. After a time he admitted that his life was lacking in 'concentration and purpose', and it was then that he joined his brother-in-law Anew McMaster's company.

Anew McMaster (1894–1962) was an actor-manager in the nineteenth century tradition. His Shakespeare presentations, for which he is best remembered and which continued until the 1960s, were unashamedly devised to display the talents of the leading actor. Many players and authors who later distinguished themselves in the Irish and British theatre gained their early experience of the stage in McMaster's tours of the Irish provinces. (Harold Pinter has written an immensely entertaining book on the subject.) McMaster was always the star, and it was McMaster whom the audience came to see. He was an outstanding Shylock,

154–6 *Left* Micheál MacLiammóir, the designer, at work on *Ring Round the Moon* by Jean Anouilh. *Top right* Hilton Edwards as Herod in *King Herod Explains*, by Conor Cruise O'Brien. *Bottom right* Anew McMaster as Oedipus.

156

Othello, Coriolanus and Oedipus, depending upon broad effects of gesture and an astonishing vocal range. He was less happy in lighter roles, though one of his early successes was in *Paddy the Next Best Thing* in which he played for over two years in the early 1920s. He was a memorable James F. Tyrone in O'Neill's *Long Day's Journey into Night* in which he toured all over the United States towards the end of his career.

McMaster possessed an insouciant disregard for 'production', and he was not greatly interested in the visual interpretation of a play. As long as the backcloths depicted the Blasted Heath or the Deck of Pompey's Galley with reasonable verisimilitude, and the costumes were more-or-less historically accurate, give or take a quarter-century, he allowed the text to speak for itself. MacLiammóir was looking for something more challenging; and when he and Edwards discussed the kind of plays in which they were interested, they found that their ideas to a great extent agreed. From its opening at the Peacock Theatre (where the company played until it found its permanent home in the Dublin Rotunda) on 14 October 1928, the Gate concerned itself very much with the visual and atmospheric aspects of production, with, for the next fifty years, Hilton Edwards directing almost all the plays, Micheál MacLiammóir designing most of them, and both partners appearing as often as their other duties permitted – Hilton Edwards, many would agree, not appearing nearly often enough.

157–8 Denis Johnston, whose first play *The Old Lady Says 'No!'* (1929) owed much of its initial success to the new techniques of production, lighting, and design which the Gate was to provide, has described the typical Abbey Theatre stage setting of the time as 'a set of warped flats lashed together with ropes and cleats'. Only at the Gate – with a few rare exceptions, such as the brief periods when Tanya Moiseiwitsch, Vere Dudgeon and Anne Yeats were employed as designers at the Abbey – could audiences expect productions in which the visual elements were treated with as much care as was the author's text.

The Gate was, inevitably, referred to with the veiled derision peculiar to Dublin as being a 'director's theatre', while the Abbey was a 'writer's theatre'. If this were so, the Gate was proud of the epithet. There was also an apocryphal story of an Abbey player remarking to a colleague from the Gate, 'You have the technique, but we have the talent'. This dismissive generalization has a ring of truth, for although the Gate did present a number of new plays by Irish writers, and although the acting was often highly polished, the company did not possess that feeling for ensemble-playing which is the hallmark of most important repertory companies. With the exception of its two founders and a few loyal adherents, actors at the Gate tended to come and go, while those at the Abbey remained, sometimes for their entire careers, giving a 'company' feeling, and providing an atmosphere of permanency and tradition – an atmosphere which could, of course, be criticized as inducing stagnation.

After the Gate had consolidated its early achievement in presenting mainly contemporary plays that had not previously been seen in Ireland, Shakespeare, Molière and the eighteenth-century Irish dramatists were added to the repertoire. This had the effect of driving the Abbey into its own backyard, so to speak, with productions of many insignificant plays which were almost a parody of the stock-in-trade; and productions of foreign and Irish classics, which had been an integral part of the Abbey repertoire, disappeared completely in the mid-1930s.

The Gate's first season had opened with Ibsen's *Peer Gynt* on the diminutive Peacock stage. This was followed by O'Neill's *The Hairy Ape* and *Anna Christie*, MacLiammóir's translation of his own play *Díarmuid agus Gráinne*, and Evreinov's

The Theatre of the Soul with the first production in the British Isles of Wilde's *Salomé*. The second season (also at the Peacock) included Tolstoy's *The Power of Darkness*, Rice's *The Adding Machine*, Čapek's *R.U.R.*, Evreinov's *A Merry Death*, Galsworthy's *The Little Man*, and three new works by Irish writers: *Juggernaut* by David Sears, a version of *Tristan and Iseult* by An Philbín, and Denis Johnston's *The Old Lady Says 'No!'*. (There was also a historical pageant presented at the Mansion House, *The Ford of the Hurdles*, which came to be known in Dublin as *MacLiammóir Through the Ages*.)

Eastern Europe and America, therefore, loomed largest, with expressionism and what is still known as the Modern Movement as the sustaining *leitmotiv*. The type of staging, which audiences found completely novel, is referred to by MacLiammóir in his autobiography *All for Hucuba*. He describes the double bill of *The Theatre of the Soul* and *Salomé*:

> It was a strange combination, and called forth a few howls, for in the Evreinov play we acted in a black set with two spotlights and a line-drawing in white and scarlet of an enormous heart rather in the manner of Joan Miró; and in *Salomé* we had a lovely set in black and silver and viperish green with the entire cast stripped almost naked. This we did partly because it is obvious the thing to do and partly for reasons of economy, for, as I pointed out, the idea of tawdry finery is unthinkable in a Wilde play: it must be Bakst and Cartier or nothing at all, and the one thing in the world that is not tawdry is the human form, provided it be of reasonable youthfulness and strength and does not gorge itself at every meal. So, naked and in a few elaborately painted head-dresses and loin-cloths, it was played on a series of black curving steps and green cube-like thrones . . .

157–8 *Left* Micheál MacLiammóir as the actor playing the part of Robert Emmet in Denis Johnston's play *The Old Lady Says 'No!'* in 1929. *Right* The playwright Denis Johnston.

The real discovery of those early seasons at the Gate was Denis Johnston, steeped as he was in the expressionist theatre of Kaiser and Toller (he collaborated with Toller on an English version of *Die Blinde Gottin*, produced as *Blind Man's Buff* in 1936).

Johnston's first play, *The Old Lady Says 'No!'*, remains at once his most characteristic and most complex work. An actor playing the part of the nineteenth-century patriot Robert Emmet in an old-fashioned melodrama sustains an accident on the stage, and the rest of the play consists of his semi-conscious ramblings (verbal and otherwise) through contemporary Dublin, with interspersed halucinatory visions of events and personalities in Irish history. The play is a scathing comedy on the 'new Ireland', with its acute parochialism, its sentimental view of history, and its society of jumped-up political and commercial leaders mingling uncomfortably with the fading ascendancy of the previous era. It is probably incomprehensible to a non-Irish audience (though it was played at the Westminster Theatre, London, in 1935) because of the local nature of the satirical allusion. Hilton Edwards remarked that it read like a railway guide and played like *Tristan and Isolde*.

Denis Johnston's second play *The Moon in the Yellow River* is a much more realistic work, in somewhat Scandinavian mood. It was produced at the Abbey – Lady Gregory had rejected *The Old Lady Says 'No!'* (hence its title), but the Abbey had generously subscribed towards its first presentation. The story concerns the building, by a German engineer, Tausch, of an electric power station, and an attempt by subversives to destroy it. The author views both technological progress and the objectives of ardent revolutionaries with some cynicism; no play better expresses the prevailing mood of the 1930s.

The Gate produced his next four plays, *A Bride for the Unicorn* (1933), *Storm Song* (1934), *The Golden Cuckoo* (1939), and *The Dreaming Dust* (1940); the latter investigates the enigma of Jonathan Swift, a subject which Johnston returned to several times. *Strange Occurrence on Ireland's Eye* (Abbey, 1956) is a courtroom drama, but unlike most plays in the genre, makes a serious examination of legal morality.

159 Denis Johnston's last play, *The Scythe and the Sunset*, was produced at the Abbey in 1958. It is set in a sleazy café overlooking the General Post Office in Dublin at the time of the Easter Rising of 1916. The café is taken over by the insurgents as a first-aid station and observation-post, and the location gives the author an opportunity to introduce several characters of widely differing background and political viewpoint who are forced to meet one another in ludicrous circumstances. A Dublin surgeon returning from a 'night on the town' provides a pointedly uncommitted obligato of sardonic comment upon the situation and the personal relationships which are established.

Johnson takes a much more objective and much less emotionally involved view of the revolution (and indeed of everything) than O'Casey in *The Plough and the Stars* (of which the title – but only the title – is a parody). The 1916 Rising, however, is only a starting point for the play's central theme, which arises from the author's preoccupation with the accidental encounters of war – those seemingly irrational meetings which take place between human beings while the destiny of nations is being indecently forged all around them.

The Gate did not have a particular policy towards the encouragement of Irish playwrights, but the very nature of the Gate's productions naturally attracted younger writers whose work was unlikely to prove acceptable at the Abbey. Mary Manning was one of these. Her *Youth's the Season –?* (1931), was what might be

159 The 1981 revival of
The Scythe and the Sunset
by the Irish Theatre
Company, directed by
Patrick Laffan, with
Denys Hawthorne and
Liam Sweeney.

described as being 'a little in advance of its time', dealing with incipient homo-
sexuality and *amer de jeunesse* in a group of well-brought-up, well-educated young
people in suburban Dublin. It is the era of the 'bright young things', of the
ubiquitous cocktail-shaker; echoes of ragtime may be discerned throughout the
play. For all this gaiety there is a terrible feeling of emptiness, of lack of purpose,
in an Ireland where there seems to be little future for the able and the gifted.

Later, immediately after the Second World War, Maura Laverty (1907–66)
wrote her plays of lower-class Dublin life specifically for the Gate. *Liffey Lane* and
Tolka Row were both produced in 1951, and *A Tree in the Crescent* the following
year. Though there is no overtly reforming message in these plays, they state by
implication that the social conditions in which the urban working-classes exist in
the new Ireland are nothing short of appalling.

Liffey Lane is set in the extreme poverty of a tenement house, such as we see in
Juno and the Paycock: but this time there is no revolution to fire the spirits and
distract the people from the apathy caused by overcrowding, starvation and disease.
The story concerns the efforts of a young girl to save her four-year-old brother
from being placed in an institution simply because the family cannot afford to
feed him. Chrissie Doyle finds a generous sympathiser in the person of a rag-man
called Billy Bunch. Billy performs the role of chorus in the play, which is cinematic
in construction.

Maura Laverty's slum characters manage to get through life with a caustic
good-humour and a warm-hearted sympathy for each other's difficulties. *Tolka
Row* shows a family which has been moved by the Corporation from the city-
centre to a desolate housing estate, and deals with the loneliness which can destroy
the soul in such an environment. In dealing with the next upward rung of the
social ladder in *A Tree in the Crescent*, Maura Laverty was less assured. Her plays,
in spite of their gloomy prognostication, are comedies, for the author deftly
captures the remarkable effervescence of life among the garrulous poor.

Twenty years later the Gate found a new and original playwright in Desmond Forristal. *The True Story of the Horrid Popish Plot* (1972) is a witty, ironic piece concerning the events leading up to the martyrdom of the seventeenth-century Archbishop of Armagh, Oliver Plunkett. His other plays are *Black Man's Country* (1974), set among Irish missionaries in an 'emerging' African state; *The Seventh Sin* (1976), which makes use of techniques of the morality play; and *Captive Audience* (1979), a claustrophobic suspense-drama.

The Gate, not enjoying State assistance (until 1970), depended upon the sale of seats and the subscription of patrons. One of its earliest supporters was Edward, 6th Earl of Longford, a Gaelic and Greek scholar, painter, and playwright. *Yahoo*, his expressionistic play about Swift, was one of the successes of the 1933–4 season. As time went on Edward Longford provided more and more funds from his private fortune to offset the theatre's deficit, and he became a member of its Board. In 1935 there was a disagreement over policy, and Longford decided to form his own company, Longford Productions, to occupy the theatre from April to September, with Edwards–MacLiammóir Productions taking over from October to March. He also generously maintained the theatre premises.

Bitter though the 'Gate split' may have been to those involved, the new arrangement benefited the Irish theatre in more general ways. When not performing in Dublin during the winter, Longford Productions toured the provinces, and gave spirited productions of the plays which Dublin had seen during the summer, before a public which had probably never seen any serious theatre other than the Shakespeare presented by Anew McMaster. Molière, Murphy, Goldsmith, Sheridan and Shaw, as well as the dryly amusing comedies of Christine Longford, were mounted in Town Halls and cinemas annually for a quarter-century.

These Longford productions had an air of rakish gentility; rarely of the first class, but always professional, they served their purpose in providing entertaining evenings during an era when there was precious little to raise the spirits. The spectacle of Edward and Christine Longford, he very pink and rotund, she as winsome as her heavy country tweeds would allow, arriving in some country town in their Ford 8 to open the hall and paste up posters, was a familiar one from 1937 until Edward Longford's death in 1961. Christine Longford remained on the board of the Gate Theatre and had the satisfaction of seeing it granted annual financial assistance from the State.

For an author who abhorred commercialism, it may seem paradoxical that MacLiammóir, the theatrical conjurer, should draw a commercial card out of his harlequin sleeve, but *Where Stars Walk* at the Gaiety Theatre, Dublin, in 1940, was an outstanding commercial success. This success may have been the reason for the kind of recognition which made Edwards and MacLiammóir into national figures rather than simply the talented leaders of a small artistic undertaking of limited public appeal.

Where Stars Walk is a comedy in which crisp dialogue packed with capricious allusion puts one in mind of the playwrights of the eighteenth-century Irish school, while its theme recalls the magic of W. B. Yeats' versions of the Celtic mythological tales: a combination of opposites, one might think. It may seem pretentious to speak of the merging of two traditions – the Anglo-Irish and the Gaelic – in what is, after all, a fairly slight comedy; yet this is precisely what MacLiammóir did in this play, where reincarnations of the lovers Etáin and Midhir appear as house-servants in the home of a famous actress; and also in *Ill Met By Moonlight* (which was revived during five seasons) where the Celtic idea of the changeling or 'stolen child' finds a counterpart in a modern writer's *ménage* in Connemara.

These plays had the benefit of their author in the main role – in both cases a country boy of captivatingly buccolic innocence and wisdom; and one is reminded of the way in which Dion Boucicault added dimension to his own Irish plays by writing the silver-tongued rural bumpkins for himself – there is certainly a parallel here, though the critics of the 1940s do not seem to have discerned it. MacLiammóirs's other plays are *The Mountains Look Different* (1948), *Home for Christmas* (1950), *A Slipper for the Moon* (1954), and *Prelude in Kazbek Street* (1973) – the latter a propaganda play which came rather too late in the history of the campaign for homosexual equality to strike an original note.

Micheál MacLiammóir's solo performances, *The Importance of Being Oscar* (1960), *I Must Be Talking To My Friends* (1963) and *Talking About Yeats* (1965), brought him on tours around the world. He published an account of his experiences in the first with characteristic humour and modesty in *An Oscar of No Importance* (1968). In *The Importance of Being Oscar* he assembled a chronological programme of the prose, poetry, correspondence and plays of Oscar Wilde, but it is in his commentary that the full resonance of one genius speaking of another truly emerges. This astonishing performance has been preserved as a telerecording and on disc.

In 1978 Denis Johnston summed up the achievement of Hilton Edwards and Micheál MacLiammóir by stating that the Dublin Gate Theatre 'has consistently stood for one fundamental principle – that it is the business of the theatre to be theatrical'. Certainly without the influence of the Gate the Irish theatre would have remained isolated from that of the Western – and indeed to a large extent from the Eastern – world, for how long one does not dare to imagine. Without its influence, too, the Abbey would probably not have renewed its production-techniques, nor would Irish actors have had the opportunity of playing so wide a variety of non-Irish roles. The Gate started as a reaction against ingrown nationalism, and emerged as a vital part of the national heritage.

160 Scene from *Witch Hunt*, a play about Dame Alice Kyteler of Kilkenny, by Christine Longford, presented by Longford Productions.

161 Dublin theatrical
conversation-piece of the
1960s – Christine
Longford, Hilton
Edwards and Micheál
MacLiammóir, painted by
Muriel Brandt.

At precisely the same time as Edwards and MacLiammóir were planning their
first season of plays in 1928, a rather different venture was being planned in
Galway. Liam O Bríain, then Professor of Romance Languages at University
College, hoped with others to inaugurate a theatre where all the plays would be
performed in the Irish language. Now that Ireland was 'a nation once again', that
nation should surely have a theatre which was truly national: and to be truly
national its language would have to be Irish. The members of the committee which
formulated the objectives of this new theatre, Taibhdhearc na Gaillimhe, aside
from their scholarly and idealistic fervour, had no practical experience of producing or writing plays; and so it came about that Liam O Bríain, having discussed
the project with Micheál MacLiammóir and having discovered that MacLiammóir had also written a play in Irish on the ancient love story of Díarmuid and
Gráinne, invited him to provide the professional expertise which was lacking.
MacLiammóir protested that he possessed no technical expertise, and so the help
of Hilton Edwards was enlisted, with the result that the first production of an
Irish-language play in the new Irish-language theatre was directed by an Englishman. MacLiammóir has described the early rehearsals in Galway:

> Sometimes Hilton and I would argue for an hour or more about the precise position
> for an actor during a speech, and to our surprise this seriousness that is commonplace
> to any stage worker drew forth cries of delighted patriotic approval from members of
> the committee. 'Dá mbeadh daoine ag plé le míonrudaí mar seo fiche blían ó shin bhí
> an Ghaelige sabháilte – 'If people had paid attention to detail like this twenty years
> ago the language would be saved', they said.

182

The Taibhdhearc opened with the benefit of an ideal first play, in what was evidently an exciting and novel style of production. A *naissance* of Gaelic theatre was proclaimed, and the Abbey was warned in the national press that it would have to look to its laurels. As matters turned out, there was no need for the Abbey to do any such thing. The Taibhdhearc flourished – but on a diet of mainly Abbey plays translated from English, interspersed with translations of French, Italian and English writers from the accomplished pen of Liam O Bríain. Local amateur actors blossomed into actors of national and sometimes international standing: but after they had done so they hardly ever returned to the Taibhdhearc.

Original plays in Irish were produced, but not many of them seemed to translate into other languages, including English; or if they did, they failed to travel further than Dublin. The sad truth of the matter is that since the foundation of the State no important new dramatist has yet emerged through the medium of the Irish language; or to put that in international terms, the Irish-language theatre has so far failed to produce a dramatist whose work could stand comparison with O'Casey or Beckett or Friel, or could hold the stage in Berlin or Stockholm or Moscow in German, Swedish or Russian translations as confidently and as plausibly as at home. Brendan Behan's *An Giall* (*The Hostage*) is an isolated exception.

Taibhdhearc na Gaillimhe continues to present plays in Irish throughout the year. It is a delightful and well-equipped small theatre, and retains the magnificent curtain designed by Micheál MacLiammóir in the neo-Celtic style of the late 1920s.

162 Neo-Celtic design by Micheál MacLiammóir for the first production of his own play *Díarmuid agus Gráinne*, at the Taibhdhearc, Galway, in 1928.

18

Conservatives
and shape-changers

After 1950

---

*Recent developments, Samuel Beckett,
contemporary writers including Hugh Leonard,
Brian Friel, Eugene McCabe, Thomas Murphy,
Thomas Kilroy and others*

The Abbey Theatre reopened in 1966 in a new building designed by Michael
Scott on the original site. The company had been playing in the charming Celtic
Revival Queen's Theatre (since demolished) for fifteen years. During this period
no new play of real stature was produced, though there were some of more than
usual interest, including *Home is the Hero* by Walter Macken (1952), *The Wood of
the Whispering* by M. J. Molloy (1953), two early plays by Hugh Leonard, *The Big
Birthday* (1956) and *A Leap in the Dark* (1957), and several comedies by John
O'Donovan and John McCann which maintained the theatre's 'popular' image.

An air of despondency pervaded the Queen's. Not only were most of the
productions unimaginative and the settings (with a very few exceptions) shoddy,
but the beauty of the building went unregarded and its interior was rarely even
clean. Lack of finance was blamed, but an enterprising management would have
made attempts to overcome such difficulties. The real obstruction to progress
seems to have been the presence of Ernest Blythe, the Managing Director. As
Minister for Finance in the first Free State government he had obtained an annual
grant for the National Theatre – a remarkable achievement: it is believed that
Ireland was the first country to provide direct State funds for such a purpose. He
was also largely responsible for persuading the Government of thirty years later
to finance the new building. These worthy activities may have diverted his attention from the sympathetic management of the company. Certainly, during his
term of office the best new Irish plays were produced elsewhere.

The principal events of the 1950s and early 1960s therefore occurred outside
the confines of the Abbey. The formation of a number of professional and semi-
professional companies in Dublin, Belfast and Cork brought several young
writers to public notice and also increased the range of productions of contemporary foreign plays, hitherto mainly the preserve of the Gate. The Dublin
International Theatre Festival, founded by Brendan Smith in 1957, was the
greatest single factor in reviving the wilting Irish theatre in more general ways.
However, the most important 'Irish' event occurred in Paris in 1953 when the
Dublin-born novelist and critic Samuel Beckett gave *En Attendant Godot* to Roger
Blin for production at the Théâtre de Babylone: the reverberations have echoed
round the world ever since.

The first of the independent or 'fringe' theatres to make a significant impact in Dublin was the Pike Theatre Club, founded by Alan Simpson and Carolyn Swift in 1953. Alan Simpson became one of the foremost Irish directors, and was Artistic Advisor to the Abbey from 1968 to 1970. He documented the Pike's brief but tumultuous history in *Beckett and Behan and a Theatre in Dublin*, published in 1962. As well as introducing a unique style of late-night revue, the Pike presented plays by Sartre, Claudel, Williams and Ionesco, as well as the first production of Brendan Behan's *The Quare Fellow* (1954) and the first production in Ireland of *Waiting for Godot* (1955).

The atmosphere of excitement encountered at the Pike was partly due to the unusually intimate actor-audience relationship and partly to the sense of expectation generated by the presentation of original work. Inevitably, the theatrical establishment sneered at the 'semi-pro' or 'experimental' ethos, but the passage of time has shown that the Pike's policy was very much in the midstream of the international theatre. Popular success, and the transfer of productions to larger theatres – such as the restaging of Williams' *The Rose Tattoo* at the Grand Opera House in Belfast after it had been closed due to court proceedings in Dublin – were factors which inhibited creativity.

The Quare Fellow was rejected by Ernest Blythe at the Abbey and taken up by Alan Simpson at the Pike. The play is a general view of life in a prison during the day and night leading up to an execution. Revealing glimpses of the characters and attitudes of prisoners and warders are given; moments of farce alternate with moments of tense drama. It is a compassionate plea for the abolition of capital punishment, but Behan is too subtle an artist to say so directly, though the audience is left in no doubt as to the nature of his message. The Abbey, to its credit, staged *The Quare Fellow* in 1956.

163 The first British production of *Waiting for Godot*, given at the Arts Theatre Club, London, 1955, directed by Peter Hall, with Paul Daneman as Vladimir, Peter Woodthorpe as Estragon, Peter Bull as Pozzo, Timothy Bateson as Lucky and Michael Wallser as the Boy.

Brendan Behan's second play for the theatre, *The Hostage*, was originally presented in Dublin as *An Giall* by Gael Linn at Halla an Damer in 1958. It was subsequently translated, and produced in altered form by Joan Littlewood at the Theatre Royal, Stratford East, London, later the same year, in her famous 'theatre workshop' series. The setting is a Dublin brothel in which a young English soldier, captured in Belfast, is held by the IRA. All the inmates of this house of ill fame grow to like him, especially the servant girl, Theresa; but he is executed nevertheless, in the cause of 'duty'. The play is full of bawdy jokes, and religious, political and national idealogies of all kinds are sharply satirized. Melodrama, farce and music-hall routines are employed, sometimes rather tediously, yet the overall effect can be deeply touching.

165   Brendan Behan (1923–64) achieved prominence as much through the publicity surrounding his own ebullient personality as through his contribution to the theatre. His early radio plays are full of boisterous good humour. A later stage play, *Richard's Cork Leg* (1972), has not endured so well. Frank McMahon's stage version of *Borstal Boy* (1967) is a superb example of the craft of the adaptor – a craft greatly called upon in the early 1960s when good new plays were a rarity. P. J. O'Connor's adaptation of Patrick Kavanagh's novel *Tarry Flynn* (1966) and Hugh Leonard's astonishing rearrangement of Joyce's *Stephen Hero* and *A Portrait of the Artist as a Young Man* as *Stephen D* (1962) are shining beacons in a genre often regarded with disdain.

The *atelier*-like atmosphere of the Pike seemed entirely suitable for the first Irish production of *Waiting for Godot*, which enjoyed a very long run there. Dubliners held their breaths in case there might be something shocking, or at least *outré*, in this work by a reclusive emigré who had so far written certain somewhat obscure novels which were said, by some, to be 'Joycean' and, by others, confusingly, to be 'Proustian'. A feature of the early audiences was their respectful attention and the absence of laughter, followed by overwhelming applause. Clearly here was something new, rich, and strange: but what was one to make of it?

164   Samuel Beckett was born in 1906 at Foxrock, an ostentatious outer suburb of Dublin full of smug 'Jacobethan' residences surrounded by tennis-courts, conservatories and clumps of pink hydrangea. He grew up in an atmosphere of material comfort, though he later remarked that he had 'little talent for happiness'. He went to Portora Royal School, Enniskillen (where Oscar Wilde had been a pupil fifty years before), and thence to Trinity College, Dublin, where he won a Foundation Scholarship in Modern Languages and distinguished himself as a cricketer.

Readers and theatregoers who share this background are perhaps in a better position to appreciate certain aspects of his writing which spring from the landscape of south County Dublin, city streets, and the college; and more especially from the authors prescribed by the college in French and Italian Literature as well as in the recondite supplementary courses which were obligatory at the time. When these elements are distilled as narrative prose or dramatic dialogue (possibly the term should be 'un-dramatic' dialogue) the speech could be nothing other than that of upper-middle-class university-educated Protestant Dublin; just as James Joyce's writing could be nothing other than lower-middle-class university-educated Catholic Dublin. These two writers, friends for years in Paris, were, socially and religiously speaking, aeons apart; but they shared a vast erudition, an irreverent wit, and they shared Dublin.

After taking his moderatorship in Trinity, Beckett taught at the Ecole Normale Supérieure in Paris, and then returned to Trinity as Lecturer in French from 1930

165 *Above* Caricature of Brendan Behan (1923–64) by Low.

164 Pencil drawing of Samuel Beckett seated, by Arikha Avigdor, 1971.

until 1932. He then moved around Europe, settling in Paris when he was thirty-one. During the war he worked for the French Resistance, fleeing with his wife from certain death at the hands of the Gestapo to Vaucluse, where he worked as a labourer. Since 1945 he has written chiefly in French, for the most part translating his own work. He has described English as 'a good theatre language, because of its concreteness, its close relationship between thing and vocable'.

Each of Beckett's plays presents a single image: a deserted road where the déclassé derelicts Estragon and Vladimir wait for another person who may not turn up and whose very existence is in question; blind motionless Hamm and restless Clov in a 'bare interior', Hamm's parents imprisoned in dustbins; Winnie, in two successive stages of burial in the encroaching earth.

En Attendant Godot (1953; *Waiting for Godot*, 1955); *Fin de Partie* (1957; *Endgame*, 1958); and *Happy Days* (1961; *Oh, les Beaux Jours*, 1963) are not conceived as a trilogy, but they are early plays which take up a full theatre-evening and are all, in some way, concerned with the condition of waiting. It may be that the waiting in *Godot* represents man's unarticulated resolve to discover the reason for his existence, however irksome the period of suspense; in *Endgame* there is the expectancy of possible departure; in *Happy Days* Winnie waits, unwittingly

163

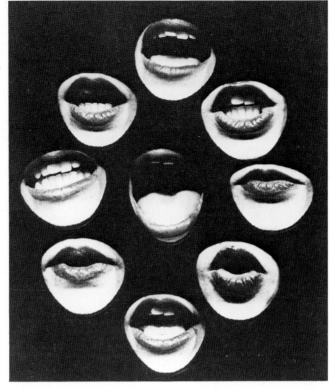

166 Patrick Magee as Hamm in *Endgame* by Samuel Beckett, in a production of 1964 by the Royal Shakespeare Company, London.

167 The mouths of the actress Deirdre Donnelly in Samuel Beckett's monologue for the theatre, *Not I*, directed by Ben Barnes at the Peacock Theatre, Dublin, in February 1981. The play was written in 1972 and first performed in New York.

trapped in inconsequential routineness of her own making, yet impelled by boundless and thoughtless energy to keep going: human will perseveres towards its undisclosed salvation.

It is surprising to find that the early critics, taking their cue perhaps from the Sartre of *Huis Clos* and the same author's essay on *L'Existentialism*, found an innate despondency in these plays. Phrases like 'post-war depression' and 'despair of the human condition' recur. Early productions – in Britain and Ireland at any rate – postulated an overall feeling of gloom. It took time for producers to recognize humour of situation and character, and impishly funny turns of phrase. The veneration-of-the-new syndrome was at work, and this heavy-handedness in interpretation took some time to evaporate. The other surprising notion which does not stand up to examination was that Beckett's plays were formless – a meandering succession of unconnected observations. For so fastidious a writer, this reads like blasphemy. Few works for the theatre are as clearly defined as *Waiting for Godot*, or (to give a totally different example) the three-minute 'dramaticule' *Come and Go* (1965): both have the symmetry of a Mozart opera, and such a framework could hardly encompass inchoateness of utterance.

Beckett's grotesque, distressed, eloquent and interdependent pairs of figures – they may be opposite halves of one personality – recall the blind and lame beggars in Yeats. He draws upon the symbolist theatre in another way in that his words, like music, must be heard: to read them on the page is insufficient – the rests between the sounds must be experienced as well. His solitary figures – Krapp* stooped over the tape-recorder unable to recognize the voice of his younger self, Joe† with his impassive countenance as he hears the Voice reminding him of incidents in his past, May‡ with her stricken ramblings, the lonely Mouth§ of the woman whose recurrent thoughts fill a listening void with memories – these

* *Krapp's Last Tape* (1958; *La Dernière Bande*, 1960).
† *Eh Joe* (1956; *Dis Joe*, 1966).
‡ *Footfalls* (1976).
§ *Not I* (1972).

solitaries bring to the theatre something of what Yeats once described as 'indefinable and yet precise emotions', emotions hitherto presented only to the single reader, as in Molly Bloom's famous soliloquy in *Ulysses* or the *memoire involuntaire* passages of *A la recherche du temps perdu* where the narrator is also the actor.

Many of Beckett's finest interpreters have been Irish actors, such as Jack McGowran who was Tommy in the first production of *All That Fall* (a play for radio, 1957) for whom *Eh Joe* was written, and whose one-man show of deftly-selected Beckett works, *End of Day*, was an international sensation; Patrick Magee, for whom *Krapp's Last Tape* was written, and who was in the original radio production of *Embers* (1959) and *Words and Music* (1962); Cyril Cusack, who was also a memorable Krapp; and Máire Kean, a superb Winnie. Since those early productions a new generation of actors and directors has arrived to whom Beckett is an established writer. It is significant that this new generation regards his work with enthusiasm and does not reject his innovations as 'old hat' or 'nineteen-fiftyish'. Indeed, he continues to be an innovator, constantly reducing his work to the barest possible essentials. As the critic Alec Reid has diagnosed, his art is the art of involvement. He presents:

> . . . the thing *itself* not something about the thing, creation not description, first hand not second, this is what makes *Godot* far more than a brilliantly original solution to a problem in play-writing . . .

Waiting for Godot changed the course of the Western theatre, in rather the same way that Giotto's frescoes in Padua changed the course of Western art. It is interesting that such a shape-changer should emerge from suburban Ireland; but Giotto, too, was born far from the world of art and artifice, or of critics and dissertation-writers, for which both evince a healthy disregard.

Another company which made inroads on the provincialism of the official theatre of the 1950s was the Dublin Globe Theatre founded by Godfrey Quigley and others in 1954. The Globe introduced many modern American plays, and also served the purpose of providing, for a few heady years, a professional repertory in Dun Laoghaire – a well-to-do seaside and dormitory borough which, being virtually a suburb of Dublin, looked (and still looks) to the capital for its cultural nourishment.

Part of the reason for the Globe's disbandment in 1960 was the very real success of many of its individual players who, for economic reasons, found it necessary to accept film, television and theatre engagements abroad. Among them were Pauline Delaney, Genevieve Lyons, Maureen Toal, Jack McGowran, Norman Rodway, Milo O'Shea and Godfrey Quigley himself. Jim Fitzgerald, the outstanding director of the era, was the creative force behind most of the Globe's stage-productions.

An independent theatre company which has survived from the late 1950s is Gemini Productions, founded by the actress and producer Phyllis Ryan and the actor Norman Rodway.

Gemini presented the first productions of many of John B. Keane's best plays, among them *The Highest House on the Mountain* (1960), *The Field* (1965), *Big Maggie* (1968) and *The Chastitute* (1980). John B. Keane (b. 1928) may not have been influenced by the work of George Fitzmaurice, but the language of his early plays shares the North Kerry quirkiness of the older writer. *Sive* (1959) was rejected by the Abbey but presented by the amateur drama group in Listowel and subsequently on Radio Eireann. It is no exaggeration to say that it caused a sensation – the rediscovery by the urbanized Ireland of the rural background from whence it had sprung was quite traumatic in the age which saw the establishment of Shannon New Town, the first jumbo jets carrying the Irish insignia, the inauguration of the television service, and the first Programme for Economic Expansion. *Sive* is a bleak and cruel story of rural poverty, in which a young girl is forced to make a match with an older man. The story was not a new one, but its treatment was new, and Keane did not feel compelled to exclude crudities of language which earlier writers of folk plays could not have used.

In Keane's *Sharon's Grave* (1960) the two grotesque brothers Jack and Dinzie Conlee have the appearance of a two-headed monster, for Dinzie is a cripple and is carried around on Jack's shoulders; instantly one is reminded of the blind and lame beggars in Yeats' *The Cat and the Moon* – with the difference that the strong, even violent, sexuality of Keane's characters introduce a force hitherto strangely muted in Irish drama.

Sharon's Grave was first produced by the Southern Theatre Group in Cork, under James N. Healy's direction. Keane's canon of plays gradually moves from the remote rural setting to the country town. He is at his best when ridiculing inhibition and hypocrisy. Many of his plays have benefited from work in production, especially by the director Barry Cassin, for Keane, once a script has been accepted for performance, seems reluctant to prune and revise.

168 James N. Healy as Moses McCoy in *The Crazy Wall* by John B. Keane, 1973. Keane's early plays, starting with *Sive* in 1959, showed that interest in the 'folk play' was still very much alive.

Several of Hugh Leonard's best plays were given their first productions by the Gemini management. Among them are *The Passion of Peter Ginty* (somewhat after Ibsen, 1961), *Stephen D* (after Joyce, 1962), *The Poker Session* (1963), *Mick and Mick* (1966), *The Patrick Pearse Motel* (1972), *Da* (1973) and *Summer* (1974). Hugh Leonard is the most prolific and the most technically assured of modern Irish playwrights. Such a statement tends to beg the question that, as a corollary, his plays must be shallow or showy, but this is far from being the case: it is the envious who see technical accomplishment as the enemy rather than the ally of talent.

Hugh Leonard has won international respect for his television adaptations of novels. In both television and stage plays he has mercilessly pilloried the twin Irish failings of chronic prudery and religiosity. He is the sternest and funniest critic of moral turpitude. A telling moment in *Irishmen* (Irish Theatre Company, 1974) occurs when a member of a subversive organization, about to perform a 'token assassination' on an innocent neighbour, dips her fingers in the holy-water font by her hall-door and blesses herself before leaving the house for this horrific assignment.

Leonard is the master of the pithy phrase and the cogent comment. He is also the master of dramatic form in his ability to reproduce without parody a chosen genre of playwriting. In *The Patrick Pearse Motel*, he uses the mechanics of late 169 nineteenth-century French farce; to this he adds a dimension of deeper social comment on the meretricious way in which Irish society has developed since the time of Pearse's idealistic vision of a pure and spotless Gaelic nation. The accepted moral values of middle-class urban Ireland come under strict scrutiny in *Mick and Mick*, in which a young woman who has been working in Britain comes home and sees her community with fresh eyes.

A vein of nostalgia runs through several of Leonard's plays. It was first manifest in *A Walk on the Water* (Globe, 1960) in which the exiled protagonist returns to Ireland for the funeral of his father and meets his companions of ten years earlier; the atmosphere of wartime Dublin is plangently evoked. A similar feeling imbues the more recent *Da, Summer* and *A Life* (Abbey, 1978), in which family relation-

169 Rosaleen Linehan, May Cluskey and John Gregson in the 1972 Dublin Theatre Festival production of *The Patrick Pearse Motel* by Hugh Leonard. The play, which is structured on the model of French farce of the belle-époque, has a darker comment to make on the development of Irish Society since the Rising of 1916.

ships are examined in a way which suggests the use of autobiographical material. As in *A Walk on the Water*, the author seems to be asking, 'What happened to us in the past?', and the answers lie in the uncovering of several strata of familial misunderstanding and unrequited love. A crispness of dialogue, and a wit which springs from character, preclude morbidity.

In retrospect, it is clear that the most important new plays of the 1960s – apart from Leonard's Joyce-adaptation *Stephen D*, which was perhaps the most satisfying – were *A Whistle in the Dark* (1961) by Thomas Murphy; *The King of the Castle* (1964) by Eugene McCabe; *Philadelphia, Here I Come* (1964) by Brian Friel; and *The Death and Resurrection of Mr Roche* (1969) by Thomas Kilroy. All these plays continue to speak for the decade in which they were written, and at the same time transcend it. It is significant that none of them was first produced at the Abbey, and that all (except Thomas Murphy's) were produced as part of the Dublin Theatre Festival.

Disappointingly, several authors of fine plays which characterized the 1960s have not maintained their promise in the theatre. From among the best plays of the time it is pleasant to recall James McKenna's poignant musical of emigration *The Scatterin'* (1959), Tom Coffey's *Them* (1962), James Douglas' *The Ice Goddess* (1964), Michael Judge's *Death is for Heroes* (1966) and Conor Farrington's *Aaron Thy Brother* (1969). Many of these playwrights have turned their talents to television and radio.

Up to 1946, when the Belfast Arts Theatre was founded by Hubert and Dorothy Wilmot, the Group Theatre was the only locally based company operating in Northern Ireland – if one excepts the heterogeneous Savoy players who occupied the Grand Opera House during the war years with a change of Broadway or West End play every week. Apart from the plays of Joseph Tomelty already noted, the Group produced very little original work of real merit. Sadly, it was a work of considerable merit which was instrumental in causing the collapse of the Group – Sam Thompson's *Over the Bridge*.

Sam Thompson (1916–65) came from a working-class background. After a successful start as a writer for radio at over forty years of age, it was speculated that he might turn out to be Belfast's answer to Sean O'Casey. Such did not prove to be the case, for he died before reaching his fiftieth birthday. *Over the Bridge* (1960) is a deeply felt plea for religious tolerance. The Board of the Group Theatre judged that the theme was too controversial, and the language too rough, to risk a production; it was in fact presented by a breakaway section of the company under the direction of James Ellis at the much larger Empire Theatre, without public protest, and subsequently in Dublin and London with the same cast. *The Evangelist* (1963) was first produced by the Dublin Gate Theatre and, ironically, only played in its author's native city as a visiting production.

Until the Group's untimely demise a relationship existed in Belfast between the Group and the Arts, somewhat akin to the relationship in Dublin between the Abbey and the Gate. The work of a very large number of contemporary European, American, British and Irish writers was presented at the Arts in an atmosphere which in Belfast was considered to be 'bohemian' and rather daring. This early promise was not fulfilled, for when the company moved to more spacious premises a more 'popular' repertoire was introduced. The theatre continues to flourish in this way, and no important new playwrights have so far emerged.

170 The playwright Brian Friel, from a painting by Basil Blackshaw.

In 1951 a young Kerrywoman, Mary O'Malley, founded the Lyric Players Theatre in the hope of establishing in Belfast a platform for a better quality of writing. A special place was given to the plays of Yeats. These early Yeats productions possessed an engaging quality of breathless reverence, later replaced by a more convincing professionalism. In 1968 a new theatre building on an attractive site overlooking the River Lagan was opened by the Governor of Northern Ireland, and the Lyric Theatre now resembles the more adventurous provincial repertory theatres of Britain rather than any specific company in Ireland. New plays by Irish writers form an extensive part of the annual programme, with the work of John Boyd (b. 1913), Patrick Galvin (b. 1927) and Martin Lynch (b. 1950) prominent in recent years. In 1980 the Grand Opera House, Belfast, was completely restored with Government assistance: it is now the most magnificent and best-equipped theatre in Ireland.

Brian Friel (b. 1929) has consistently proved himself to be Ireland's most substantial dramatist – Samuel Beckett apart – over two decades. His first play for the stage, *The Francophile* (1960), was presented at the Ulster Group Theatre, unfortunately just after the fragmentation of that company. Friel is an Ulsterman by birth, temperament, and residence; born in Omagh, yet chiefly connected with Derry where he was educated and where he taught up to 1960 when he took up writing as a full-time occupation, he now lives outside the city in Co. Donegal, just over the border in the Republic, yet still in the Province of Ulster. He is therefore an Irishman in the fullest and most obvious sense: but as a dramatist he is in no sense insular.

The Enemy Within (1962), a play about St Colmchille (Columba), was produced at the Abbey, and *The Blind Mice* (1963) by Gemini Productions at the Eblana in Dublin. It was *Philadelphia, Here I Come!* (1965), directed by Hilton Edwards, which proved him to be a dramatist far surpassing the ordinary. The transfer of

171–2 *Top* Joe Dowling, Artistic Director of the Abbey Theatre, and *above* Tomás MacAnna, the Theatre's former Artistic Director.

the production to New York established Friel as a leading playwright in the United States – he did not achieve comparable acclaim in London until much later.

Philadelphia, Here I Come! concerns the isolation of those who cannot convey their true feelings to each other – exemplified here as failure of communication among the members of a small-town family. Gar O'Donnell, offered the alternative of emigration to the USA or unchallenging work in his father's store, is constitutionally unable to respond openly to the emotions which his decision to emigrate stir in his own mind, and in the minds of his intractable father, his aunt Lizzie, his girlfriend, his mates, and the housekeeper Madge who is the all-understanding maternal figure. The technical device of introducing two actors to portray Gar and his *alter ego* – between whom there are pithy exchanges of dialogue – gives the play additional psychological point, most subtly when Gar Private's 'unheard' comments contradict the actual remarks of Gar Public. The brisk country humour of the dialogue tellingly underscores the anguish of unexpressed personal dislocation.

The Loves of Cass Maguire (1966) gives a laceratingly sad picture of the loneliness of an Irish-American woman who returns to the family which has no interest in her oft-recalled past, or in herself. *Lovers* (1967) contains two stories: *Winners*, in which two school-leavers (the girl pregnant) fantasize about their future, though the audience is made subtly aware that they are to die in a boating-accident before the day is over; the suffocating small-town atmosphere is amusingly and tenderly suggested; and *Losers*, in which a middle-aged bachelor attempts to woo an equally unprepossessing spinster, while keeping his intentions from her pietistic bedridden mother; the comedy is continuously hilarious, the situation all too real in provincial Ireland.

Crystal and Fox (1968) is a drama set in a travelling theatre in which the speech of the virtually inarticulate members of what one normally presumes to be a most articulate profession is convincingly reproduced. *The Mundy Scheme* (1969) is a macabre satire on the extremes to which empty-headed politicians will go in the interests of expediency. An Irish government, bankrupt of both finances and ideas, decides to sell parcels of 'the old country' as graves to sentimental (presumably American) émigrés.

In most of Friel's plays time is a great healer. In *The Freedom of the City* (1973) the author seems to be less detached, more concerned with the particularities of contemporary affairs in Northern Ireland, or, indeed, in Derry itself. The waste of human energy and creativity occasioned by the local conflict, and its brutalizing effect on the attitude and daily habits of the citizens, are presented with unusual pessimism, for Friel is normally the observer who discerns good in the midst of evil. Another play with a topical application is *Volunteers* (1975), a metaphorical comment on the Irish propensity for self-destruction.

Brian Friel is a conventional dramatist in that he generally employs a linear plot. He does, however, make some startling experiments with that form: the physically-split personality of Gar O'Donnell, which affects the structure of *Philadelphia, Here I Come!* is a case in point. Such effects surprise the audience into a different kind of awareness, and cause its members to listen more closely. In *Translations* (1980), a play with a completely conventional structure, he introduces a linguistic contrivance which affects the play on all levels: the complete dialogue is written in English, but a convention is established whereby the 'Irish-speaking' characters cannot be understood by the English-speaking characters. Without this highly original device the play succeeds in various ways – as an observation on one of the causes for the decline of the Gaelic cultural tradition, as a tale of Donegal in the

era of the hedge-schools, or as a love story of social and racial opposites; but it is really about language – about the destruction of a language by that of a superior colonial power, about the basic notion of language as a means of conveying thought, and about the nature of words.

An earlier play, *Faith Healer* (1976), is also concerned with language, though in a different way. In this instance, Friel abandons the linear plan. The story is narrated by three players, each giving a diverging interpretation of certain shared incidents which took place in the past; the Faith Healer returns in a fourth monologue to give the final *coup-de-grâce*. There is virtually no dramatic action, except the drama of the recounted occurrences. Yet *Faith Healer* is intensely dramatic in another sense – possibly in the way it unites the art of the *seanchai* with the craft of the stage. A great deal is demanded of the audience, especially as the text is exceptionally compact. Much depends upon the quality of the production and the casting; the play's comparative failure in New York may be attributed to failure in these departments. When produced four years later at the Abbey by Joe Dowling, it emerged triumphantly.

When forming a company of players to produce *Translations* in Derry in 1980 Brian Friel spoke of the need for 'a brave and violent theatre that in some way expresses the country'. In fact, he had already created a brave and violent theatre through his own writing.

If *Philadelphia, Here I Come!* is one of the most important plays of the 1960s, Eugene McCabe's *The King of the Castle* is the one which best expresses the

173 A scene from the 1973 Abbey Theatre production of *The Freedom of the City* by Brian Friel, directed by Tomás MacAnna. The play speaks very directly of the 'Northern troubles', and specifically of the troubles in Derry.

The King of the Castle, by Eugene McCabe, first produced in 1964 at the Gaiety Theatre, Dublin, directed by Godfrey Quigley, and subsequently (*above*) on RTE television, directed by Louis Lentin, with Niall Toibín as Scober, Fionnuala Flanagan as Treasy, and Tony Doyle as Lynch. It gives a more honest and uncompromising view of Irish society than any other play of its period.

viciousness and rapacity of the affluent but spiritually impoverished new middle classes in the period of economic expansion which occurred under the Government of Sean Lemass. Like Friel, McCabe lives in Ulster. His plays for television, distilled from experience of sectarian animosity and violence in the border counties, are outside the scope of a monograph on the theatre, but it is worth remarking that his trilogy *Cancer*, *Heritage* and *Siege* (1974–5), directed by Deirdre Friel under the generic title *Victims*, are probably the finest plays ever written in Ireland for that medium.

The King of the Castle is set on a large farm. Scober has bought the 'big house' – once inhabited by local gentry – but neither the handsome surroundings nor the installation of luxurious modern amenities can raise him or his shrewish wife Treasy to the social level of its previous occupants. Scober's obsession is with the procreation of an heir: in the most skilful scene, psychologically speaking, in any modern Irish play, he bargains with a vigorous young labourer, Lynch, to sire a child for him: in other words, to copulate with his wife. The action of the play takes place in the fall of the year, and the dialogue is suffused with ironic imagery of harvest and seed-time. The conversation of the men hired for the annual threshing is laced with innuendo regarding Scober's apparent sterility; there is much allusion to grosser animal functions. The raw humour vented at the harvest-tea reminds one of the elder Bruegel's paintings of peasant festivities.

The King of the Castle is in the tradition of the Irish Ibsenite play in so far as it treats a domestic situation in a given social climate; but McCabe eschews polite circumlocution and speaks directly of matters usually only hinted at. In spite of the passions generated by the subject-matter, McCabe manages to avoid turgidity.

Eugene McCabe's other notable plays for the stage are *Breakdown* (1966), a rather more conventional piece in the Ibsen mould, and *Swift* (1969), which

investigates the personal enigma of the author of *Gulliver*. It was directed by
Tyrone Guthrie in its first production at the Abbey Theatre.

Thomas Murphy was born in Co. Galway in 1936. Several of his plays –
particularly *The White House* (1972) and a superb duo of one-acters *On the Outside*
and *On the Inside* (1974), reflect the *acidie* of small-town existence in that part of
Ireland at mid-century. The young people meet in dance-hall or pub; their self-
delusion is accurately observed and all the more frightening for its absurdity.

The White House takes its name from the pub whose owner, J. J., models himself
both physically and – or so he would believe – mentally on John F. Kennedy.
When the President is assassinated, J. J.'s self-esteem and his stature as a local
quasi-hero are instantly diminished; and the whole sham of Ireland's claim to the
reflected glory of the Kennedy charisma is forcefully exposed. The style of these
plays is (to use a term from art criticism) hyper-realism: every detail is painted
with an extraordinary clarity. Yet Murphy has written in a variety of styles. His
earliest stage play, *A Whistle in the Dark*, is a naturalistic drama, set among
immigrant Irish workers in Coventry. It was first produced in London in 1961.

A Whistle in the Dark explores the sense of social and racial inferiority of the
'Fighting Carney' family, and the circumstances of their home-background in
Ireland. Michael Carney has married an Englishwoman and, through diligence at
work, is integrating himself with his new community. The frustration of life in
the Irish ghetto, which leads to violence and death, are impressively realized by
this author in one of the outstanding plays of the decade.

Famine (1966), set at the time of the 'great hunger' of 1846, deals as much with
spiritual as with material famine in an Ireland where the people accept disasters
of the natural as well as the socio-political kind far too meekly. *The Morning After
Optimism* (1971) is written in an allegorical mode. There are four characters: a

175 *The White House* by
Thomas Murphy. First
produced at the Abbey
Theatre, Dublin, in 1972,
directed by Vincent
Dowling, with Máire ní
Dhomhnaill and Dan
O'Herlihy.

middle-aged whore and a gigolo, an innocent orphan girl and a chivalrous young poet of *amour-courtois* demeanour, who encounter one another in a romantic forest. Sleazy decadence triumphs over storybook purity. Illusions are humorously destroyed; virtue is lyrically debased. Hugh Hunt's original production at the Abbey, with Colin Blakeley and Eithne Dunne as the older couple, would be difficult to emulate, and perhaps this is why the play is so rarely revived.

Thomas Murphy has said that his plays attempt to produce 'something that can be identified with or recognized rather than understood or explained', but this statement is more true of plays like *The Morning After Optimism* and *The Blue Macushla* than *A Whistle in the Dark*. *The Blue Macushla* (1979), set in a mythical Chicago gangsterland, was not as successful as it should have been at its first appearance, and deserves reappraisal. Murphy's other plays which have entered the national or international repertoire are *The Orphans* (1968), *A Crucial Week in the Life of a Grocer's Assistant* (1969) and *The Sanctuary Lamp* (1975).

Of the five Irish playwrights who came to prominence in the 1960s, it is probable that Thomas Kilroy (b. 1934) has the most still to contribute, for his work in the theatre – he is also a novelist – has not yet reached a phase of crystallization: it is not possible to identify the archetypal Kilroy play. This, indeed, may be a great advantage to the writer, for he can evade the irritating adherence of critical labels.

Thomas Kilroy is the most literate of Irish playwrights. Allusive material of all kinds crams his texts. As with the Friel of *Faith Healer*, a great deal is demanded of the audience, and it is encouraging to note in parenthesis how Irish audiences are again prepared to make the effort to receive plays like *The Morning After Optimism*, *Faith Healer* and *Tea and Sex and Shakespeare* outside the studio theatres; and it is largely due to the new spirit of enterprise manifest at the Abbey Theatre since the late 1960s that such a situation has been reached. Presentation of the work of an intellectual playwright like Kilroy would not have been conplated at the Abbey during the twenty years following the death of Yeats.

The Death and Resurrection of Mr Roche (1968) is an absorbing drama in a naturalistic style from which one senses the characters are trying to escape. *Tea and Sex and Shakespeare* (1976) brings to mind an animated version of a painting by Dominique Appia; it is a surrealist comedy full of visual as well as verbal antics. *Talbot's Box* (1977) is Kilroy's most considerable play to date. Matt Talbot (1856–1925) was a Dublin labourer, a reformed alcoholic who devoted the last thirty years of his life to charitable work and mortification of the flesh. Kilroy uses Talbot's eccentric career for a seemingly incongruous series of observations presented in a rich array of literary and vernacular styles. The effect is totally

176 cohesive, however, and in Patrick Mason's production at the Peacock Theatre, with John Molloy adding a macabre quality to the character of Talbot, this (by turns) wildly comical and touching work was the 'theatrical event' of its year.

Kilroy's achievement in this mode springs not only from natural talent, but also from professional discipline. All too many 'free expression' plays express nothing so much as their author's confusion of mind and self-indulgence. The 'experimental theatre' can only be of value when there is a fixed base from which to experiment; and the 'total theatre' can only live up to its name if the author and collaborators are totally in charge of their material. Thomas Kilroy's clarity of mind, his ear for nuance, accent and inflexion, his understanding of dramatic architecture, leave no doubts as to his supremacy among Irish dramatists who would break from the straitjacket of literary and structural conventions; and yet, as a 'literary' writer of extreme sensibility, it would seem that he is possibly the leading Irish dramatist in *any* conveniently discernible category.

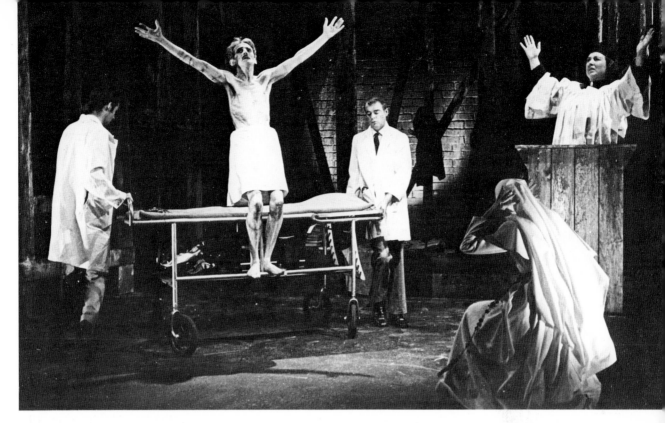

Beckett, of course, is the great innovator and Beckett (if for this reason alone) has to be regarded as a case apart. Those not so *rarae aves*, the existentialist theatre, the theatre of the absurd, the theatre of cruelty, as well as the agit-prop theatre, have only brushed Ireland lightly with their wings. Nevertheless, several writers have produced exciting innovatory (if hardly revolutionary) work, among them Wesley Burrowes (who writes superbly for television), Tom McIntyre (who is also a leading novelist), Stewart Parker (a musician and journalist of distinction), and Joe O'Donnell (who writes excellently for children).

The Project Arts Centre in Dublin, founded by Colm O Briain in 1967, has done much to encourage both the presentation and appreciation of new forms of theatre, but, disappointingly, an original school of writers has not as yet emerged. Some good new plays with a rather watery socialistic message have been produced, but one would like to have seen something more radical as a reaction to the over-whelming conservatism of the Irish psyche.

The most heartening aspect of the Irish theatre of the last ten years has been the growth of professionalism outside Dublin. Several new theatre-buildings have been erected, and some older provincial theatres – notably those in Waterford and Wexford – have been restored. The Arts Councils of the Republic and of Northern Ireland have taken an increasingly important part in the encouragement of theatrical enterprise outside the main centres.

In Tralee, in 1968 Pat Ahern founded Síamsóirí na Ríochta, incorporated in 1974 as Síamsa Tíre, the National Folk Theatre. This company, which uses traditional music, mime and dance to interpret Irish folklore in theatrical terms, has toured extensively abroad. A new theatre was opened in 1978 to house the company's activities, and also to serve as a centre in Kerry for recitals, concerts and visits from touring theatre and ballet companies. In 1976 the Riverside Theatre in the New University of Ulster at Coleraine was opened to serve the local community in the same way.

176 *Talbot's Box*, by Thomas Kilroy, directed by Patrick Mason at the Peacock Theatre, Dublin, 1977 (above), and subsequently at the Royal Court Theatre, London, with Stephen Brennan, John Molloy, Clive Geraghty, Ingrid Craigie and Eileen Colgan. The play is a surrealistic and highly comic comment on the life of a famous Dublin labourer and reformed alcoholic.

177

In Cork, James N. Healy's Group Theatre flourished from 1958 until 1974 as a forum for smaller local and visiting companies. The Southern Theatre Group, notable for its early productions of John B. Keane, was reformed as Theatre of the South Ltd in 1971; under James N. Healy's direction it plays at the Cork Opera House and throughout the Munster counties. The Opera House, accidentally destroyed by fire in 1955, was rebuilt to a design by Michael Scott ten years later. The Everyman Playhouse, a comfortable theatre of medium size, was opened in 1972 by the enterprising amateur society of the same name to house its own very varied repertoire, and also to receive visiting companies.

In Galway, the Taibhdhearc continues to present plays in Irish. In 1975 the Druid Theatre Company was formed by Gary Hynes; lively productions of experimental as well as established plays are presented in its diminutive auditorium. Public response has been so encouraging that a new purpose-built theatre or arts centre may be inaugurated in Galway before long. In Limerick – a city once known as a theatrical cemetery – the Belltable Arts Centre has been drawing more than satisfactory attendances since its opening in 1981. A new theatre in Sligo, imaginatively named The Hawk's Well after Yeats' play, opened in 1982.

This expansion of the physical facilities for play presentation could not have taken place without the enterprise of a large number of voluntary societies, or without the pioneering work of the Irish Ballet Company (1973) and the Irish Theatre Company (1975). 'Pioneering' is the correct term, for the older touring companies had disappeared, and it had become economically impossible for commercial managements to operate outside Dublin, Belfast and Cork. The Irish Ballet and Theatre companies are State-assisted; they have developed their own touring circuits, and have created new audiences.

It would be invidious to single out the work of individual players, directors or designers, for a number of reasons – the principal one being that the number of

177 Síamsa Tíre, the National Folk Theatre, is primarily a music theatre. The company, which is resident in its own theatre in Tralee, Co. Kerry, also performs on tour in Ireland and abroad. This scene, in which an itinerant poet makes an unwelcome visit, is similar in content to Douglas Hyde's play *Casadh an tSugáin* (1901).

professionals who, through their ephemeral art, and their dedication, ensure the continuance of the Irish theatre, is large. It would be wrong, however, not to mention the two artistic directors whose work has re-established the Abbey as the centre of creative activity in the theatre in Ireland, north or south: Tomás MacAnna and Joe Dowling.

In 1974 Mícheál O hAodha noted in his book *Theatre in Ireland* that, at the time, the better new plays were adaptations from other literary works, and that there existed 'a decay of invention, and a dearth of original material'. All theatre depends upon its writers, and the Irish theatre has always been pre-eminently a writers' theatre. Since 1974 Brian Friel, Thomas Kilroy, Hugh Leonard and Thomas Murphy have consolidated their positions; and several highly talented younger writers have (principally on account of the Abbey's imaginative encouragement) appeared, so to speak, on the scene. It is far too early to say if the promise already manifest by Neil Donelly, Bernard Farrell, Martin Lynch, Liam Lynch, Heno Magee, J. Graham Reid and others will bear further fruit; but there is an atmosphere of buoyancy, and it is difficult to envisage the early dissipation of such talent and energy.

Since the end of the seventeenth century, Irish writers have stood in the vanguard of the English-speaking theatre; from Boyle and Farquhar to Samuel Beckett, Irish dramatists – whether they remained at home or became a part of the great Irish literary diaspora – have interpreted, led and innovated in their own particular ways. In the present climate of optimism it is impossible to believe that this splendid tradition will not continue.

178 Malcolm Douglas and Ciarán Hinds in a scene from *Krieg*, by Liam Lynch, directed by Patrick Mason, in 1981. Set mainly in a psychiatric hospital, this proved to be one of the most powerful and stimulating new plays presented by the Project Arts Centre in Dublin.

178

Acknowledgments

A number of private individuals, as well as several public institutions, have been most helpful in the preparation of this book. I would like to thank the Director of the National Library, Dublin, An t-Uasal Alf MacLochlainn, and the Assistant Director, Mr Michael Hewson, particularly for assistance regarding visual material. The Librarian of Trinity College, Dublin, Mr Peter Brown, as well as the Keeper of Printed Books, Miss M. Pollard, and the Assistant Librarian, Mr Charles Benson; the Curator of Marsh's Library, Dublin, Mrs Muriel McCarthy; the former Irish and Local Studies Librarian at the Belfast City Library, Mr John Gray; the County Librarian for Longford-Westmeath, Miss Marian Keaney; the County Librarian for Cavan, Mr Donal O'Gorman; Miss Nodlaig Hardiman of the Dublin Public Libraries; and Miss Mary Clark of the Irish Theatre Archive, have all been very helpful indeed.

I would also like to express my gratitude to Sir Roy Strong, Director of the Victoria and Albert Museum, London, and my thanks to Mr C. M. Kauffman, Keeper of the Department of Prints and Drawings, and Miss Christina Huntley of the same Department; also to Mr Alexander Schouvaloff, Keeper of the Theatre Museum at the same institution, as well as Miss Janet Steen, Research Assistant, Miss Carolyn Tuckwell, Senior Museum Assistant, and Miss Eileen Robinson, Museum Assistant. The Raymond Mander and Joe Mitchenson Theatre Collection in London also possesses a great deal of material of Irish interest, and I would like to express my admiration and thanks to its joint founders.

I also wish to thank Mr Joe Dowling, Artistic Director of the Abbey Theatre, Dublin, and Miss Deirdre McQuillan, Publicity Manager, whose help with material from the photographic archive has been invaluable; Miss Mary Canon, Managing Director at the Dublin Gate Theatre, and Miss Patricia Turner, Public Relations Officer; Mr Phelim Donlon, General Administrator of the Irish Theatre Company, and Miss Polly O'Loughlin, its Secretary; Mr John Boyd, Literary Advisor to the Lyric Players Theatre, Belfast; Mr Michael Barnes, General Administrator and Artistic Director of the Belfast Grand Opera House, and Mr Robert Agnew, its Publicity Manager; and Mr James N. Healy, Managing Director of Theatre of the South Ltd., Cork.

Both Tourist Boards in Ireland have been most helpful; thanks are due to the Photographic Officer and Librarian of the Irish Tourist Board, Dublin, Mrs Margaret McGahon; and to the Publicity Manager of the Northern Ireland Tourist Board, Belfast, Mr Ian Hill, and the Film/Photographic Librarian, Miss Betty Wilson.

Others who gave useful advice for which I am most grateful were Mrs Mary Boydell, Major Congreve, Mr Leo Daly, Mr John Finnigan, Mr Aiden Grennell, Mr Denis Johnston, Dr John McCormick, Mr Patrick Mason, Mr Richard Pine, an t-Uasal Micheál O hAodha, and Miss Shelah Richards.

I acknowledge with gratitude the assistance of the Tyrone Guthrie Centre at Annaghmakerrig, and of its Resident Director Mr Bernard Loughlin.

Finally, I wish to thank my wife for her continual encouragement, and also for helping to read proofs and compile the index.

Christopher Fitz-Simon
Dublin – Annaghmakerrig – London

Select bibliography

General

BOYLAN, HENRY, *A Dictionary of Irish Biography*, Dublin 1978.
DE BLACAM, AODH, *Gaelic Literature Surveyed*, Dublin 1929.
DILLON, MYLES, *Early Irish Society*, Dublin 1954.
FITZ-SIMON, CHRISTOPHER, *The Arts in Ireland: a Chronology*, Dublin 1982.
HARMON MAURICE, *A Select Bibliography for the Study of Anglo-Irish Literature*, Dublin 1977.
LEECH CLIFFORD and T. R. CRAIK, *The Revels History of English Drama*, London 1975.
MARTIN, AUGUSTINE, *Anglo-Irish Literature*, Dublin 1980.
MARTIN, F. X. and T. W. MOODY, *The Course of Irish History*, Cork 1967.
NICOLL, ALLARDYCE, *A History of English Drama*, Cambridge 1952.
O'BRIEN, CONOR CRUISE, *The Shaping of Modern Ireland*, London 1960.
O'FAOLÁIN, SEÁN, *The Irish*, London 1948.
O HAODHA, MICHEÁL, *Theatre in Ireland*, Oxford 1974.
SHARE, BERNARD, *Irish Lives*, Dublin 1971.
USSHER, ARLAND, *The Face and Mind of Ireland*, New York 1950.

Chapter 1

BLISS, ALAN, *Spoken English in Ireland, 1600–1700*, Cambridge 1929.
CHAMBERS, E. K., *The Mediaeval Stage*, Oxford 1903.
CLARK, W. S., *The Early Irish Stage*, Oxford 1955.
LARDNER, DIONYSIUS, *James Shirley*, London 1838.
SCHUCHARD, MARGRET, *John Ogilby*, Hamburg 1976.
SEYMOUR ST JOHN, *Anglo-Irish Literature, 1200–1582*, Cambridge 1929.

Chapter 2

CLARK, W. S., *Roger Boyle*, Cambridge, Mass., 1937.
DOBRÉE, BONAMY, *Restoration Tragedy*, London 1929.
HIRST, DAVID, *The Comedy of Manners*, London 1979.
LANSON, G., *Esquisse d'une Histoire de la Tragédie française*, Paris 1920.
ORGEL, VERA, *A New View of Racine*, London 1948.
STANFORD, W. B., *Ireland and the Classical Tradition*, Dublin 1976.

Chapter 3

ANSELMENT, WILLIAM A. (Ed.), *George Farquhar*, London 1977.
DOBRÉE, BONAMY, *William Congeve*, London 1963.
FARMER, A. J., *George Farquhar*, London 1966.
HODGES J. C., *William Congreve the Man*, New York 1941.

HOLLAND, NORMAN N., *The First Modern Comedies*, Cambridge, Mass. 1959.
MORRIS, BRIAN, *William Congreve*, London 1972.
WILKES, THOMAS, *A General View of the Stage*, London 1759.

Chapter 4

ANON., *The Life of Mr James Quin, Comedian*, London 1887.
DUNBAR, HOWARD H., *The Dramatic Career of Arthur Murphy*, New York 1946.
DUNBAR, JANET, *Peg Woffington and her World*, London 1968.
STOCKWELL, LA TOURETTE, *Dublin Theatre and Theatre Customs*, Kingsport, Tenn. 1938.

Chapter 5

BELLAMY, GEORGE ANN, *An Apology for the Life of George Ann Bellamy*, Dublin 1785.
BOAS, FREDERICK S., *An Introduction to Eighteenth Century Drama*, London 1981.
CHETWOOD WILLIAM R., *A General History of the Stage*, London 1749.
SHELDON, ESTHER K., *Thomas Sheridan of Smock Alley*, Princeton 1967.

Chapter 6

BEVIS, RICHARD, *The Laughing Tradition*, London 1981.
GINGER, JOHN, *The Notable Man*, London 1977.
JEFFARES, A. NORMAN, *Oliver Goldsmith*, London 1959.
LYTTON SELLS, A., *Oliver Goldsmith*, London 1974.
QUINTANA, RICARDO, *Oliver Goldsmith*, London 1969.
TASCH, PETER A., *The Dramatic Cobbler: the Life and Work of Isaac Bickerstaff*, Lewisburg 1971.
WARDLE, A. M., *Oliver Goldsmith*, London 1957.

Chapter 7

ANON., *Sheridaniana*, London 1826.
BINGHAM, MADELEINE, *Sheridan: the Track of a Comet*, London 1972.
GIBBS, LEWIS, *Sheridan*, Port Washington 1947.
LE FANU, WILLIAM (Ed.), *Betsy Sheridan's Journal*, London 1960.
MOORE, THOMAS, *Life of Sheridan*, London 1825.

Chapter 8

CLARK, W. S., *The Irish Stage in the County Towns*, Oxford 1965.
DAVIES, THOMAS, *Dramatic Miscellanies*, London 1784.
KAVANAGH, PETER, *The Irish Theatre*, Tralee 1946.
O'KEEFE, JOHN, *Recollections*, London 1826.

Chapter 9

ANON., *The Private Theatre of Kilkenny*, Kilkenny 1819.

BARRETT, WILLIAM ALEXANDER, *Balfe: his Life and Work*, London 1882.

BOOTH, MICHAEL R., *English Plays of the 19th Century*, Oxford 1969.

FLOOD, HENRY GRATTAN, *William Vincent Wallace*, Waterford 1912.

Chapter 10

DUGGAN, G. C., *The Stage Irishman*, New York and London 1937.

FAWKES, RICHARD, *Dion Boucicault*, London 1979.

KRAUSE, DAVID (Ed.), *The Dolmen Boucicault*, Dublin 1976.

SILLARD, R. M., *Barry Sullivan and his Contemporaries*, London 1901.

RAHILL, FRANK, *The World of Melodrama*, Pennsylvania State University 1967.

Chapter 11

GAUNT, WILLIAM, *The Aesthetic Adventure*, London 1945.

HARDWICK, MICHAEL, *The Osprey Guide to Oscar Wilde*, Reading 1973.

HOLLAND, VYVYAN, *Oscar Wilde and his World*, London 1966.

HYDE, H. MONTGOMERY, *Oscar Wilde*, London 1976.

MacLIAMMÓIR, MICHEÁL, *The Importance of Being Oscar*, Dublin 1973.

PEARSON, HESKETH, *Oscar Wilde*, London 1946.

Chapter 12

BENTLEY, ERIC, *Shaw: a Reconsideration*, New York 1947.

HARTNOLL, PHYLLIS, *Who's Who in Shaw*, London 1975.

HOLROYD, MICHAEL (Ed.), *The Genius of Shaw*, London 1979.

McCARTHY, DESMOND, *Shaw: the Plays*, London 1951.

PEARSON, HESKETH, *Bernard Shaw, his Life and Opinions*, London 1961.

PURDOM, C. B., *A Guide to the Plays of Bernard Shaw*, London 1963.

Chapter 13

BROWN, MALCOLM, *George Moore*, Seattle 1955.

COFFEY, DIARMUID, *Douglas Hyde*. Dublin 1938.

COURTNEY, MARIE THÉRÈSE, *Edward Martyn and the Irish Theatre*, New York 1952.

COXHEAD, ELIZABETH, *Lady Gregory*, London 1961.

ELLIS-FERMOR, UNA, *The Irish Dramatic Movement*, London 1939.

FLANNERY, JAMES W., *W. B. Yeats and the Idea of a Theatre*, Toronto 1976.

HOGAN, ROBERT and JAMES KILROY, *The Modern Irish Drama* (and subsequent volumes), Dublin 1976.

HONE, JOSEPH, *W. B. Yeats*, London 1943.

HUNT HUGH, *The Abbey Theatre*, Dublin 1980.

ROBINSON, LENNOX, *Ireland's Abbey Theatre*, London 1951.

TAYLOR, RICHARD, *The Drama of W. B. Yeats*, New Haven 1976.

Chapter 14

BOURGEOIS, MAURICE, *John Millington Synge and the Irish Theatre*, New York 1913.

CORKERY, DANIEL, *Synge and Anglo-Irish Literature*, Dublin 1931.

GREENE, DAVID and EDWARD M. STEPHENS, *J. M. Synge*, New York 1961.

GRENE, NICHOLAS, *Synge*, London 1975.

HARMON, MAURICE (Ed.), *J. M. Synge Centenary papers*, Dublin 1972.

Chapter 15

DOYLE, PAUL A., *Paul Vincent Carroll*, Lewisburg 1972.

HOGAN, ROBERT, *After the Irish Renaissance*, London 1968.

O'NEILL, MICHAEL J., *Lennox Robinson*, New York 1964.

PORTER, RAYMOND J., *Brinsley McNamara and George Shiels*, Lewisburg 1973.

ROBINSON, LENNOX, *The Irish Theatre*, London 1939.

Chapter 16

ARMSTRONG, W. A., *Sean O'Casey*, London 1967.

HUNT, HUGH, *Sean O'Casey*, Dublin 1980.

KRAUSE, DAVID, *Sean O'Casey, the Man and his Work*, London 1960.

O'CASEY, EILEEN, *Sean*, London 1971.

O hAODHA, MICHEÁL (Ed.), *The O'Casey Enigma*, Dublin 1980.

Chapter 17

CLARKE, BRENNA KATZ and HAROLD FERRAR, *The Dublin Drama League*, Dublin 1979.

LUKE, PETER (Ed.), *Enter Certain Players*, Dublin 1968.

MacLIAMMÓIR, MICHEÁL, *All for Hecuba*, London 1946.

RONSEY, JOSEPH (Ed.), *Denis Johnston: a Retrospective*, Gerrard's Cross 1981.

Chapter 18

BAIR, DEIRDRE, *Samuel Beckett*, London 1978.

BELL, SAM HANNA, *The Theatre in Ulster*, Dublin 1972.

MAXWELL, D. E. S., *Brian Friel*, Lewisburg 1973.

O'CONNOR, ULICK, *Brendan Behan*, London 1970.

REID, ALEC, *All I Can Manage, More than I Could*, Dublin 1968.

SIMPSON, ALAN, *Beckett and Behan and a Theatre in Dublin*, London 1962.

WORTH, KATHLEEN (Ed.), *Beckett the Shape-Changer*, London 1975.

——, *The Irish Drama of Europe from Yeats to Beckett*, London 1978.

VINSON, JAMES (Ed.), *Contemporary Dramatists*, New York 1977.

Index

Sources of Illustrations

Courtesy Abbey Theatre, Dublin: XV, XVIII, XIX (*photo* Rex Roberts), XXIV (*photo* Fergus Bourke), 57 (*photo* Fergus Bourke), 94, 112, 117, 129–30, 136, 144–5 (*photo* Fergus Bourke), 151–2, 167 (*photo* Fergus Bourke), 171–3, 175–6 (*photo* Fergus Bourke); The Arts Council: IX; Belfast Central Library: X, 90; courtesy Basil Blackshaw: 170; British Library, London, 65, 71, 122; British Museum, London: 87; Fergus Bourke: 131, 139; Collection Seamus de Burca: XI; by permission of the Syndics of Cambridge University Library: 8; Conacht Tribune photo, Galway: 116; Collection Major Congreve, Newbury, Berks: II; Crawford Municipal Art Gallery, Cork: VIII; From *Scenes from the Nineteenth-Century Stage* by Stanley Appelbaum, Dover Publications Inc., 1977: 88, 91–2; Dublin City Library: 7; Dublin Gate Theatre Productions Ltd: XX, 157–8, 161; G. A. Duncan, Dublin: 118; Gaiety Theatre, Dublin: 156 (*photo* John Brooks, Jarrold Colour Publications); Garrick Club, London: VI (*photo* John Brooks, Jarrold Colour Publications); courtesy Aiden Grennell: 66, 115, 160; courtesy James N. Healy: 168; Irish Theatre Company: XVI (*photo* Chris Hill), XXII (*photo* Fergus Bourke), 1 (*photo* Amelia Stein), 159; Irish Tourist Board: XXIII, XXIV, 58–9, 98, 108, 154, 177; Jarrold Colour Publications: 12 (*photo* John Brooks), 97 (*photo* John Brooks); Hugh Lane Municipal Gallery of Modern Art, Dublin: 120–1, 124, 134; The London Tara Hotel: 147; Longford-Westmeath County Library: 50 (*photo* Leo Daly); Lyric Theatre, Belfast: 30, 106 (*photo* Chris Hill), 132–3; The Raymond Mander and Joe Mitchenson Theatre Collection: IV, 42 (engraving after I. Roberts, 1776), 62 (painting by Samuel de Wilde, 1799), 85, 95, 113, 123, 126–7, 135, 148–9, 163; courtesy Liam Miller: 138, 140; Minister for Posts and Telegraphs: 107; National Library of Ireland, Dublin: 1, 2, 5, 9, 11, 13,

16, 17, (engraving after painting by Kneller), 23, 43 (engraving after J. Roberts, 1776), 44–5, 47, 49, 67, 70, 72–3 (engraving after painting by Ensign Dighton), 74, 79, 82, 84 (engraving after George Petrie, 1821), 125 (drawing by Ben Bay), 128, 137; National Gallery of Ireland, Dublin: III (*photo* John Brooks, Jarrold Colour Publications), 119, 142; National Portrait Gallery, London: 31, 51, 60, 75, 101, 133, 164–5; The National Trust: XIV (painting at Shaw's Corner, Ayot St Lawrence, Herts); Northern Irish Tourist Board: XVII; courtesy Richard Pine: 155, 162; private collection 99, 100; Project Arts Centre: 178 (*photo* Amelia Stein); Radio Telefis Eireann: 111, 114, 174; courtesy Shelah Richards: 146; Tate Gallery, London: V, 37; The Theatre Archive, Dublin: 169; Enthoven Collection, courtesy Theatre Museum, London: 54 (engraving after Wheatly, 1791), 81, 89, 93, 102–3, 105, 109; Harry R. Beard Collection, courtesy Theatre Museum, London: 22 (mezzotint after painting by Thomas Lawrence, 1783), 28 (mezzotint after painting by Zoffany), 33, 46, 63–4, 69 (engraving after Saxon, 1804), 78 (engraving after painting by George Petrie), 80 (from *The Illustrated London Times*, 1861), 83, 86 (lithograph by Count D'Orsay, 1839); The Board of Trinity College, Dublin: 14, 18, 35; courtesy Victoria and Albert Museum, London: VII, XII, XIII, XXI, 6, 15 (engraving after Hamilton, 1791), 20 (engraving after Dayes, 1795), 21 (engraving after Barralet, 1776), 24 (engraving of 1816), 25 (engraving after Craig, 1796), 26 (engraving after painting by Singleton), 27 (engraving of 1816), 34, 38 (engraving after painting by Singleton), 40 (engraving after Craig), 48 (engraving after Graham, 1796), 52–3 (engraving after Stodhart), 56, 61 (engraving after painting by Singleton), 104, 110; courtesy Eve Watkinson: 29; Reg Wilson: 76, 166.